Table of Contents

MATH   Page

Getting Ready for Math I 2
> Dot-to-dots, coloring, and cutting-and-pasting activities will help your child begin to learn
> about counting, writing numbers, and putting numbers in the correct order.

Getting Ready for Math II 35
> More matching, coloring, cutting-and-pasting, and dot-to-dots plus hidden pictures,
> number rhymes, and games will help your child begin to learn numbers to 10, all
> about 0, "more" and "less," money, and time.

Math Around the House 67
> Cutting-and-pasting, coloring, drawing, tracing, dot-to-dots, and matching will
> help your child practice counting things in the house and writing numbers. He or she will
> also learn about "big - small" and "long - short," while having some special
> fun with counting cards and a cooking activity.

Beginning Counting with Mother Goose 99
> The fun of learning these rhymes will help your child practice counting, writing numbers,
> and putting numbers in the correct order.

LANGUAGE

Motor Skills 131
> These pages will help your child develop fine motor skills. There are lots of fun
> activities with sand, clay, and paper to help children get used to using their fingers to draw
> with crayons, cut with scissors, and learn to trace.

Think & Do 165
> Your child will learn to match things that go together; compare things and then decide
> how they are alike and different; and show how to put pieces of a picture
> together so that they make sense.

Trace & Write 194
> These pages are all about helping your child practice writing letters.

Draw & Talk 226
> The drawing and coloring activities in this book are springboards for getting your child
> to talk about specific things, just like students have to do in school!

Colors & Shapes 257
> These pages will help your child learn all the colors of the rainbow, and they'll also
> help him or her learn about circles, squares, triangles, and other shapes.

What Comes Next? 289
> Things happen in a certain order, and the cut-and-paste fun in this book will
> help your child practice putting pictures of events in the right sequence.

Is there a hat for each clown?   yes   no

Understanding one-to-one relationships

Note: Help your child discover that the items in the picture correspond to the numbers being practiced.

Trace and write.

| 1 | 2 | 3 |

Color the set of 1 green.
Color the set of 2 blue.
Color the set of 3 orange.

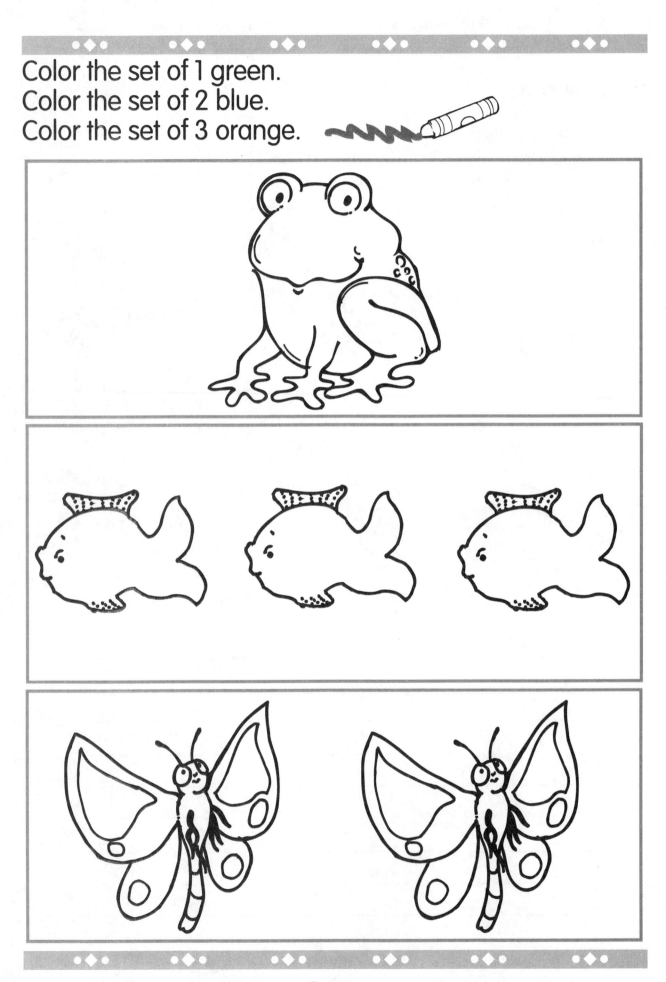

Counting

Cut out the bees.
Paste them on the correct hives.

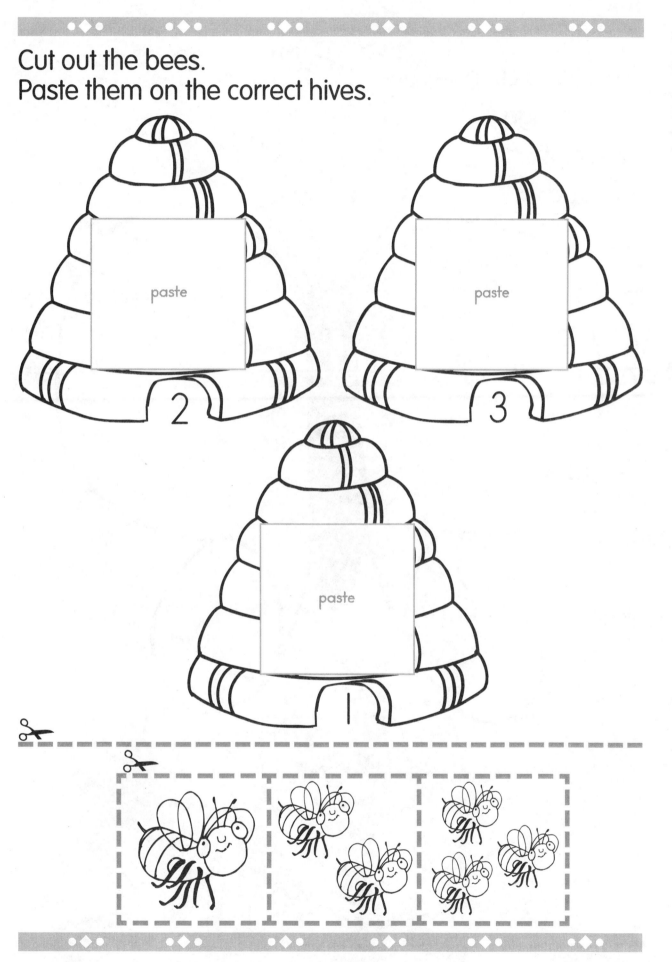

Color the picture.

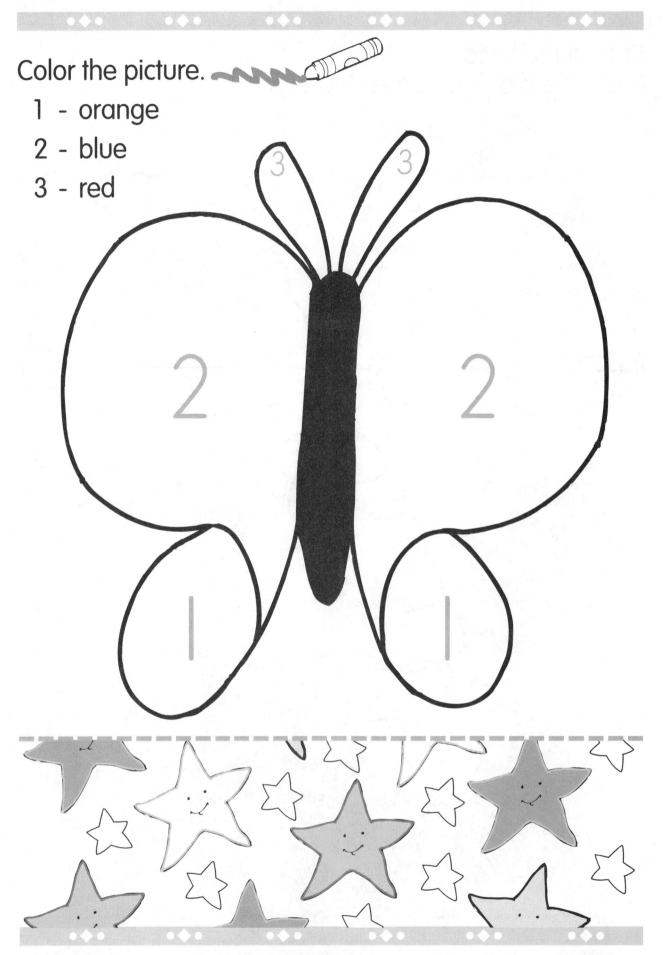

1 - orange
2 - blue
3 - red

Recognizing numbers; following directions

Connect the dots.

How many are in each set?

1   2   3

1   2   3

2   3   1

2   3   1

3   2   1

3   2   1

Counting objects and matching with a number

Note: Help your child discover that the items in the picture correspond to the numbers being practiced.

Trace and write.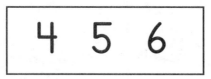

4 5 6

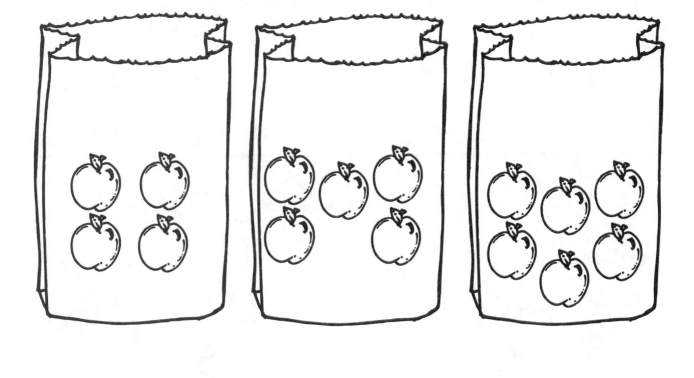

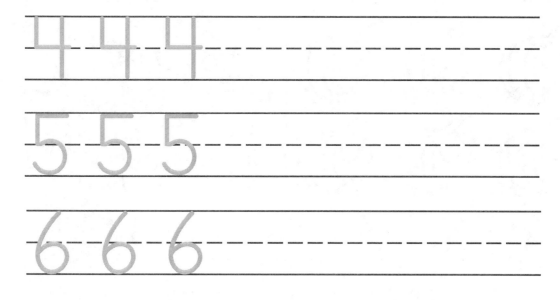

Tracing and writing numbers; understanding one-to-one relationships

How many are in each set?

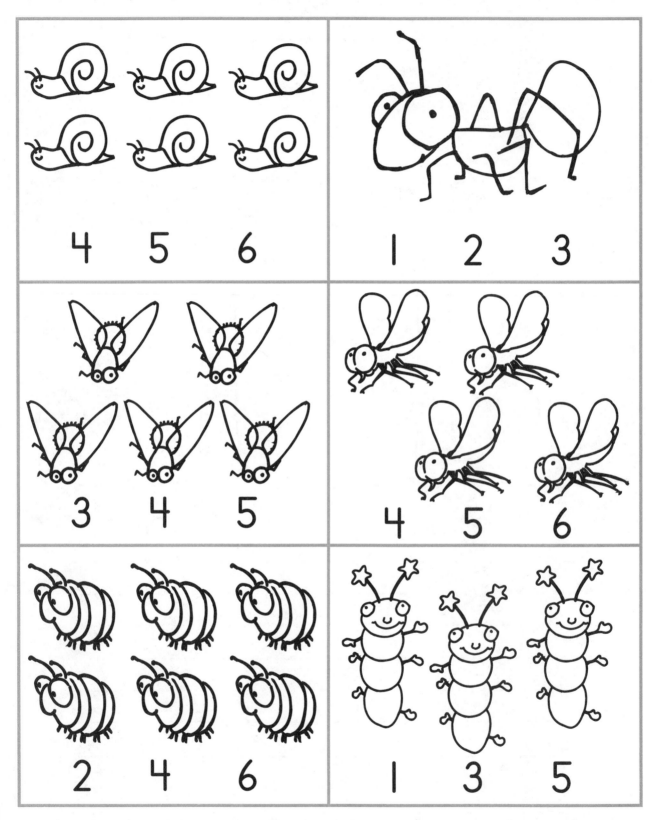

Counting objects and matching with a number

Draw the correct number of dots on the clown hats.

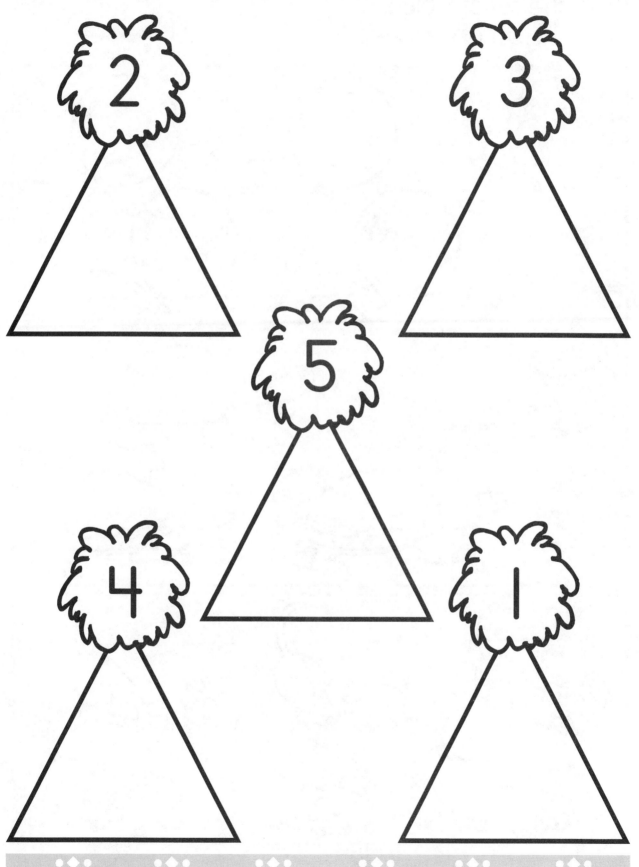

Color the set of 4 green.
Color the set of 5 blue.
Color the set of 6 brown.

Counting

Cut out the apples.
Paste them on the correct trees.

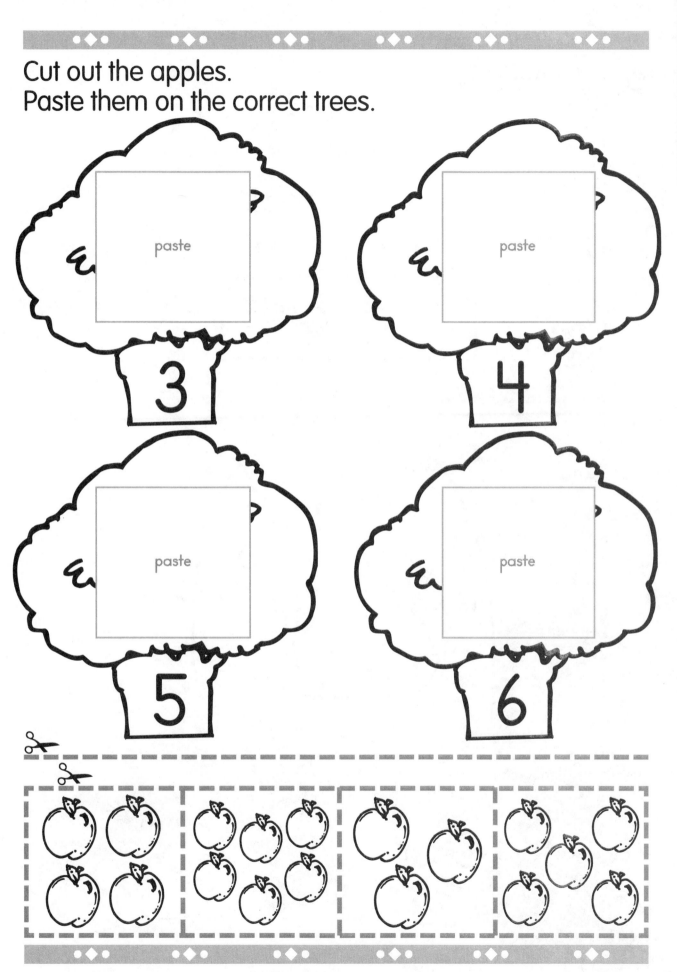

Connect the dots.

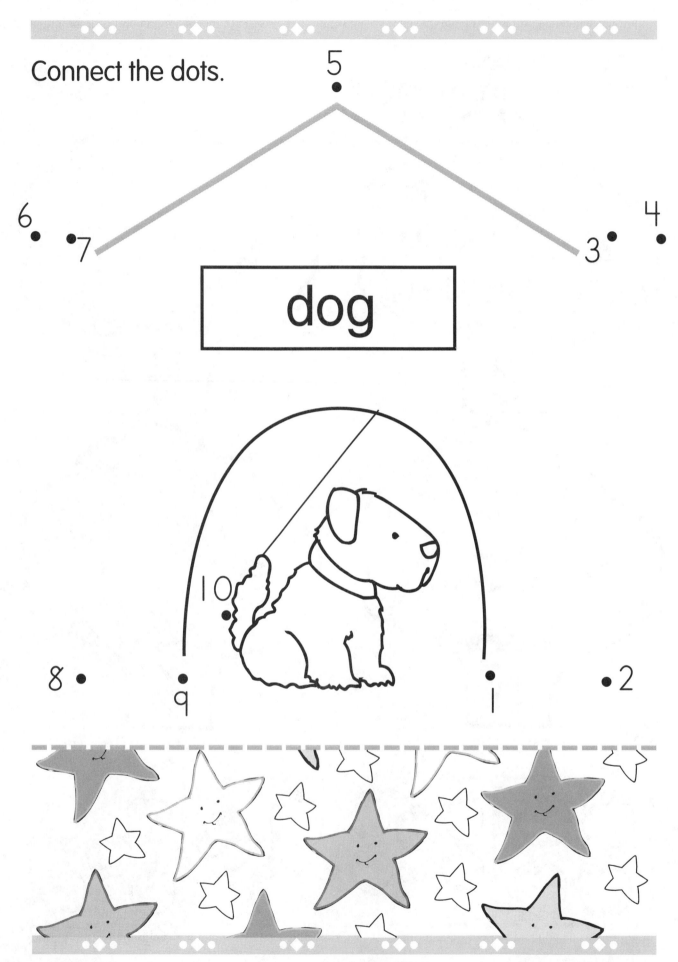

dog

Understanding number order

Color the picture.

1 - green
2 - yellow
3 - orange

white

white

black

black

How many are in each set?

Counting objects and matching with a number

Cut out the numbers.
Paste them in order.

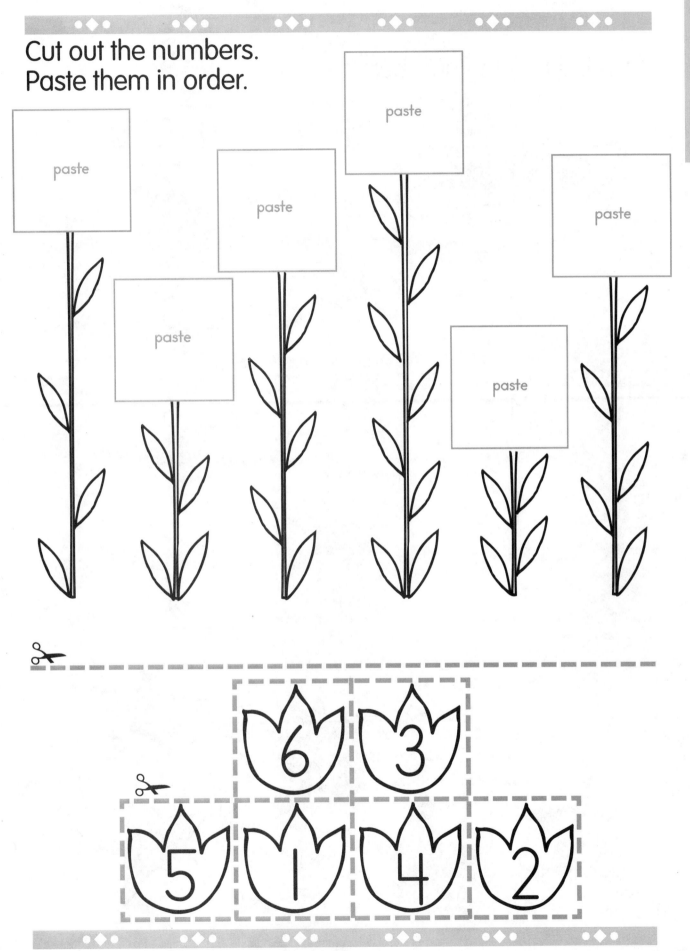

Fill in the missing numbers.

1 2 3 4 5 6

2 _3_

4 __

1 __

5 __

__ 3

__ 6

__ 4

__ 2

Understanding number order

Draw the correct number of petals on the flowers.

Trace and write.

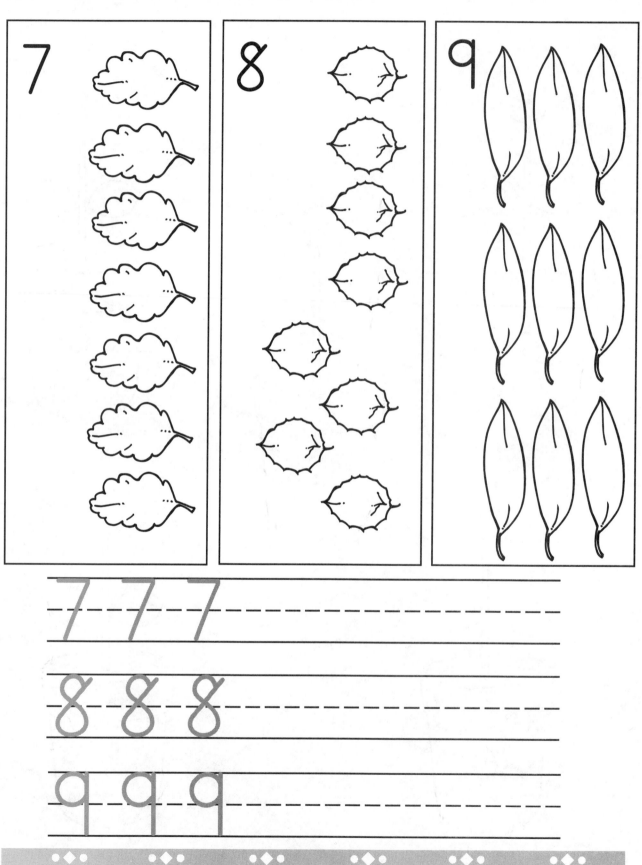

Tracing and writing numbers; understanding one-to-one relationships

Color the set of 6 purple.

Color the set of 7 orange.

Color the set of 8 yellow.

Color the set of 9 red.

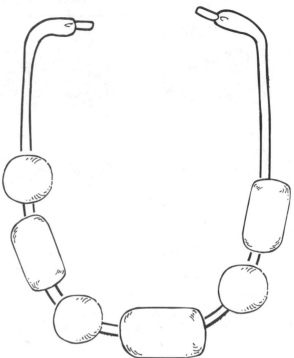

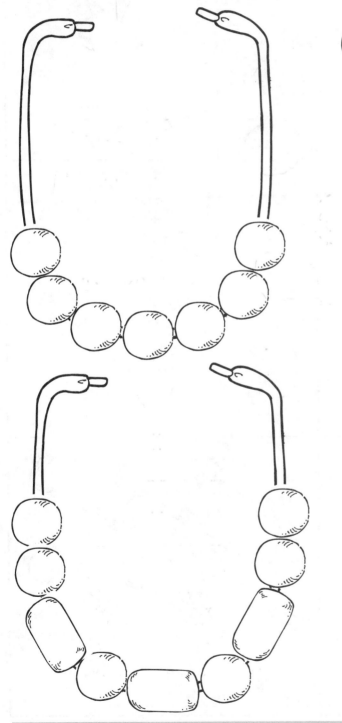

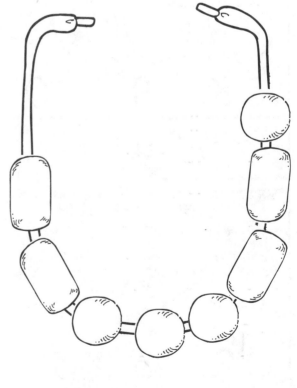

Understanding quantities represented by numbers

How many are in each set?

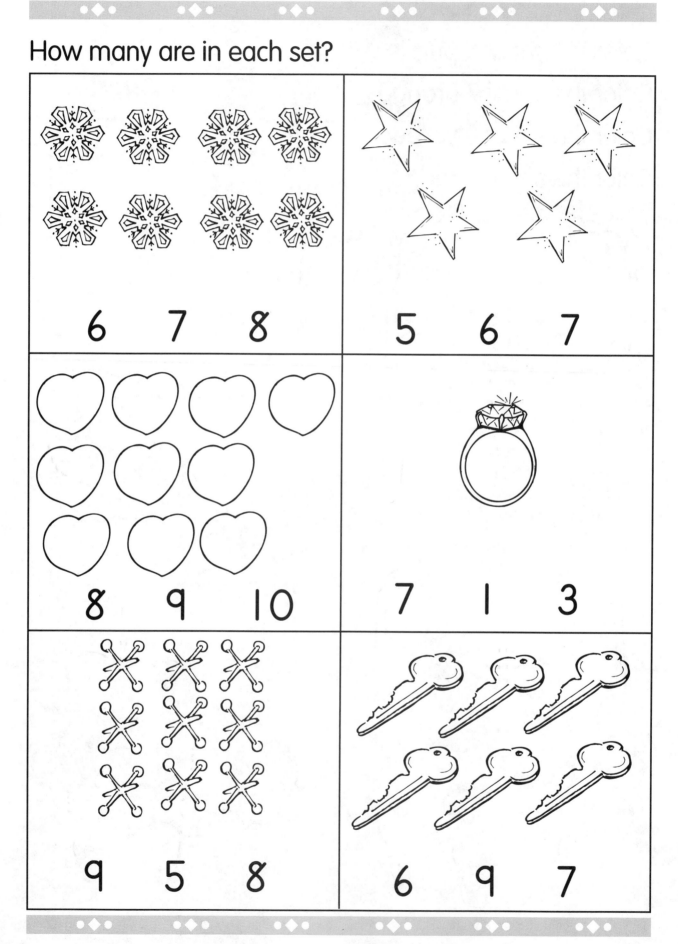

6   7   8

5   6   7

8   9   10

7   1   3

9   5   8

6   9   7

Counting objects and matching with a number

Cut out the fish.
Paste them in the correct bowls.

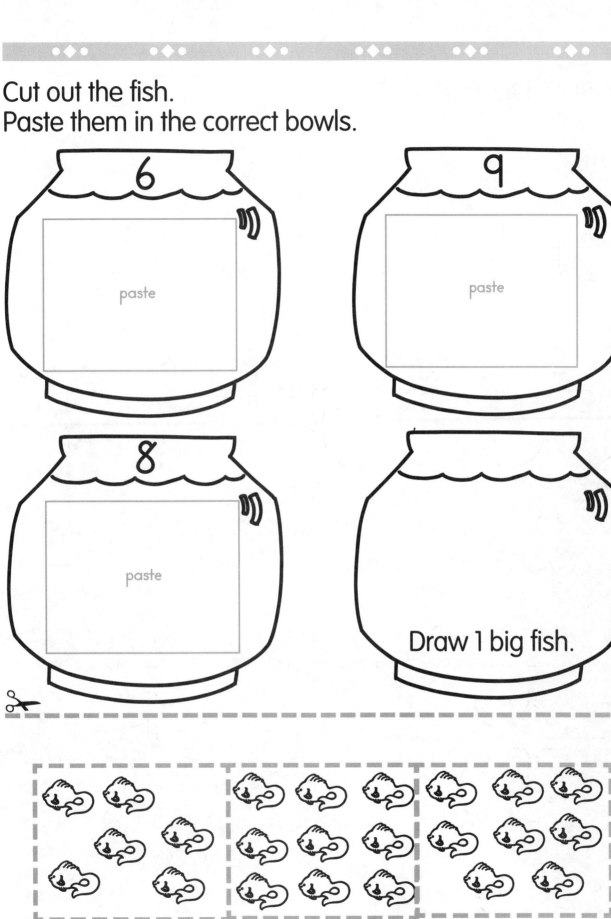

6

paste

9

paste

8

paste

Draw 1 big fish.

Connect the dots.

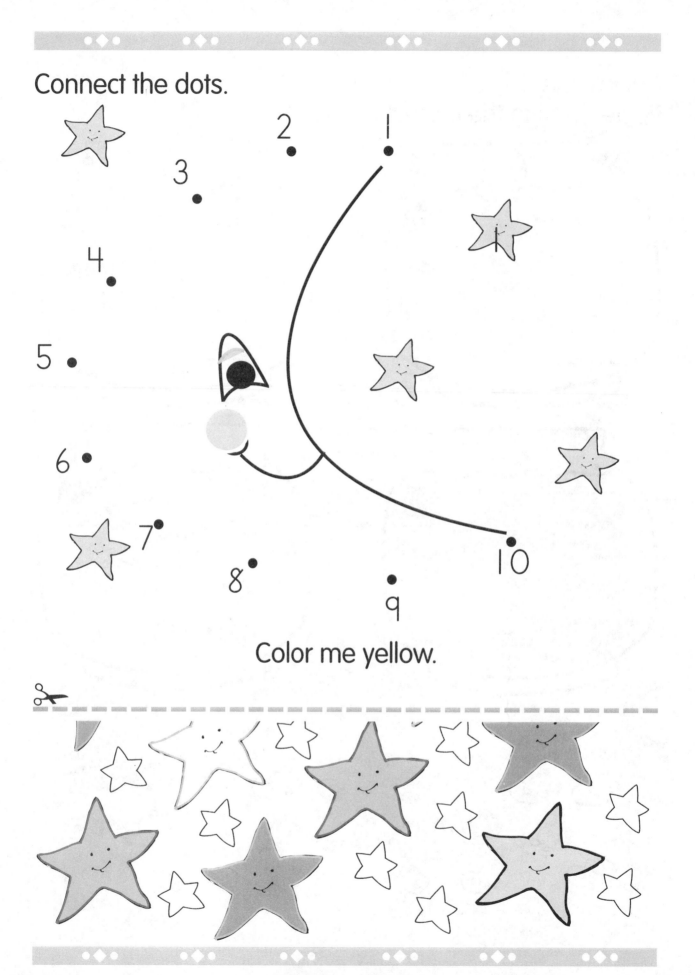

Color me yellow.

Match.

6

7

8

q

Draw the correct number of spots on the dogs.

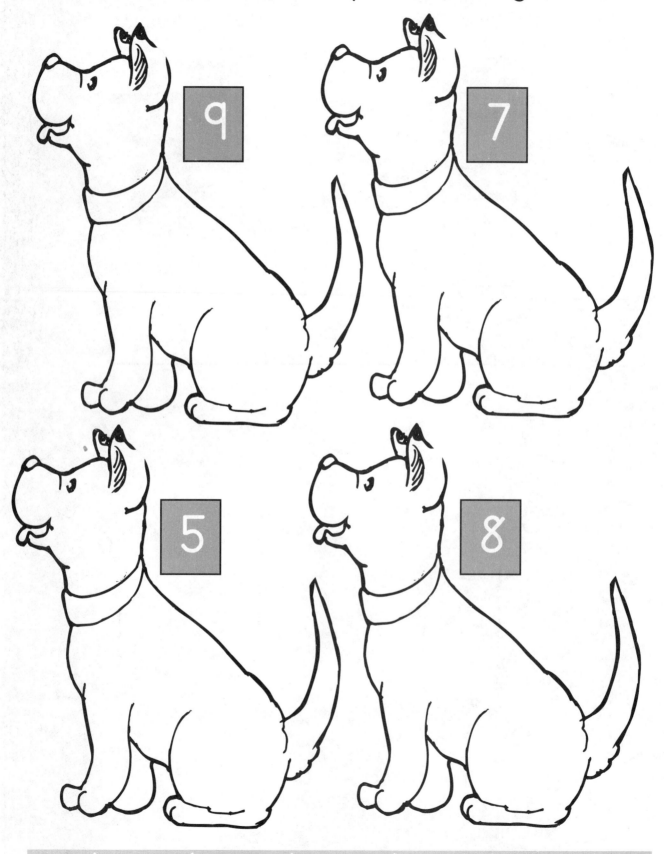

Understanding quantities represented by numbers

Cut out the numbers.
Paste them in order.

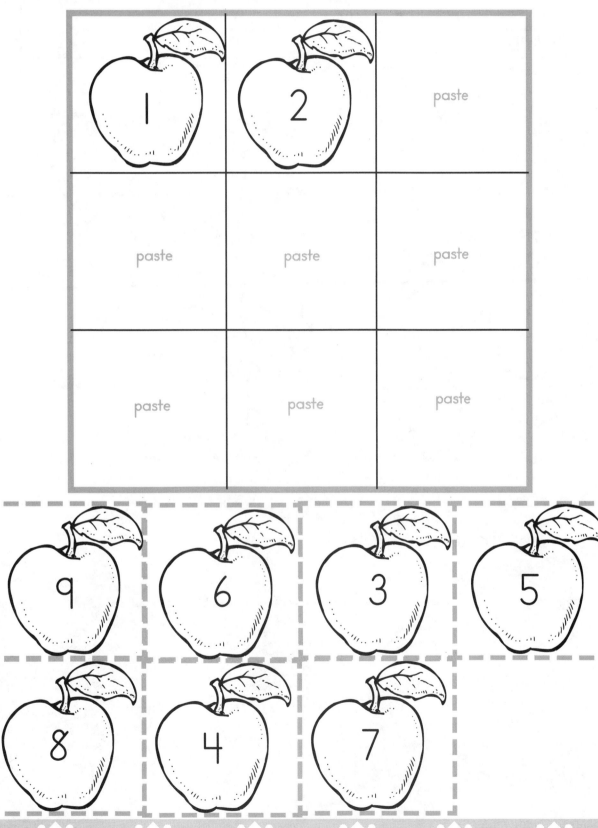

Fill in the missing numbers.

1 2 3 4 5 6 7 8 9

3 _____

7 _____

5 _____

8 _____

Trace and write. _____

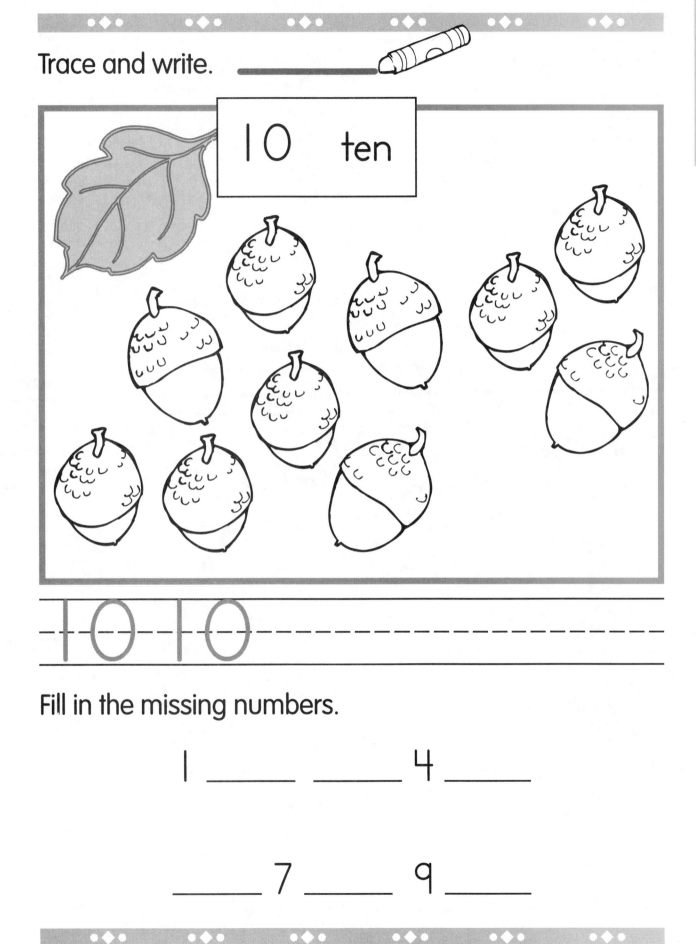

10   ten

Fill in the missing numbers.

1 ____ ____ 4 ____

____ 7 ____ 9 ____

Connect the dots.

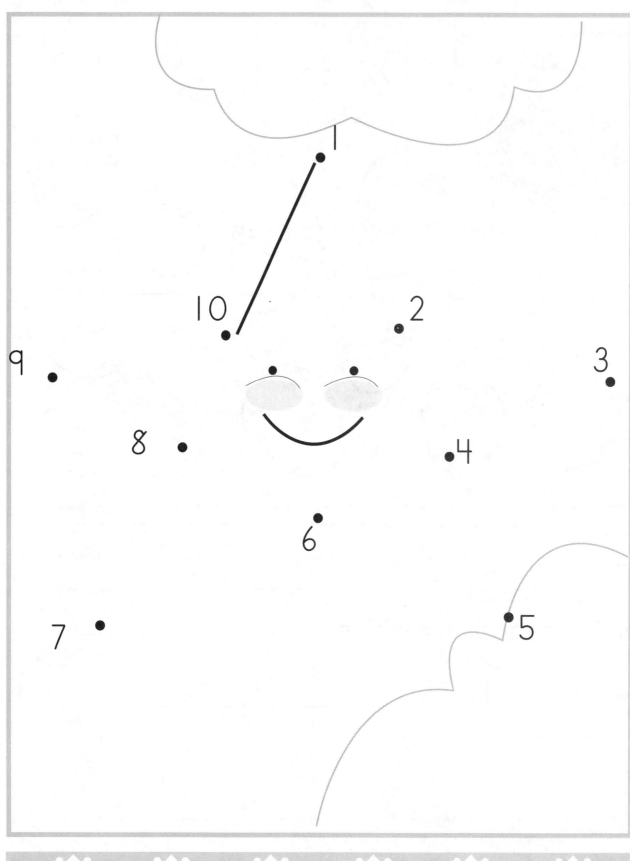

Understanding number order

Cut out the numbers.
Paste them in order.

Fill in the missing numbers.

1 2 3 4 5 6 7 8 9 10

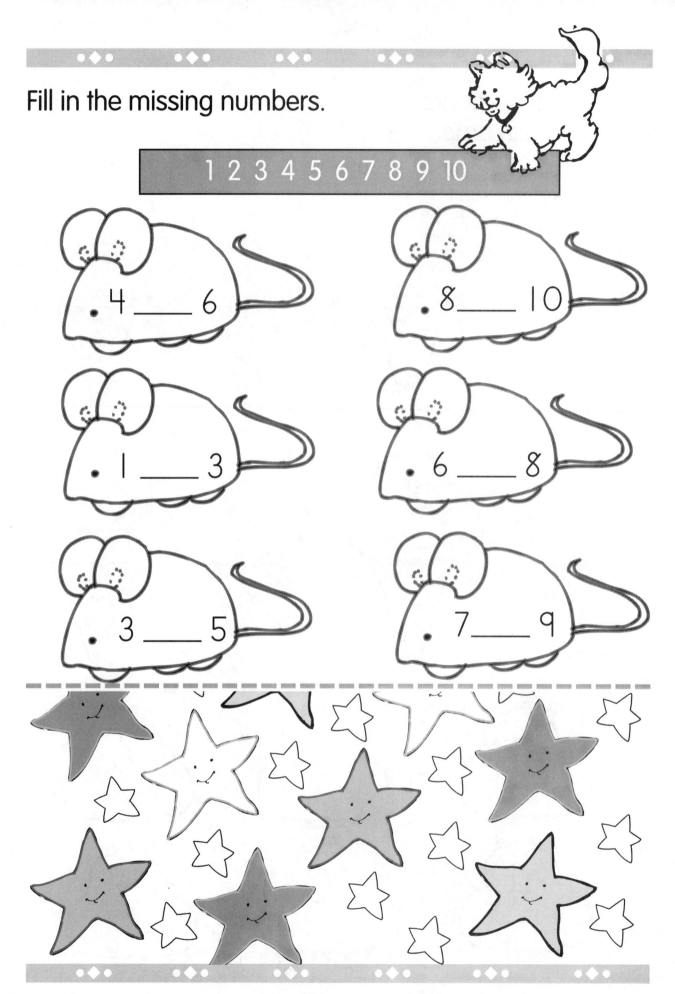

4 ___ 6

8 ___ 10

1 ___ 3

6 ___ 8

3 ___ 5

7 ___ 9

Understanding number order

Answer Key

Please take time to go over the work your child has completed. Ask your child to explain what he/she has done. Praise both success and effort. If mistakes have been made, explain what the answer should have been and how to find it. Let your child know that mistakes are a part of learning. The time you spend with your child helps let him/her know you feel learning is important.

page 2

NO

page 4

first row = green
second row = orange
third row = blue

page 5

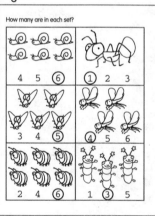

page 8

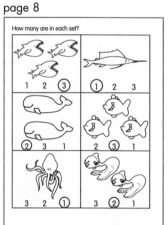

page 10

page 11

page 12

first row = blue
second row = green
third row = brown

page 13

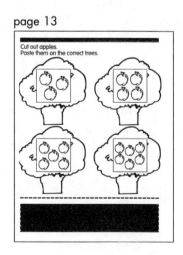

page 14

page 16

How many are in each set?

4 (5) 6   1 (2) 3

(3) 4 5   6 2 (4)

(1) 3 5   5 2 (6)

page 17

Cut out the numbers.
Paste them in order.

1 2 3 4 5 6

page 18

Fill in the missing numbers.

1 2 3 4 5 6

2 2   1 3

4 5   5 6

1 2   3 4

5 6   1 2

page 19

Draw the correct number of petals on the flowers.

5   2   3

6   4

page 22

How many are in each set?

6 7 (8)   (5) 6 7

8 9 (10)   7 (1) 3

(9) 5 8   (6) 9 7

page 23

Cut out the fish.
Paste them in the correct bowls.

6   9

8   Draw 1 big fish.

page 25

Match.

6
7
8
9

page 26

Draw the correct number of spots on the dogs.

9   7

5   8

page 27

Cut out the numbers.
Paste them in order.

1 2 3
4 5 6
7 8 9

page 28

Fill in the missing numbers.

1 2 3 4 5 6 7 8 9

3 4   7 8

5 6   8 9

page 29

Trace and write.

10 ten

10 10

Fill in the missing numbers.

1 2 3 4 5

6 7 8 9 10

page 31

Cut out the numbers.
Paste them in order.

3 4 5 6

7 8 9 10

page 32

1 2 3 4 5 6 7 8 9 10

4 5 6   8 9 10

1 2 3   6 7 8

3 4 5   7 8 9

Parents: One–to–one matching requires your child to compare sets of objects to see if they are the same or if one is larger than the other.

Can you feed all of the dogs a bone?

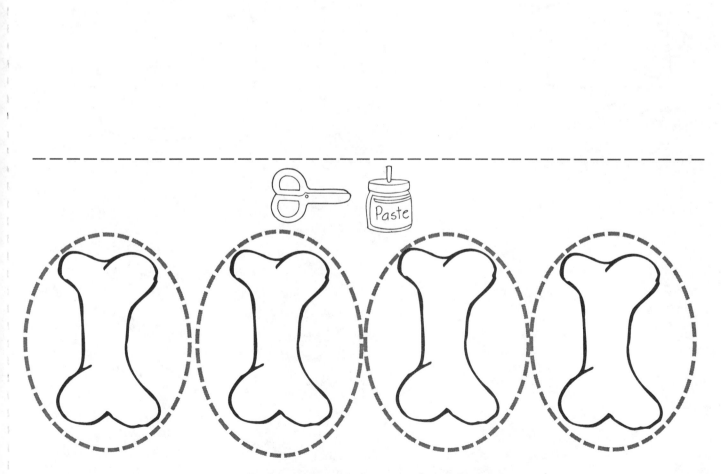

Understanding one-to-one relationships

Can you put a fish in every bowl?

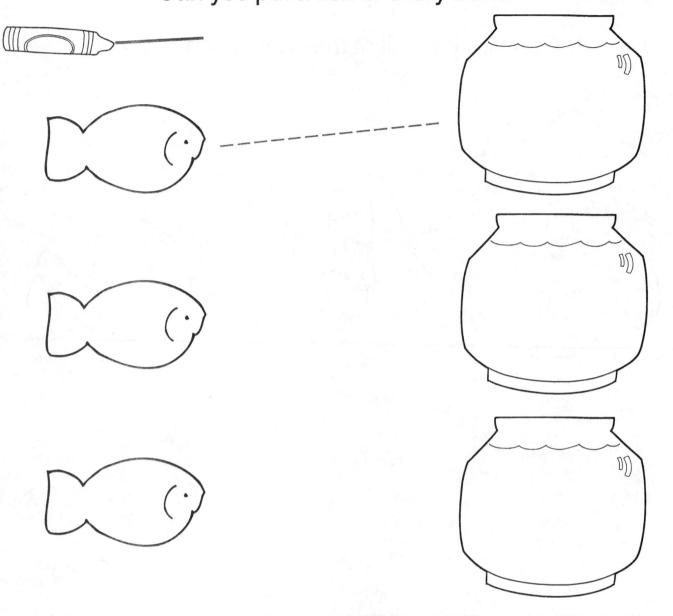

Understanding one-to-one relationships

Parents: Your child needs to learn to recognize and name items by their sizes. Point out objects and talk about their sizes. Ask your child to make size comparisons and encourage him/her to use size words. For example: "Which spoon is the longest?" "Am I taller or shorter then you?" "Which box is the biggest?"

What is big?

Color the big picture.

Understanding big

Big or Small?

big

small

Understanding big and small

Long or Short?

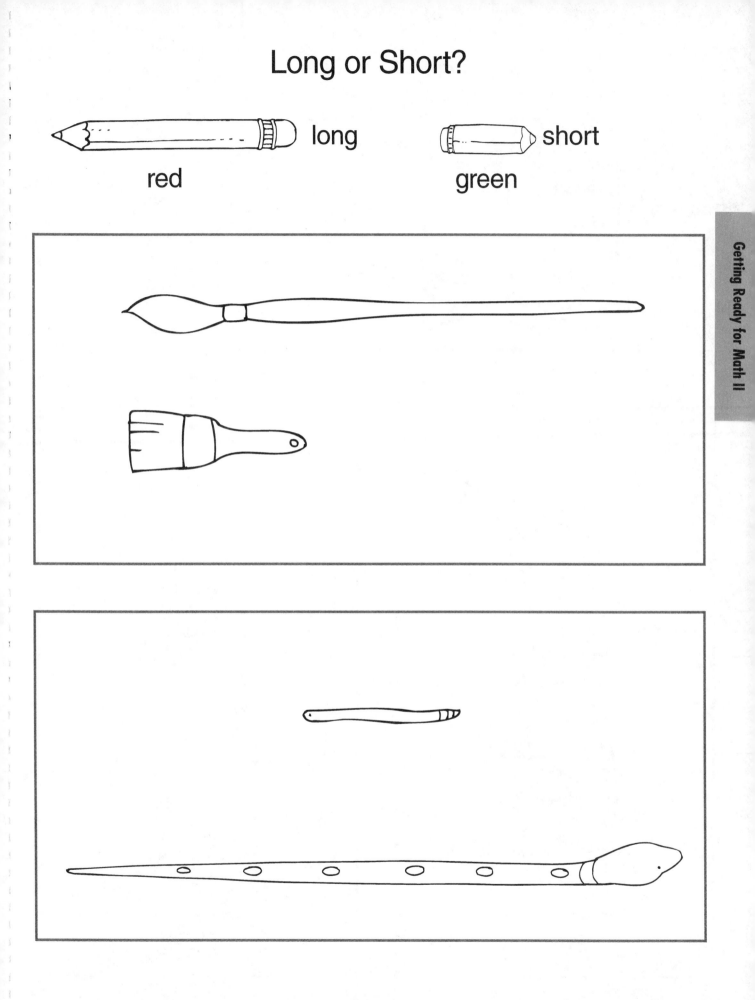

long — red

short — green

Tall or Short?

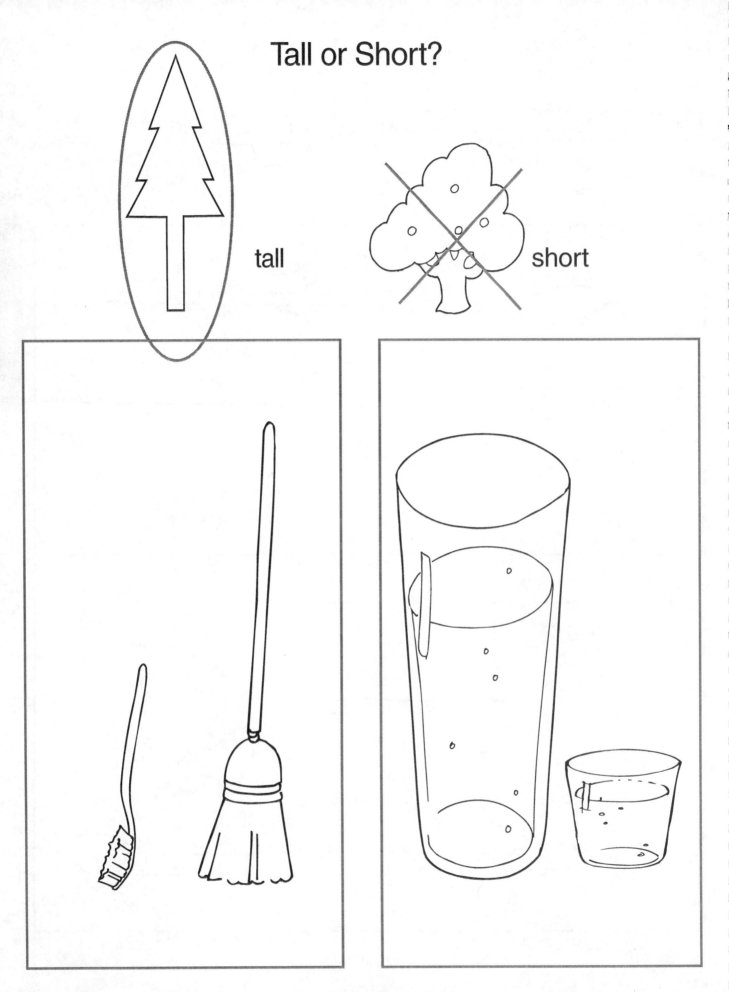

tall

short

Understanding tall and short

Parents: Help your child become aware of numbers in the world around us. When you are driving around, point out numbers on signs, cars, buildings, etc. Go on a "number walk" at home to find numbers around the house. Have your child find and circle numbers in newspapers and magazines. Point to some of the numbers and ask your child to name them.

Circle.

Find the numbers.

Find the numbers hiding in this picture.

Did you find these numbers? I 2 3 4 5

Recognizing numbers

Numbers 0 to 10

1. Begin with the numbers 1–5. Hold up a card and have your child count the set of objects. Point to the number and have your child say it.

2. When your child is comfortable with the numbers 1–5, add in one or two new numbers each time you practice.

3. Add in zero after you have done the poem on page 53.

Getting Ready for Math II

Recognizing numbers and counting

43

Getting Ready for Math II

Playing with Number Cards

1. **Put the Cards in Orde**r – Ask your child to put the cards in order from 1 to 10.

2. **What Comes Next?** This skill is more difficult than putting the cards in order. Put out all of the cards your child has practiced. Pick up one card. Have your child name it. Ask "what comes next?" Your child picks up the correct card. When your child can do this easily you can play **What Comes Before?**

How many do you see?

1

2

3

4

5

Counting objects and matching with a number

Parents: Explain to your child that he/she is to draw a line between the numbers in order. Start at 1.

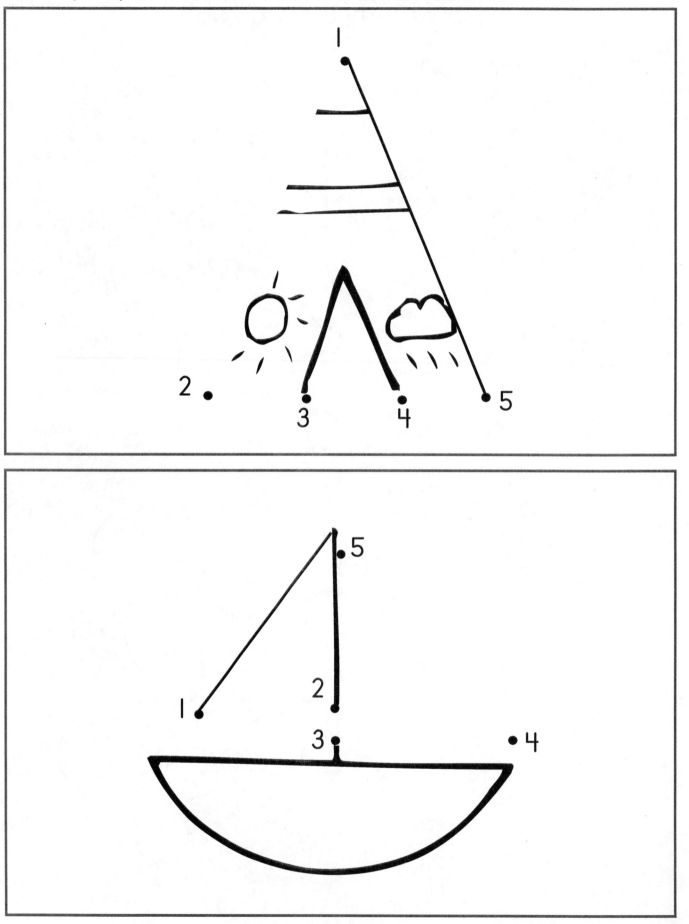

Understanding number order

How many do you see?

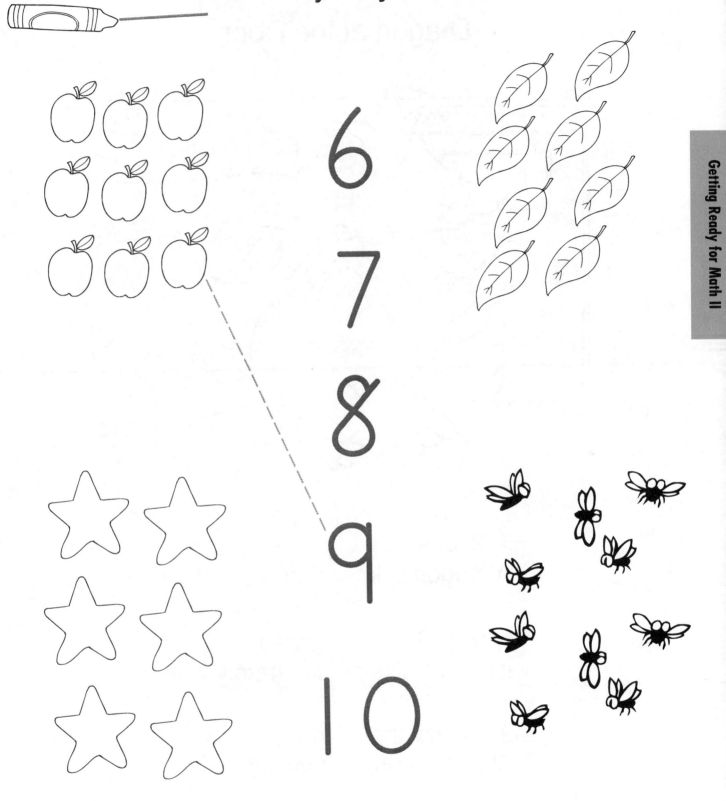

Counting objects and matching with a number

Dragon at the Door

1, 2, 3, 4
A dragon is knocking at my door.

5, 6, 7, 8
It sounds like he can hardly wait.

9 knocks, then 10
Shall I go and let him in?

Find the numbers hiding in this picture.

Did you find these numbers? 6 7 8 9 10

Connect the dots.

Start at 1.

Understanding number order

Zero

How many striped elephants
Are dancing on your knees?

How many purple chimpanzees
Are swinging from the trees?

We use a special number
For creatures so very rare.

It's *zero* – fat and round
That tells us none are there.

Parents: Point to each shape on this page and ask your child to name it. If he/she doesn't know the name, say it. Walk around the house and help your child locate objects that are these shapes.

Color the shapes.

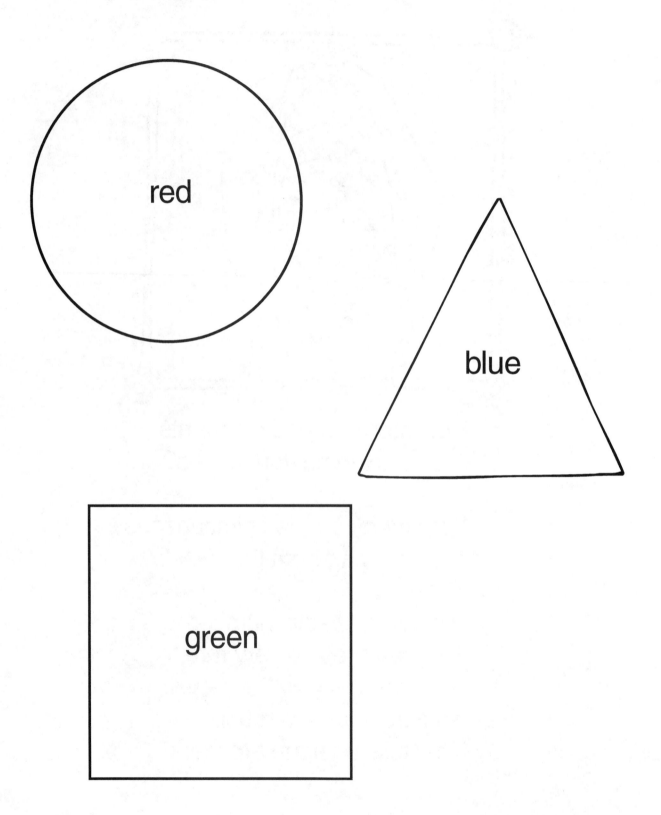

red

blue

green

Recognizing shapes

Match the shapes.

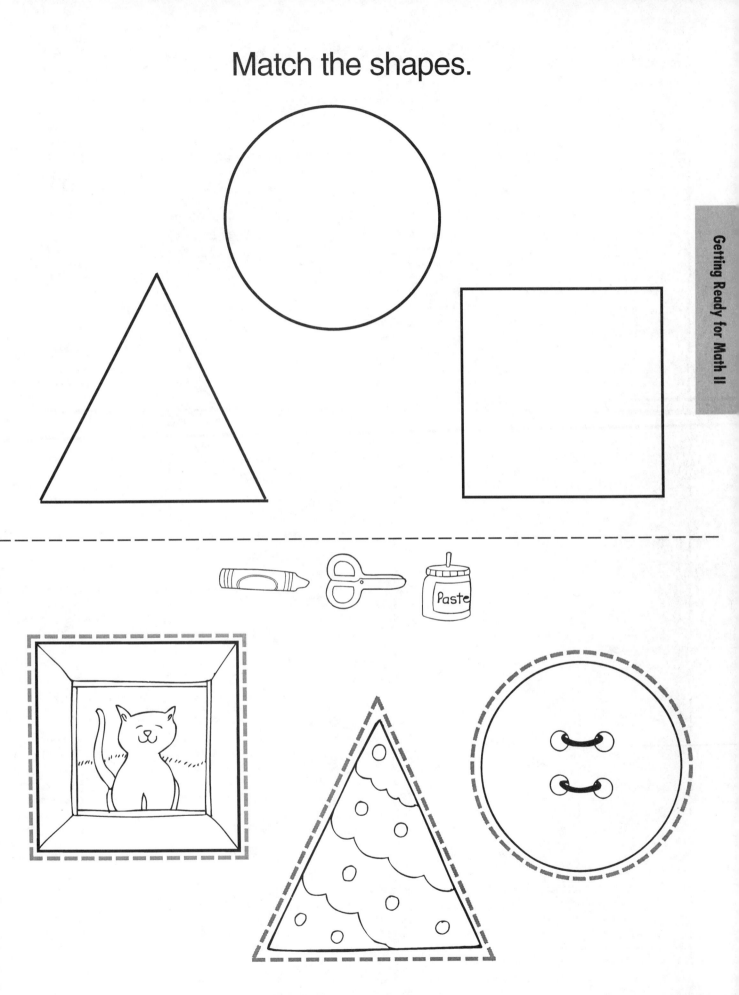

Paste

Matching shapes

Connect the dots.

Start at 1.

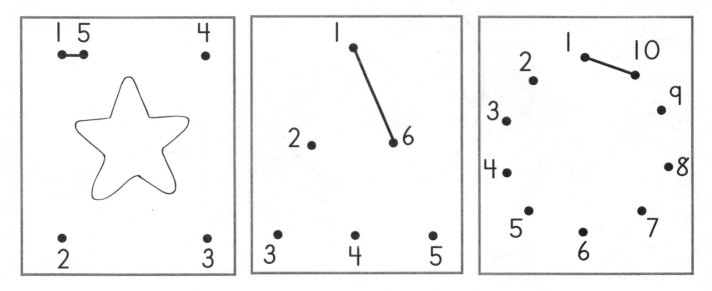

Understanding number order

Let's Play a Game

Follow Me:
Put your hands in various positions around your body. Have your child copy what you do, repeating what you say.

"I put my hands **over** my head."
"I put my hands **under** my chin."
"I put my hands **between** my knees,"
"I put my hands **behind** my back."
"I put my hands by my **left** side."
"I put my hands on my **right** shoe."

Put It Away:
Hand your child an object and give directions telling your child where to put it.

"Please put this book **on** the table."
"Please put this spoon **in** the drawer."
"Please put my slippers **under** the bed."
"Please put this towel **over** the towel rack."
"Please put this box **under** the table."
"Please sit down **between** your brother and sister."

Where Is It?
Look at pictures in magazines and ask questions about location.

"Where is the airplane flying?" (It is flying **up** in the sky.)
"Where is the cereal?" (It is **inside** the box.)
"Where did the dog go?" (It ran **behind** the house.)
"Where is the red car?" (It is **between** the blue car and the green truck.)

Parents : Point to each bear and ask your child to tell you where the bear's balloon is located.

Where is bear's balloon?

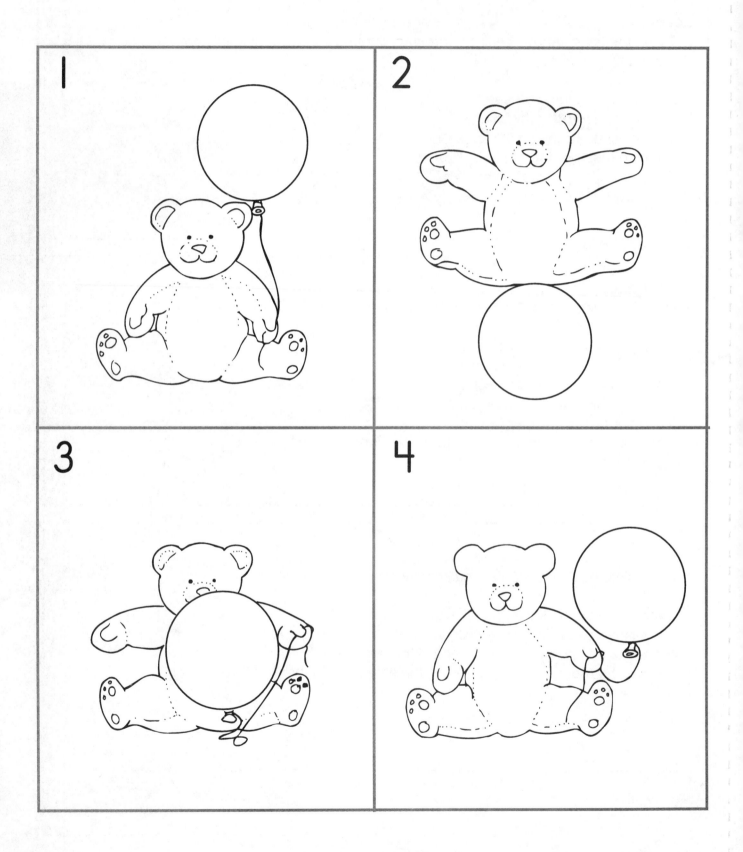

Understanding position words

Parents: Work with your child on this page to help him/her begin to understand the idea of "more" and "less." Point to the first box. Ask your child to look at the two sets of objects. Ask "Are there more ladybugs or more honeybees?" Have him/her color the set that is more. Point to the next two sets of objects. Ask "Are there more cats or more dogs?" Have him/her color the set that is more.

More or Less?

Understanding more and less   **59**

Parents: Your child needs to understand the idea that if you add some to what you have, it is "more" and if you take some away, it is 'less." This is setting a foundation for learning to add and subtract. Point to the first set. Ask your child to draw another ball. Ask, "Do you have more or less now?" Repeat this with each set of objects. Go back to the first set. Have your child cover up two. Ask "Do you have more or less now?" Repeat this with each set. Repeat the activity using real objects around the house.

Add and Take Away

Understanding more and less

Parents: Use real coins to help your child learn the name and value of a penny and nickel. Explain that both one nickel and five pennies equal "five cents." Point to a pocket. Ask "How many cents are in this pocket?."

Pocket Money

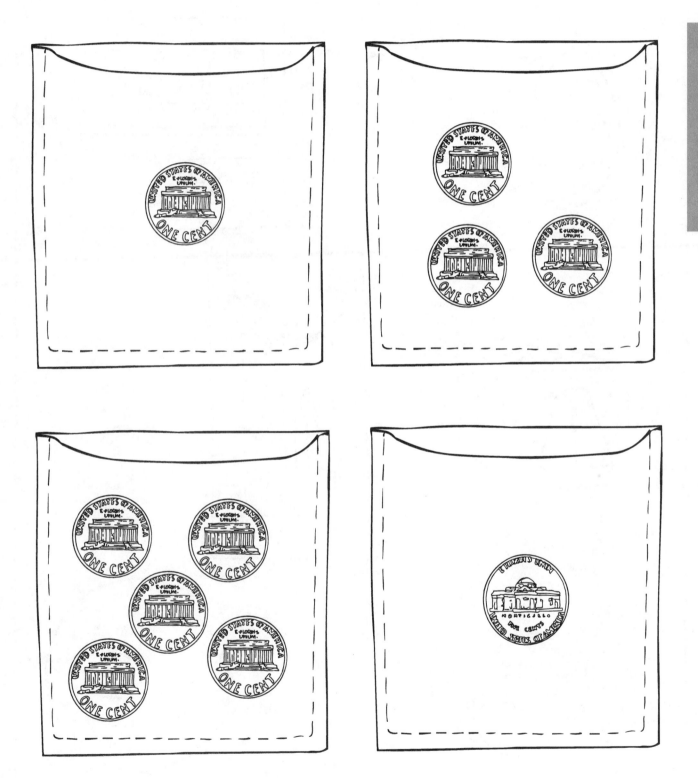

Understanding coin amounts

What tells the time?

Circle.

Parents: Patterning is a skill that is used in both math and reading. You can use real objects to build the same kinds of patterns your child will practice on pages 63-64. Have your child copy a pattern you build, continue a pattern you start, or build his/her own patterns using objects such as blocks, silverware, buttons, seashells, rocks, and other "real–life" objects.

Copy the pattern.

Color.

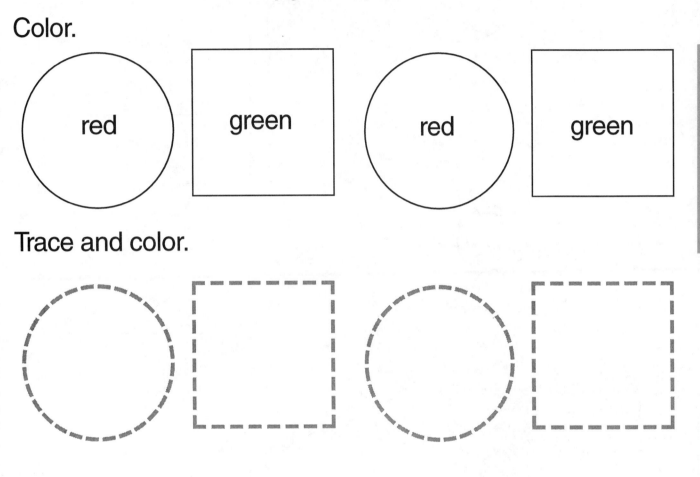

Trace and color.

What Comes Next?

paste

paste

paste

Completing patterns

Answer Key

Please take time to go over the work your child has completed. Ask your child to explain what he/she has done. Praise both success and effort. If mistakes have been made, explain what the answer should have been and how to find it. Let your child know that mistakes are a part of learning. The time you spend with your child helps let him/her know you feel learning is important.

page 35
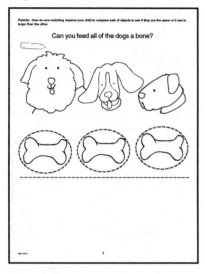

page 36
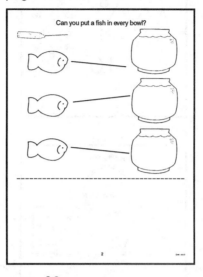

page 37

page 38
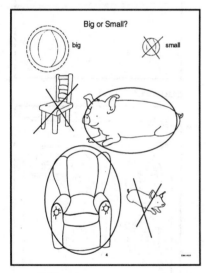

page 39
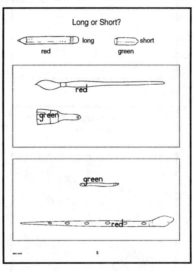

page 40
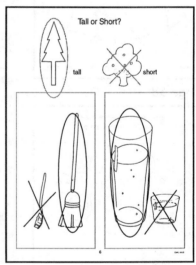

page 41
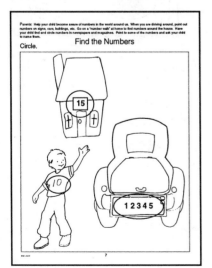

page 42
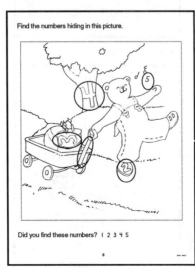

page 47
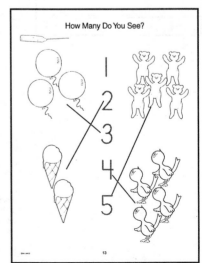

Answers

page 48

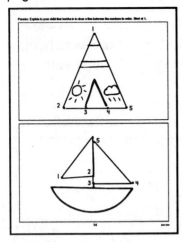

page 49

How Many Do You See?

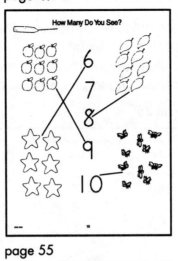

page 51

Find the numbers hiding in this picture.

Did you find these numbers? 6 7 8 9 10

page 52

Connect the Dots

Start at 1.

page 55

Match the Shapes

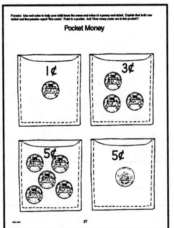

page 56

Connect the Dots.

Start at 1.

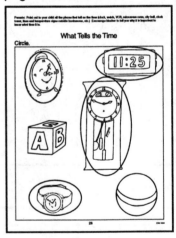

page 58

Where is Bear's Balloon?

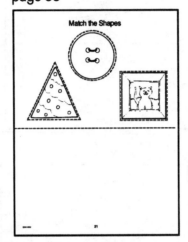

page 61

Pocket Money

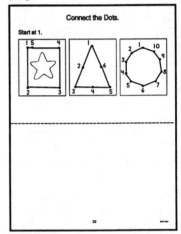

page 62

What Tells the Time

Circle.

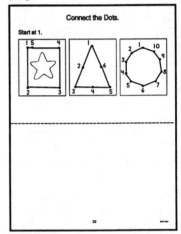

page 64

What Comes Next?

Parents: A pattern is a design that repeats over and over again. This skill is helpful to children in many learning areas. Help your child practice by making patterns together using things around the house such as dried beans, nuts and bolts, buttons, etc.

What Comes Next?

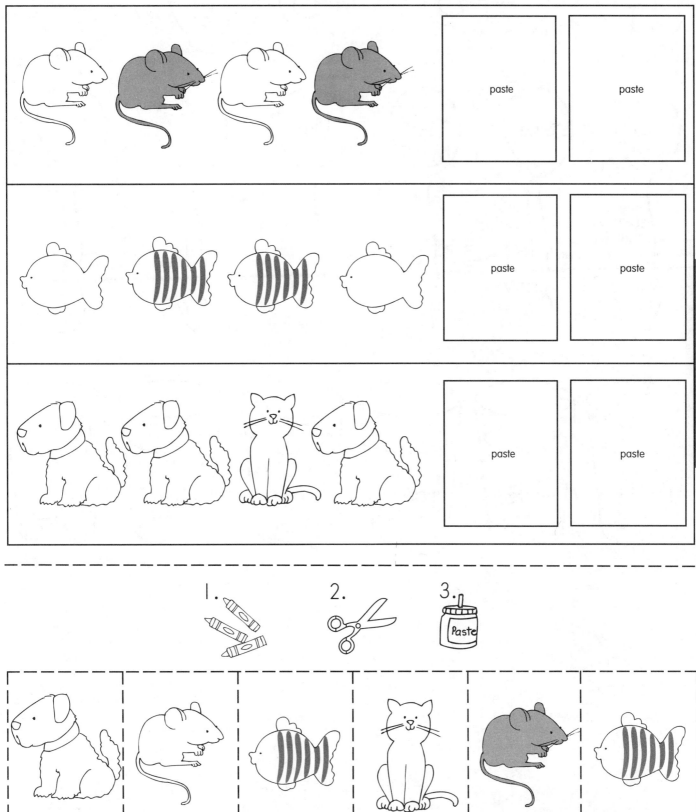

1. (crayons)
2. (scissors)
3. (paste)

Color the Pattern

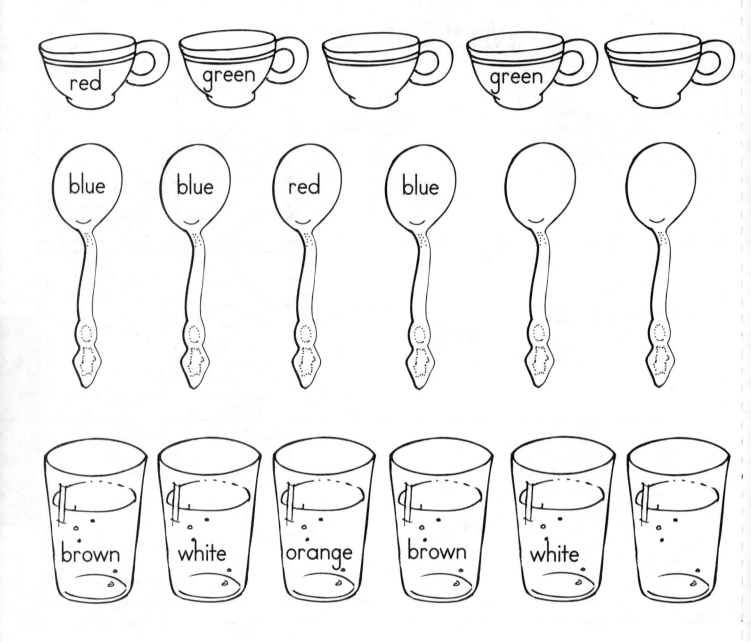

red   green   green

blue   blue   red   blue

brown   white   orange   brown   white

Completing patterns

What Comes Next?

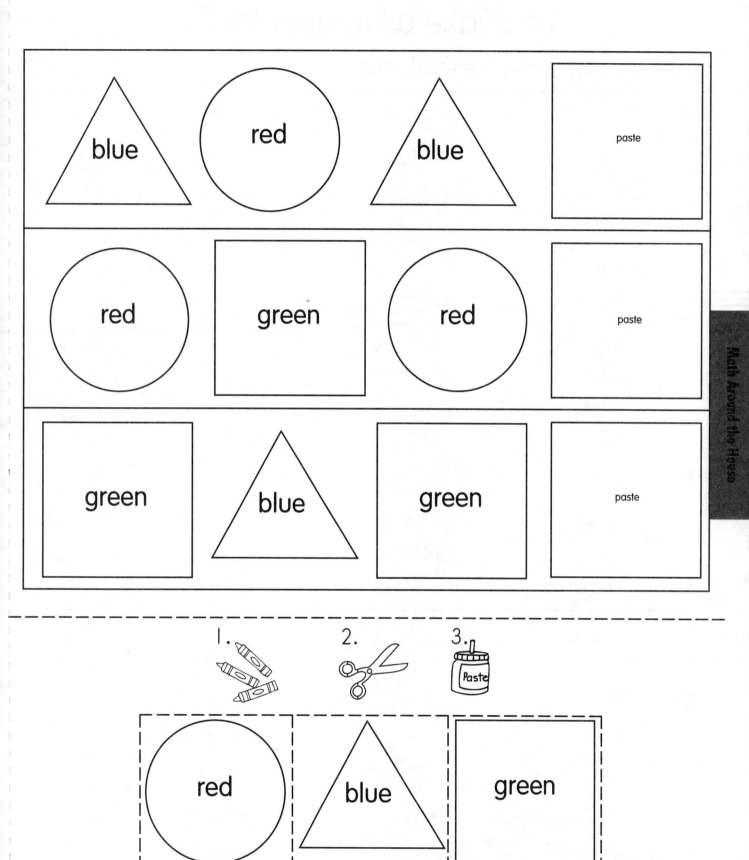

blue	red	blue	paste
red	green	red	paste
green	blue	green	paste

1. 2. 3.

red	blue	green

Parents: Take a walk around the house with your child. Help him/her find all the places numbers can be found. Have him/her draw some of the places below.

Let's Take a Number Walk

I found numbers in these places.

Recognizing numbers

Trace the Numerals

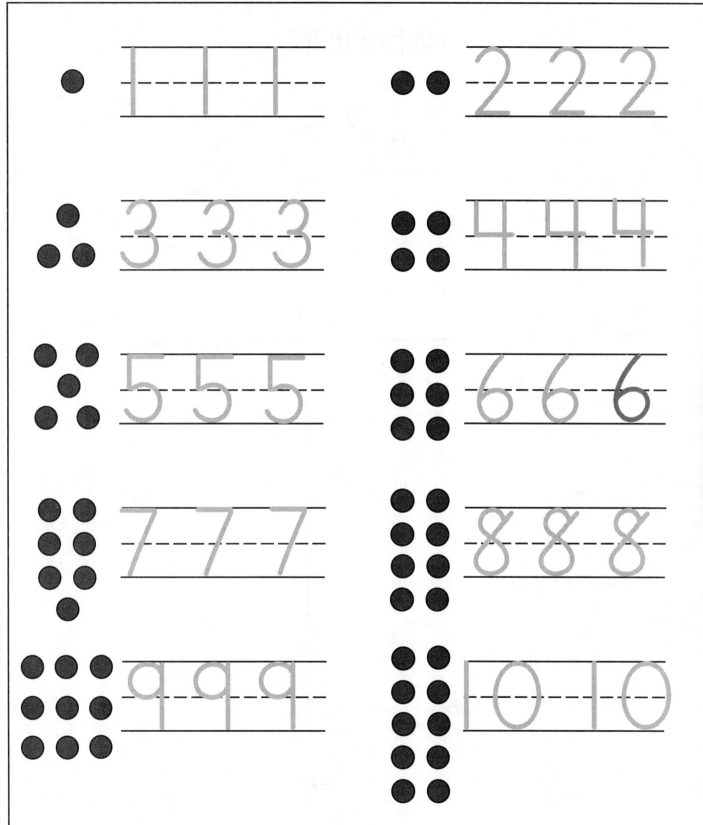

Parents: Explain to your child that he/she is to draw a line from the dot by each number in the correct order to find the picture hiding here.

What Is It?

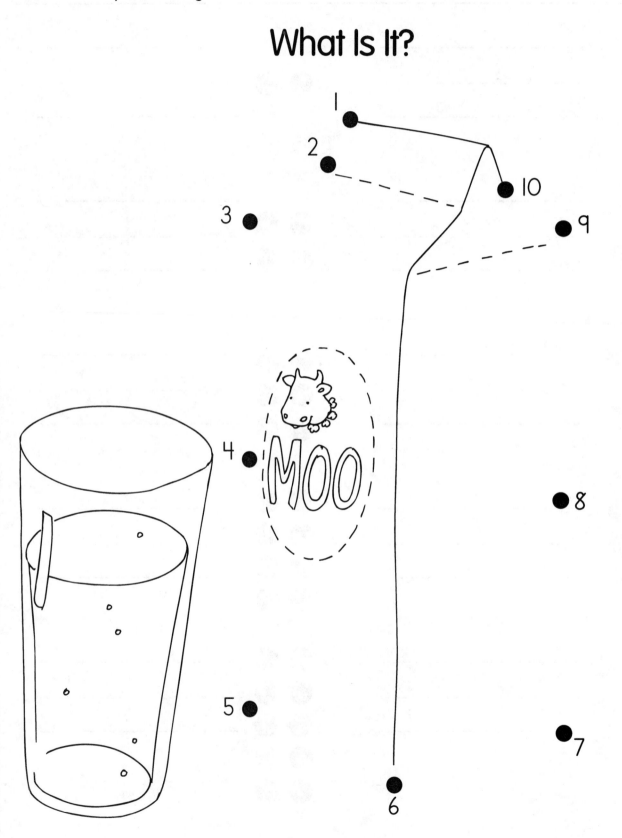

Understanding number order

How Many Can You Find?

 rooms in your home   _____ rooms

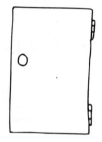 doors in your home   _____ doors

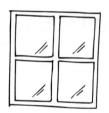 windows in your home   _____ windows

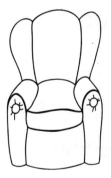 chairs in your home   _____ chairs

 light switches in your home_____ light switches

Math Around the House

How Many Can You Find?

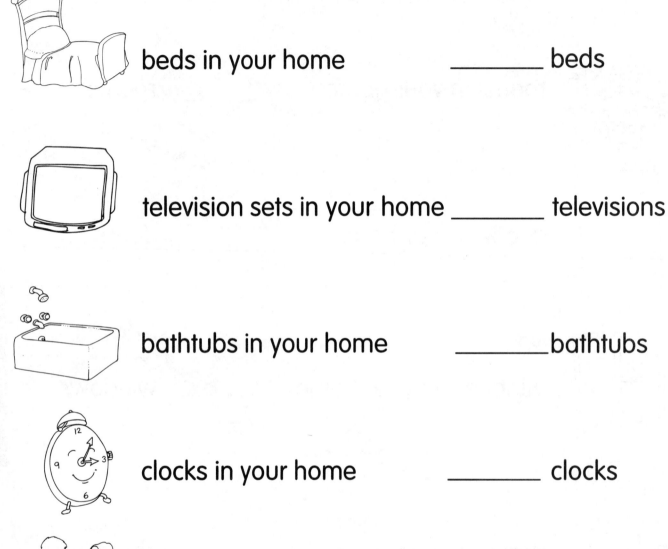

beds in your home   _____ beds

television sets in your home _____ televisions

bathtubs in your home   _____ bathtubs

clocks in your home   _____ clocks

people in your home   _____ people

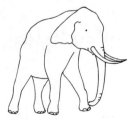

elephants in your home   _____ elephants

Let's Count in the Kitchen

Find 3 of something. Draw them here.

Find 5 of something. Draw them here.

Find 7 of something. Draw them here.

How Many Do You See?

Counting objects and writing the number

Parents: Help your child find something in the bedroom for each of the numbers listed below. Have him/her draw what is found.

Let's Count in the Bedroom

Find 1 of something. Draw it here.

Find 8 of something. Draw them here.

Find a **pair** of something. Draw it here.

How Many Do You See?

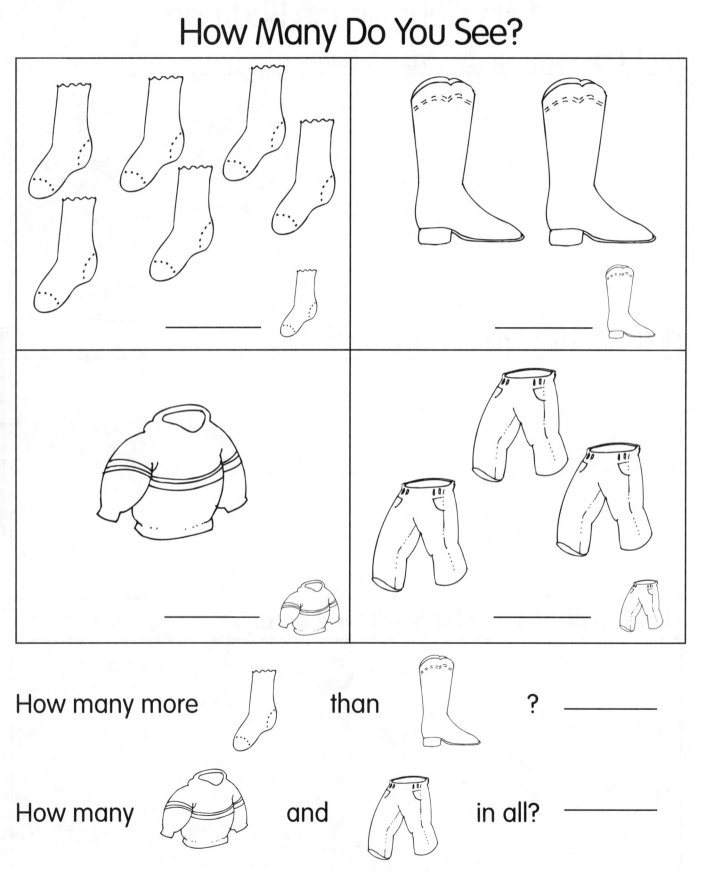

How many more [sock] than [boot] ? _____

How many [sweater] and [pants] in all? _____

Counting objects and writing the number

Parent: Talk to your child about things that come in pairs (shoes, socks, gloves, etc.). Put all of his/her shoes in a pile and ask your child to put match them by pairs.

Find a Pair

Match.

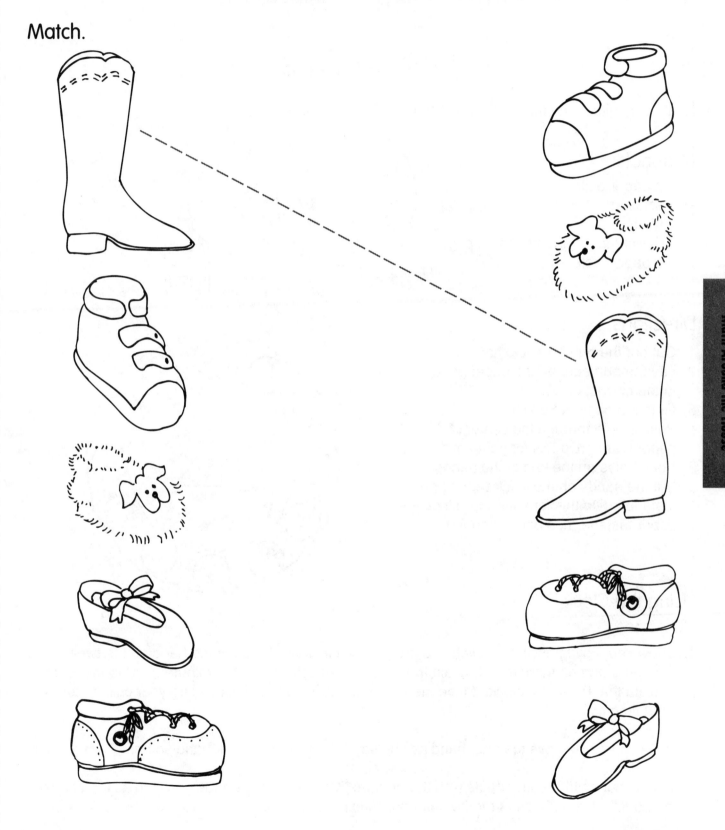

Math Around the House

Parents: Take a walk around the house with your child looking for all the places you find things that tell the time. Point out places your child overlooks such as the oven or VCR. Help your child understand why we need to know how to tell time (to leave for school, to know when a favorite television show is on, at bedtime, etc.) Every once in a while, have your child look at a clock and see if he/she can tell the time (stick with just the hour in the beginning.)

Telling Time

Help your child make this clock to use to practice telling time.

Materials

- a paper plate
- scissors
- glue
- the numbers and hands on page 81
- a paper fastener

Directions

1. Cut out the numbers and hands.
2. Lay the numbers on the paper plate in the correct order.
3. Glue the numbers down.
4. Poke a hole through the center of the paper plate. (Do this for your child.)
5. Poke holes on the end of the hands.
6. Put the hands on the clock with a paper fastener. (Do this for your child since the paper fastener has pointed ends.)

Using the Clock

1. Show your child how the hands move around the clock. Put the minute hand on the twelve and the hour hand on the three. Explain that this is 3 o'clock. Move the minute hand to the four. Explain that this is 4 o'clock. Move the hour hand around the clock asking your child to tell you what time it is.

2. Have your child move the hour hand as you say "Show me 2 o'clock." and so on.

3. When your child is comfortable with the hour, explain where the hands go when it is "half past the hour." Use both terms for the half hour (half past 6, 6:30.)

Making a teaching clock

Making a teaching clock

Parents: Your child will need small objects such as cereal, dried beans, macaroni, etc. to count. Have your child put ten objects in each box, then go back to the first box and count all the way to 100. Some children need to touch each object while saying the number.

Can You Count to 100?

100

83

Parents: You can see how much your child knows about money by taking change out of your pocket and asking your child to name each kind of coin and to tell you how much it is worth. Gradually help your child count small groups of money.

How Much Is It?

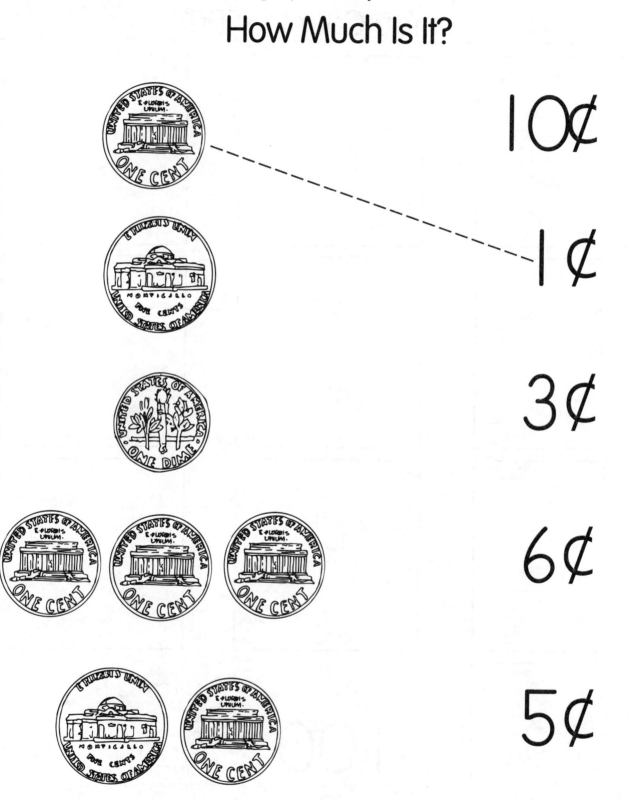

10¢

1¢

3¢

6¢

5¢

Understanding coin amounts

How Much Is in the Bank?

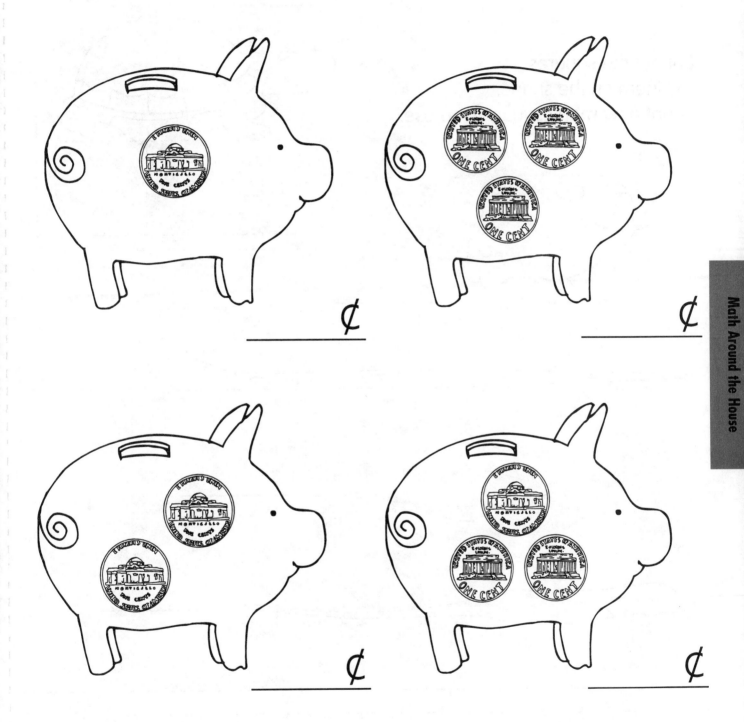

Understanding coin amounts

85

How Long Is It?

Cut out the squares.
Lay them on the shape.
Count how many squares you use.

_____

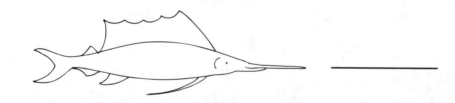

_____

_____

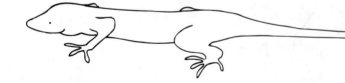

_____

　　　　Counting to measure

Parents: A good way to help your child learn about measurement in the kitchen is to have him/her help with simple cooking tasks. Name the measuring tools you are using and let your child fill and dump the ingredients into a bowl for you. Provide the items necessary for your child to do these simple "cooking" jobs. Help him/her follow these simple recipes requiring measurement.

Let's Cook

Instant Pudding

You Need:
- measuring spoons
- measuring cup
- jar with lid
- paper cup
- spoon
- 4 level teaspoons (60 ml) pudding mix
- 1/2 cup (125 ml) milk

Steps:

1. Put the pudding mix and milk in the jar.

2. Put the lid on the jar. Shake the jar as you count ot 50.

3. Pour the pudding into the paper cup. Let it sit for one minute.

4. Eat your pudding

5. Clean up your work area.

Peanut Butter and Jelly Sandwich

You Need:
- plastic knife
- measuring spoon
- 1 slice of bread
- 2 level tablespoons (30 ml) peanut butter
- 2 teaspoons (10 ml) jelly

Steps:

1. Spread peanut butter on the bread.

2. Spread jelly on the bread.

3. Cut the bread in half like this. What shape did you make?

4. Eat your sandwich.

5. Clean up your work area.

Parents: You can increase your child's ability to observe and describe size and other differences by doing the same activity shown below using items you collect from around the house. Lay out two or three items at a time and ask the same questions as the ones used below.

Which One Is It?

Look at the dogs.
Circle the one that is bigger.
X the one that is smaller.

Look at the flowers.
Circle the one that is the tallest.
X the one that is the shortest.

Look at the pictures.
Circle the one that is heavier.
X the one that is lighter.

Look at the glasses.
Circle the one that is full.
X the one that is almost empty.

Understanding sizes

Parents: Show your child something big and then something small. Explain that he/she is to put an X on the big things on this page and circle around the small things.

Is It Big or Small?

X - big
O - small

Understanding big and small

Parents: Show your child two different sized spoons. Have him/her tell you which one is longer and which one is shorter. Explain that he/she is to put an X on the longer thing in each set and circle around the shorter thing.

Is It Long or Short?

X - long
O - short

Understanding long and short

Parents: You can have your child practice the skill of one-on-one correspondence by having him/ her do something as simple as get forks from the drawer and put one by each plate at the dinner table. Have your child cut out the cookies and paste one to each on the plates on this page, then circle "yes" or "no" to answer the question.

Cookies for Everyone?

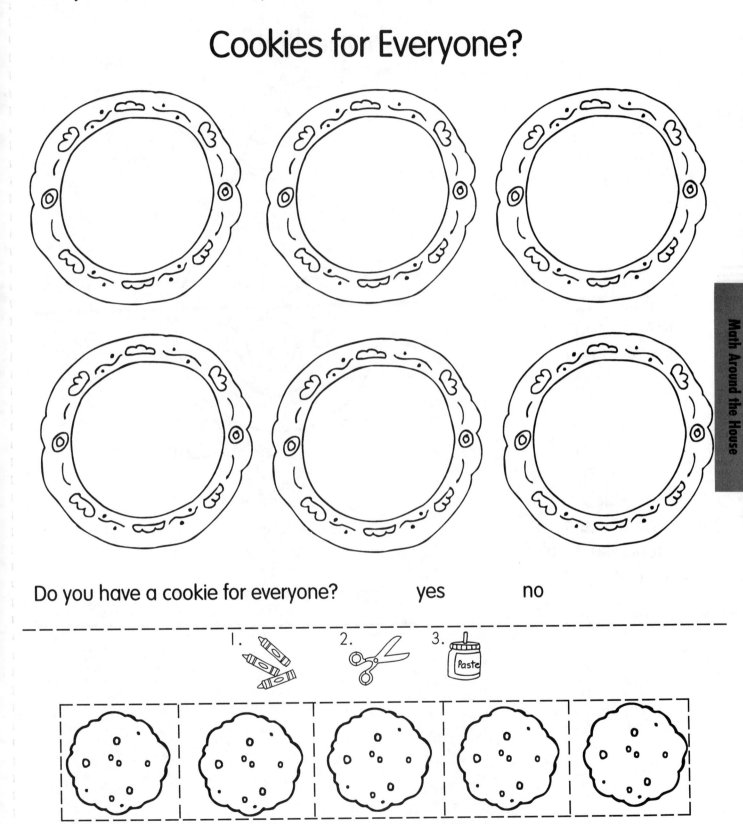

Do you have a cookie for everyone?   yes   no

1.   2.   3.

Parents: Talk with your child about these basic shapes: circle, square, triangle. Point out the number of sides and corners each has. Help him/her find things around the house that are these shapes. Then read the shape riddles below and have your child find and color the answers.

Which Shape Is It?

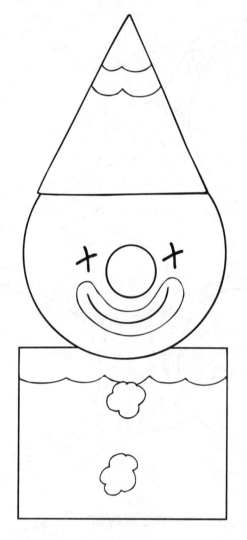

It has four sides.
It has four corners.
Color it green.

It has three sides.
It has three corners.
Color it orange.

It has no sides.
It has no corners.
It is round like a ball.
Color it red.

Parents: Have your child cut apart these cards for practicing the numbers from 1 to 12. Start by putting out a set of small objects starting with one. Ask "How many do you see?" "Can you find the number for this many?" Repeat with all the numbers.

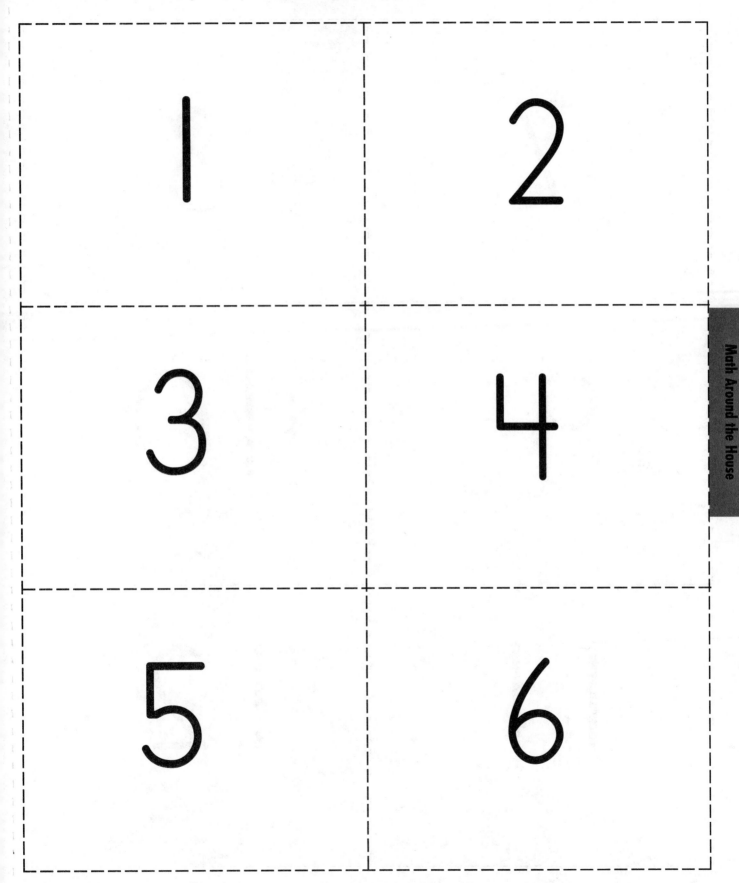

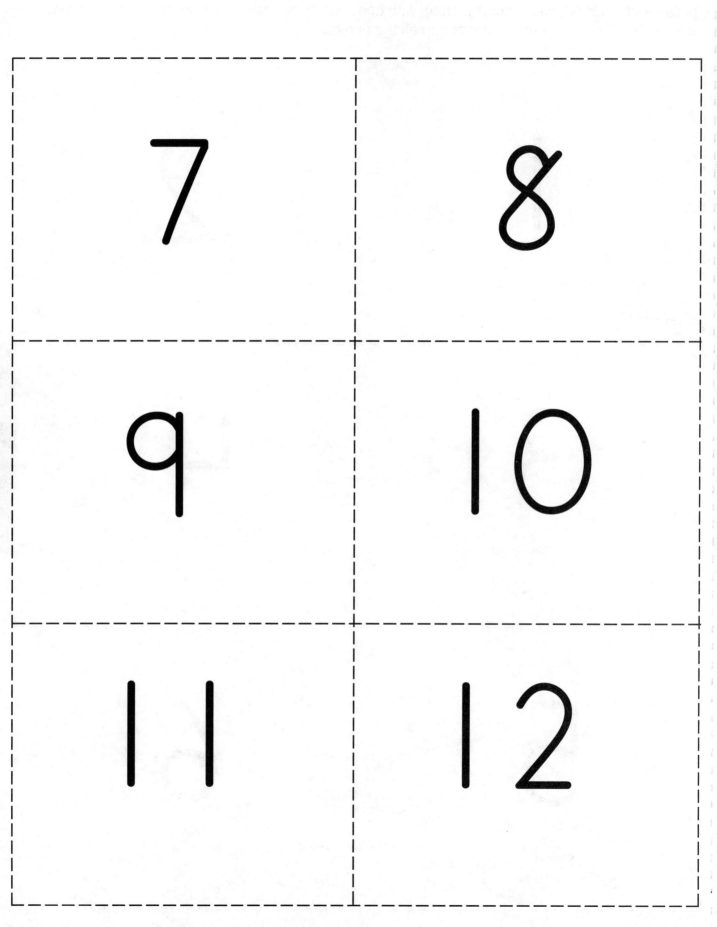

Recognizing numbers 1-12

Parents: You can help your child begin to understand what addition and subtraction are by playing "Feed My Dog" using the dog dish and bones on page 96. (Or use real dog bones and a bowl for extra fun.) Give the directions and ask the questions. Your child will count and answer the questions. Use numbers equaling no more than nine.

 # Feed My Dog.

Say "Put three bones in the dog dish."

(Your child will place three of the dog bones in the dog dish.)

Say "A hungry puppy ate one of the bones.

(Your child will remove one bone.)

Say "How many bones are left in the dog dish?"

(Your child counts all of the bones and answers.)

Say "Now put five more bones in the dog dish."

(Your child will put in five more bones.)

Say "How many bones does that make in all?"

(Your child counts all of the bones and answers.)

Continue the game for several minutes asking more questions, but using different numbers. You can make the game more challenging by moving on to questions such as "I have four bones. I want to give them to two dogs. How many bones will each dog get?"

Feed My Dog

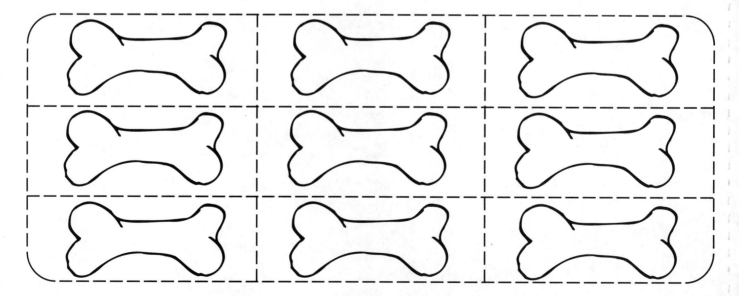

Beginning to understand addition and subtraction

Answer Key

Please take time to go over the work your child has completed. Ask your child to explain what he/she has done. Praise both success and effort. If mistakes have been made, explain what the answer should have been and how to find it. Let your child know that mistakes are a part of learning. The time you spend with your child helps let him/her know you feel learning is important.

page 67

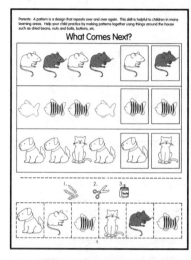

page 68

page 69

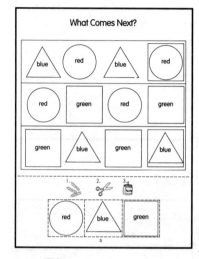

page 72

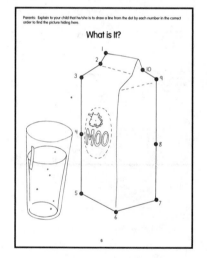

page 76

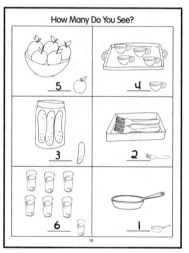

page 78

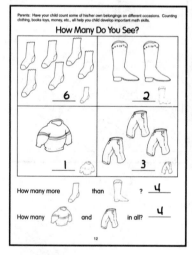

page 79

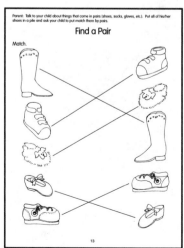

page 84

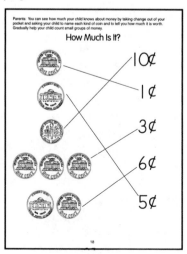

page 85

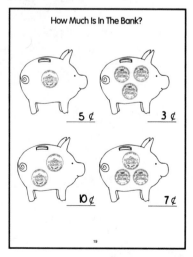

page 86

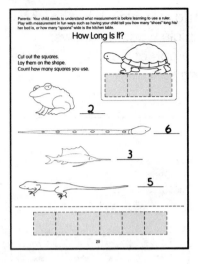

page 88

page 89

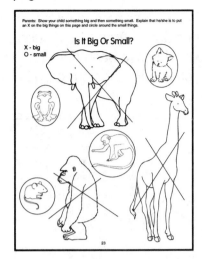

page 90

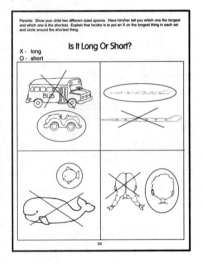

page 91

page 92

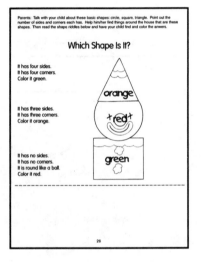

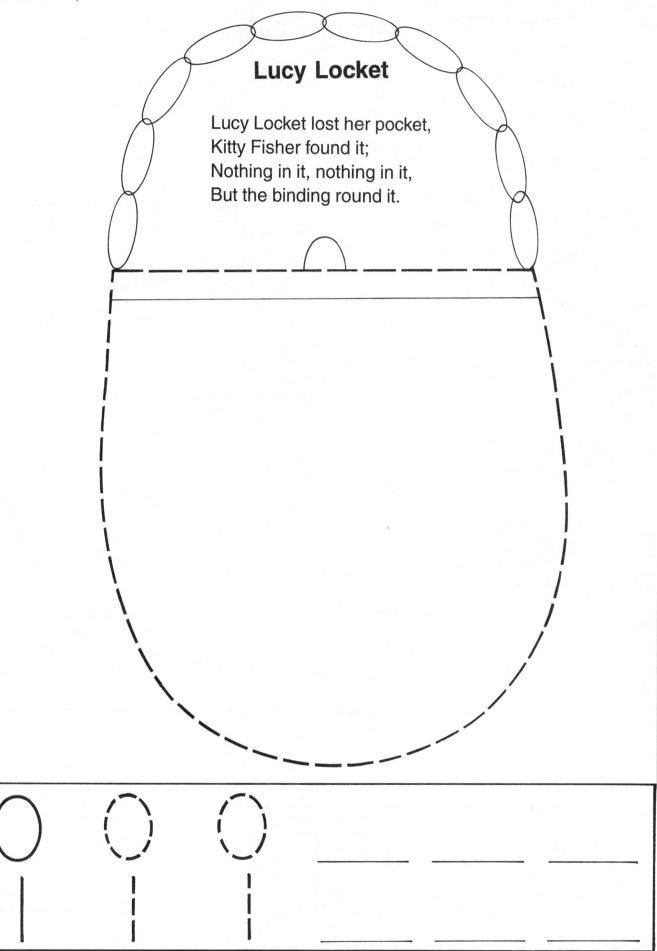

Lucy Locket

Lucy Locket lost her pocket,
Kitty Fisher found it;
Nothing in it, nothing in it,
But the binding round it.

Beginning Counting with Mother Goose

Hot Cross Buns!

Hot cross buns!
Hot cross buns!
1 a penny, **2** a penny,
Hot cross buns!

If you have no daughters,
Give them to your sons.

Tracing and writing numbers

Rub-a-Dub-Dub

Rub-a-dub-dub
Three men in a tub
And who do you think they be?
The butcher, the baker,
    the candlestick maker
And they all set out to sea.

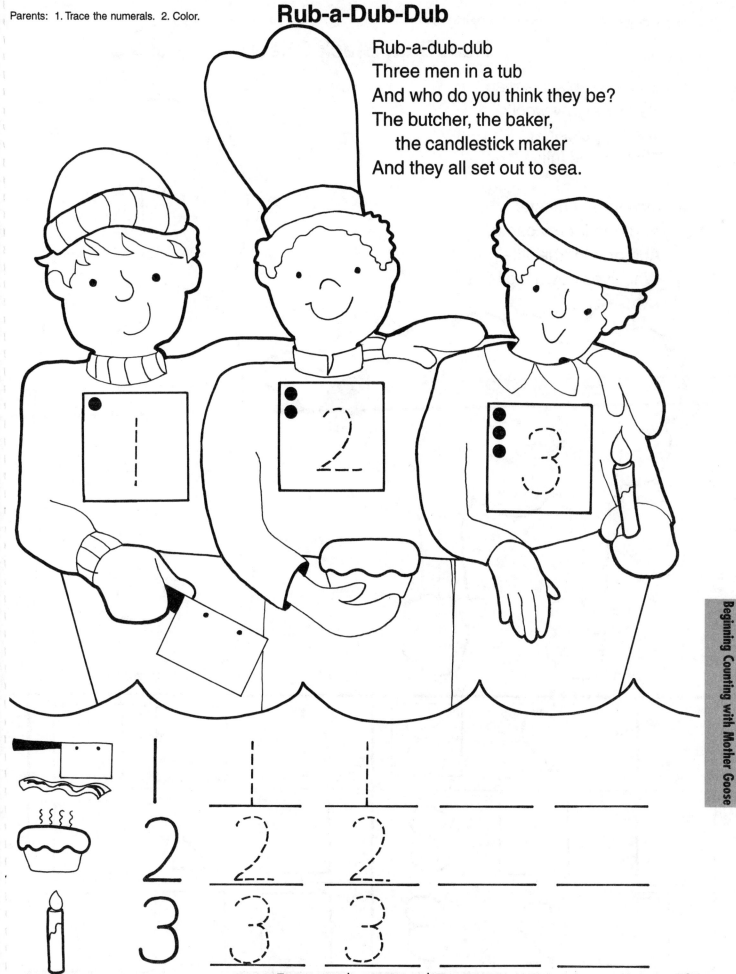

Tracing and writing numbers

101

Baa, Baa, Black Sheep

Baa, baa, black sheep,
Have you any wool?
Yes sir, yes sir,
Three bags full;

One for my master,
And one for my dame,
And one for the little boy
Who lives down the lane.

1	2	3	1	☐	☐
1	☐	3	☐	2	☐
☐	2	3	☐	☐	3

Understanding number order

Parents: Color and find Mother Goose.

Mother Goose

0 - red   2 - green

1 - orange   3 - blue

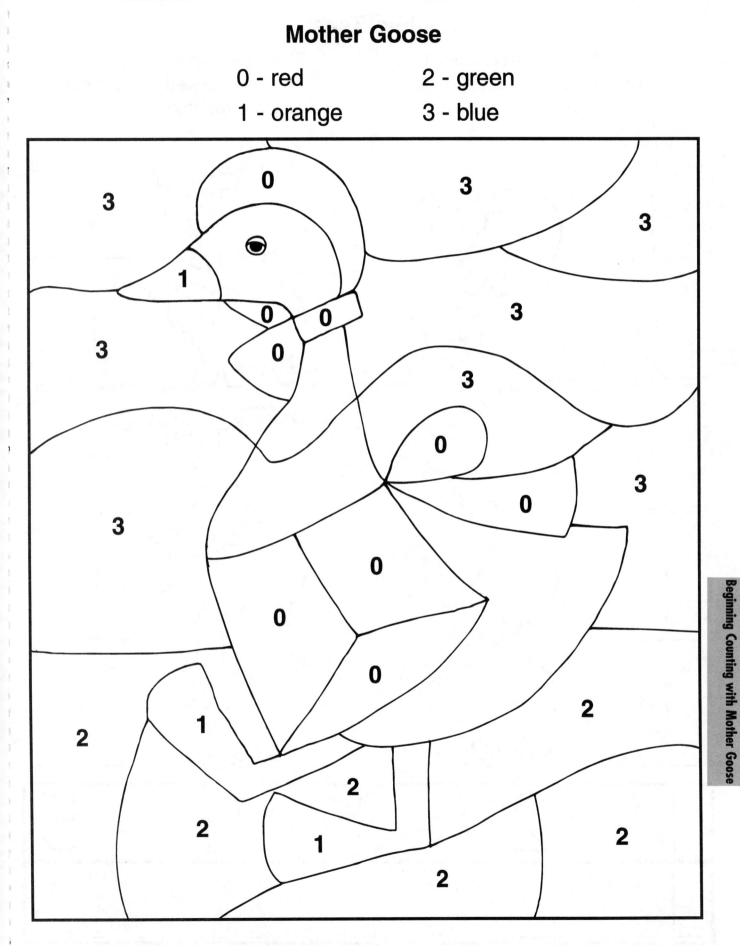

Five Toes

This little pig went to market;
This little pig stayed at home;
This little pig had roast beef;

This little pig had none;
This little pig said, "Wee, wee!"
All the way home.

1

2

3

4

5

5

4

3

2

1

1   2   3   4   5

1

Parents: 1.Trace the trees and color them green. 2. Do the dot-to-dot and find the sheep for Bo-Peep.

Little Bo-Peep

Little Bo-Peep has lost her sheep,
And can't tell where to find them;
Leave them alone, and they'll come home,
Wagging their tails behind them.

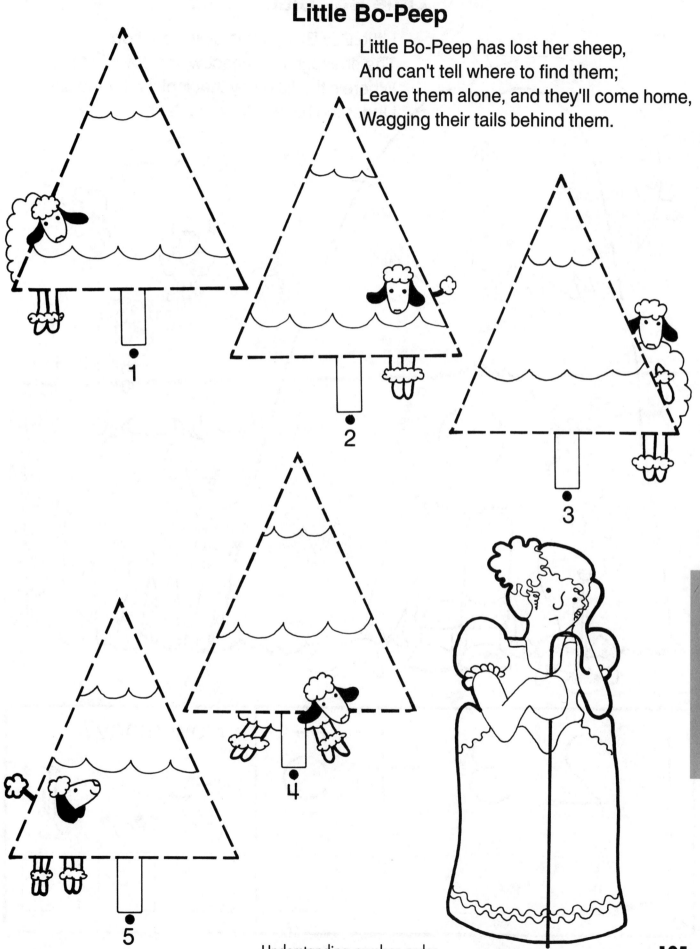

1

2

3

4

5

Understanding number order

Little Boy Blue

Little Boy Blue, come blow your horn!
The sheep in the meadow, the cows in the corn.
Where's the little boy that looks after the sheep?
Under the haystack, fast asleep!

1 2 3 4 5

How many?

Counting and writing the number

Wee Willie Winkie

Wee Willie Winkie runs through the town,
Upstairs and downstairs, in his nightgown.
Rapping at the window, crying through the lock,
"Are the children in their beds? Now it's eight o'clock."

Counting objects and matching with a number

107

The Little Girl with a Curl

There was a little girl who had a little curl
Right in the middle of her forehead;
When she was good, she was very, very good,
And when she was bad she was horrid.

Understanding number order

One to Eight

1,   2,   3,   4,
Mary at the cottage door.

5,   6,   7,   8,
Eating cherries off a plate.

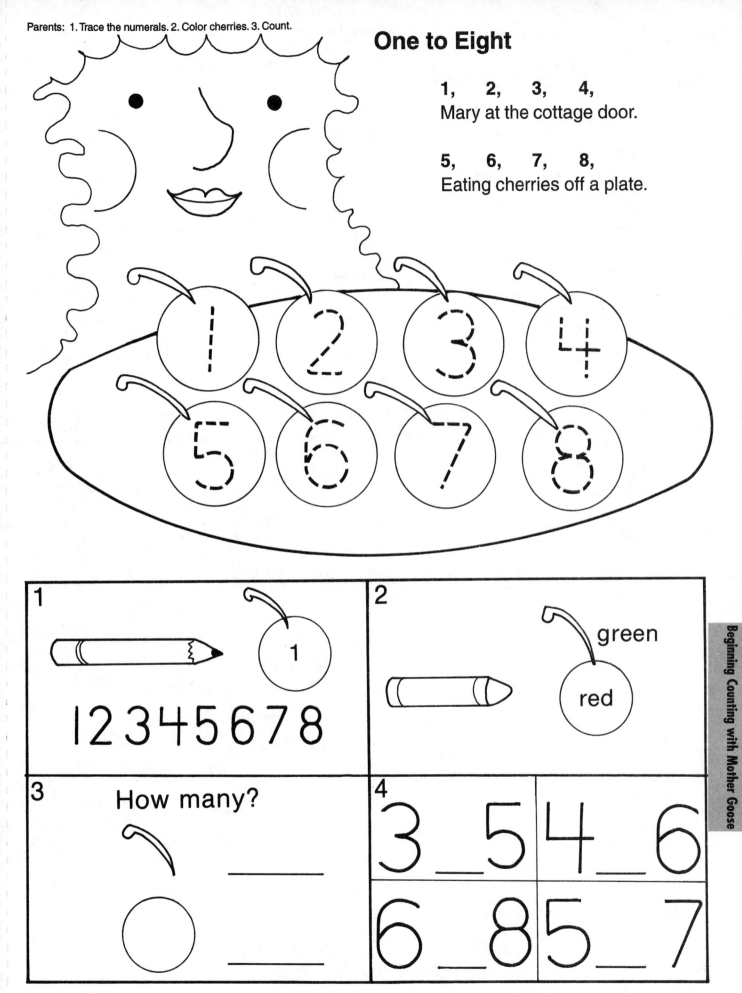

1

1 2 3 4 5 6 7 8

2

green

red

3 How many?

____

____

4

3 _ 5   4 _ 6

6 _   8 5 _ 7

Tracing and writing numbers

109

Mary, Mary, Quite Contrary

Mary, Mary, quite contrary,
How does your garden grow?
Silver bells and cockle-shells,
And pretty maids all in a row.

1 2 3 4 5 6 7 8 9

Circle the ones you found.

1 2 3 4 5 6 7 8 9

Tracing numbers and recognizing hidden numbers

Pease Porridge

Pease porridge hot,
Pease porridge cold,
Pease porridge in the pot,
Nine days old.

Some like it hot,
Some like it cold,
Some like it in the pot,
Nine days old.

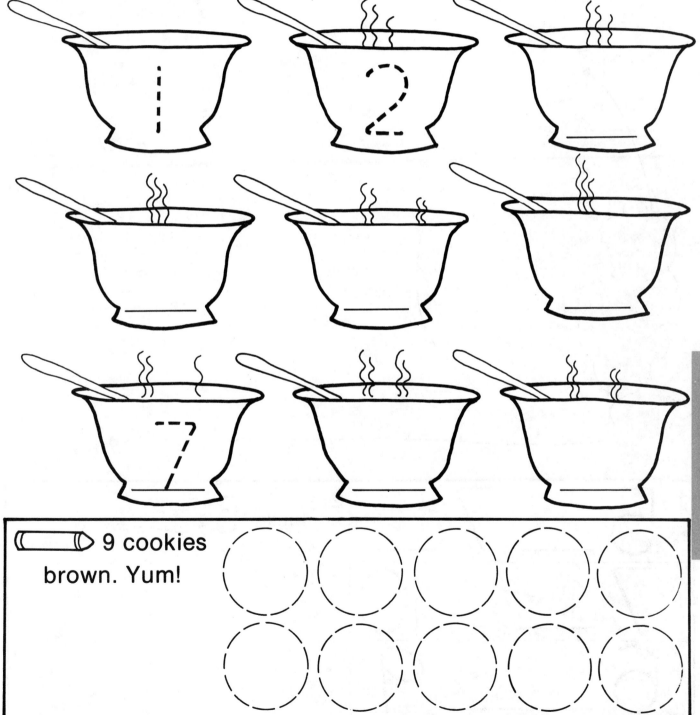

9 cookies brown. Yum!

Beginning Counting with Mother Goose

Writing numbers in order

One To Ten

1,   2,   3,   4,   5,
I caught a hare alive;

6,   7,   8,   9,   10,
Then I let her go again.

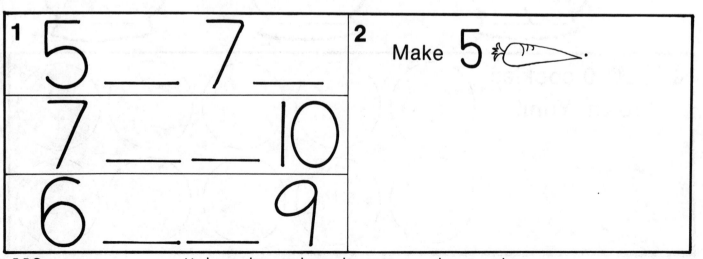

1

5 __ 7 __

7 __ __ 10

6 __ __ 9

2

Make 5

112   Understanding number order; writing numbers in order

The Little Bird

Once I saw a little bird
Come hop hop, hop;
So I cried, "Little bird,
Will you stop, stop, stop?"

I was going to the window
To say, "How do you do?"
But he shook his little tail,
And far away he flew.

1

5

7

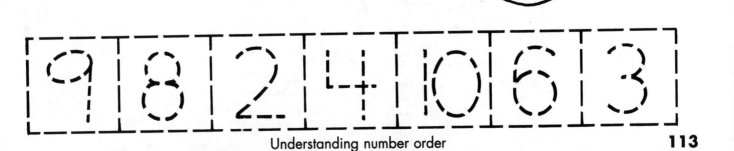

Beginning Counting with Mother Goose

The Mouse and The Clock

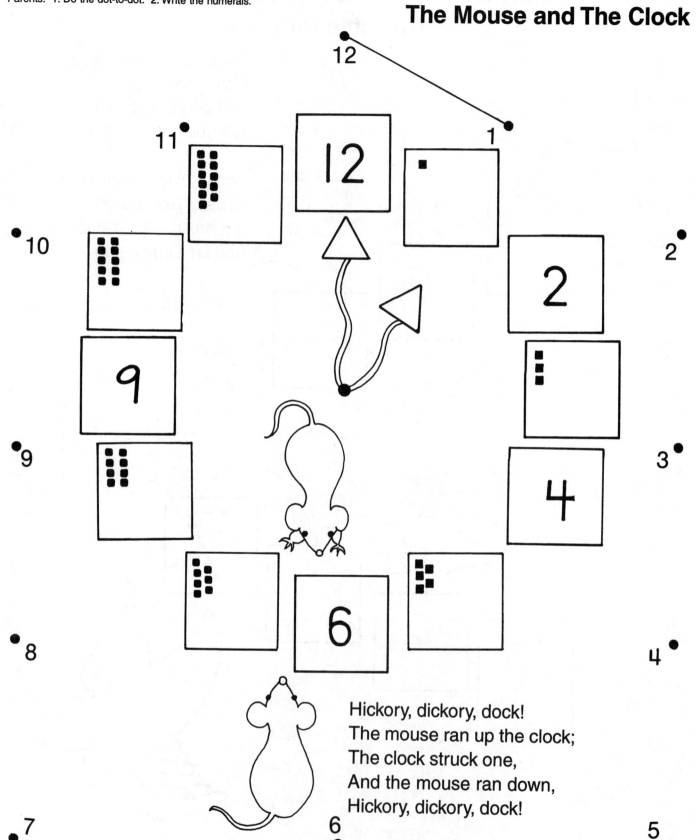

Hickory, dickory, dock!
The mouse ran up the clock;
The clock struck one,
And the mouse ran down,
Hickory, dickory, dock!

Writing numbers in order

The Pumpkin-Eater

Peter, Peter, pumpkin-eater,
Had a wife and couldn't keep her;
He put her in a pumpkin shell,
And there he kept her very well.

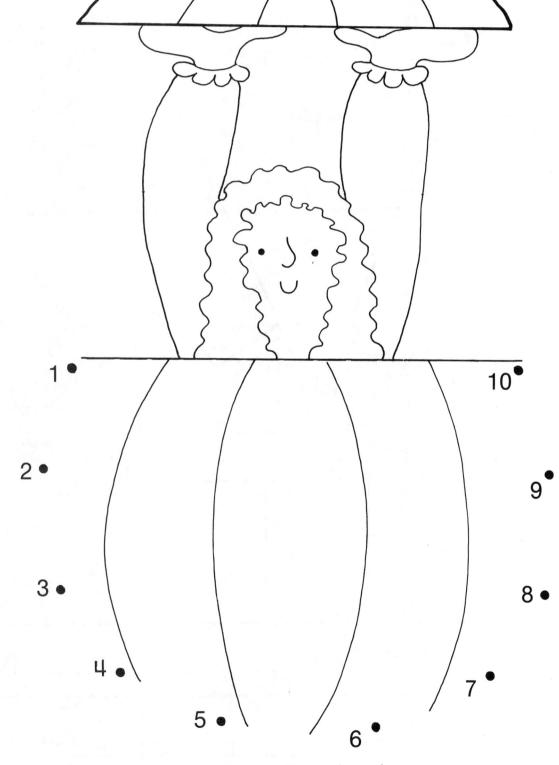

1 •

10 •

2 •

9 •

3 •

8 •

4 •

7 •

5 •

6 •

Understanding number order

Beginning Counting with Mother Goose

Rain

Rain, rain, go away,
Come again another day;
Little Johnny wants to play.

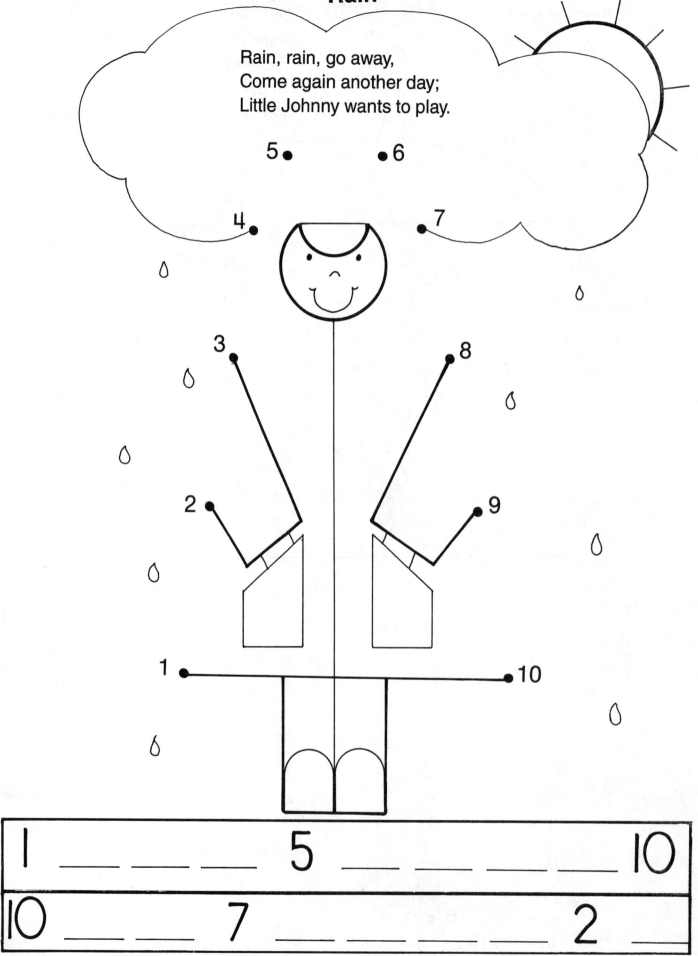

Understanding number order; writing numbers in order

Banbury Cross

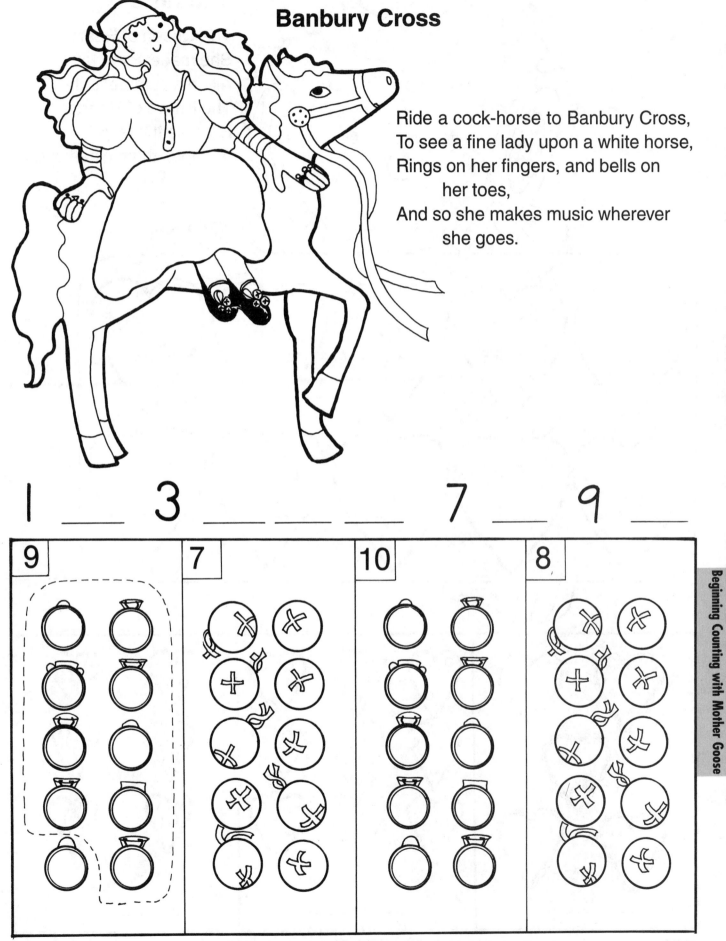

Ride a cock-horse to Banbury Cross,
To see a fine lady upon a white horse,
Rings on her fingers, and bells on
her toes,
And so she makes music wherever
she goes.

1 __ 3 __ __ __ 7 __ 9 __

| 9 | 7 | 10 | 8 |

Writing numbers in order; counting objects to match a number

The Tarts

The Queen of Hearts,
She made some tarts,
All on a summer's day;
The Knave of Hearts,
He stole the tarts,
And took them clean away.

1 ___ 3 ___ ___

6 ___ ___ ___ ___

___ ___ ___

118   Writing numbers in order; counting objects and writing the number

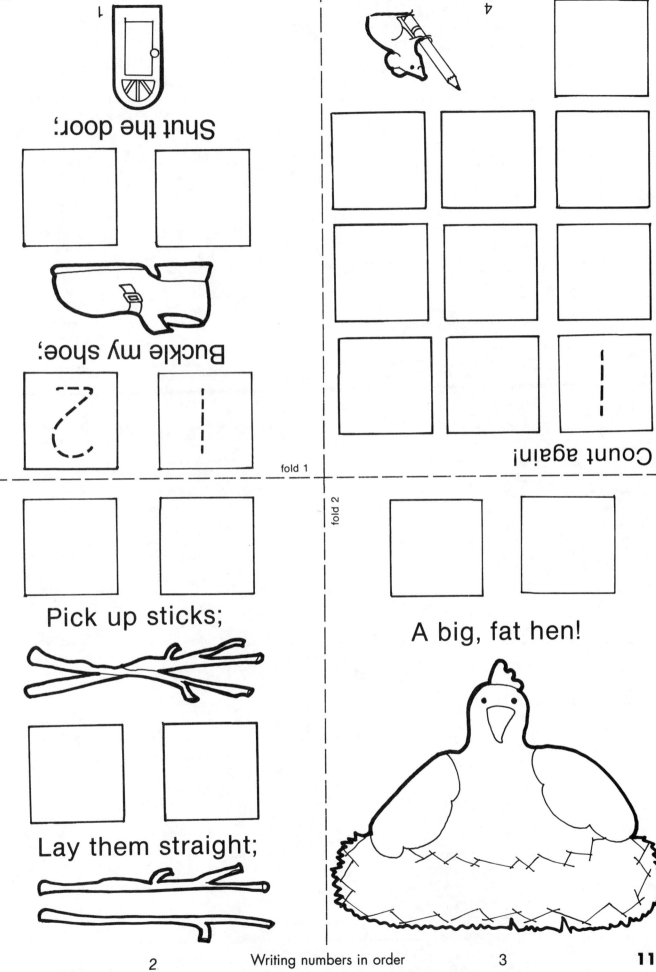

Shut the door;

Buckle my shoe;

fold 1

Count again!

fold 2

Pick up sticks;

Lay them straight;

A big, fat hen!

Beginning Counting with Mother Goose

The Black Hen

Hickety, pickety, my black hen,
She lays eggs for gentlemen;
Gentlemen come every day
To see what my black hen doth lay.

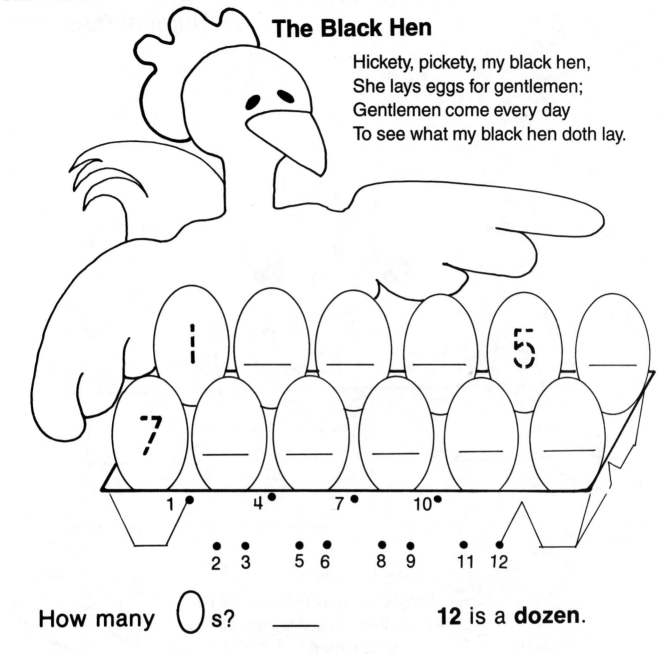

How many ◯s? ___

12 is a **dozen**.

6 __ __ 9	8 __ __ __
__ 10 __ 12	__ __ 6 __
5 __ 7 __	__ 8 __ __

Writing numbers in order

Parents: 1. Do the dot-to-dot. 2. Fill in the missing numerals.

Humpty Dumpty

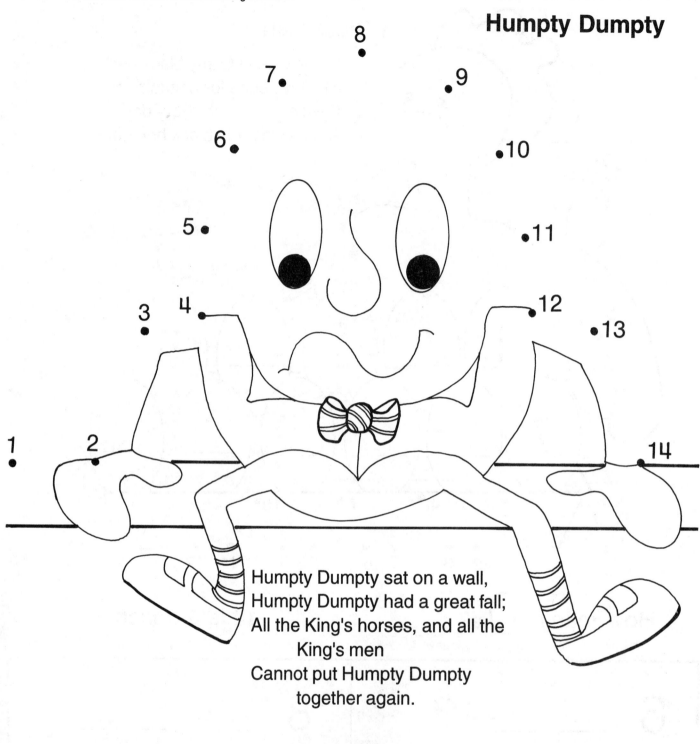

Humpty Dumpty sat on a wall,
Humpty Dumpty had a great fall;
All the King's horses, and all the
King's men
Cannot put Humpty Dumpty
together again.

1				5		
8						13

122   Writing numbers in order

Parents: 1. Do the dot-to-dot 2. Fill in the missing numerals.

The Cat and The Fiddle

15

14

13

12

11

10

9

8

3

2

1

4

5

6

7

Hey, diddle, diddle
The cat and the fiddle,
The cow jumped over the moon;
The little dog laughed
To see such sport,
And the dish ran away with the
    spoon.

11 ___ 13	9 ___ 11	13 ___ 15

Writing numbers in order

123

Jack

Jack be nimble,
Jack be quick,
Jack jump over
the candlestick.

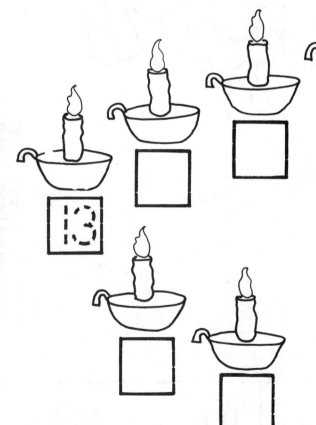

1

3

7

9

13

Writing numbers in order

Miss Muffet

Little Miss Muffet
Sat on a tuffet,
Eating her curds and whey;

There came a big spider,
And sat down beside her,
And frightened Miss Muffet away.

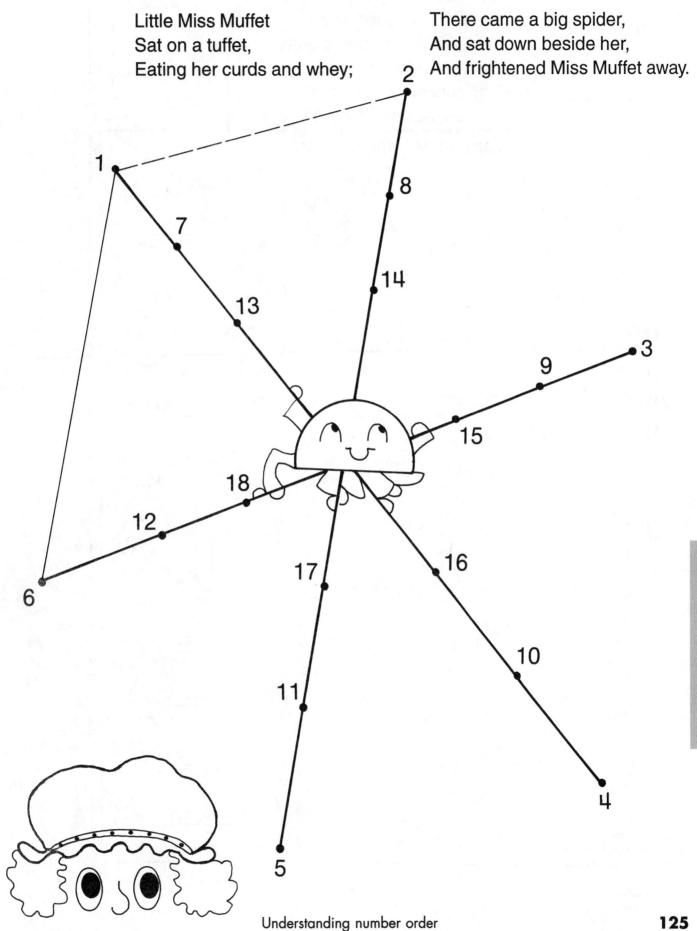

Understanding number order

125

Parents: 1. Fill in the missing numerals. 2. Color.

Old Mother Hubbard
Went to the cupboard,
To give her poor dog a bone
But when she got there
The cupboard was bare,
And so the poor dog had none.

Fill up the cupboard for Mother Hubbard.

Writing numbers in order

The Flying Pig

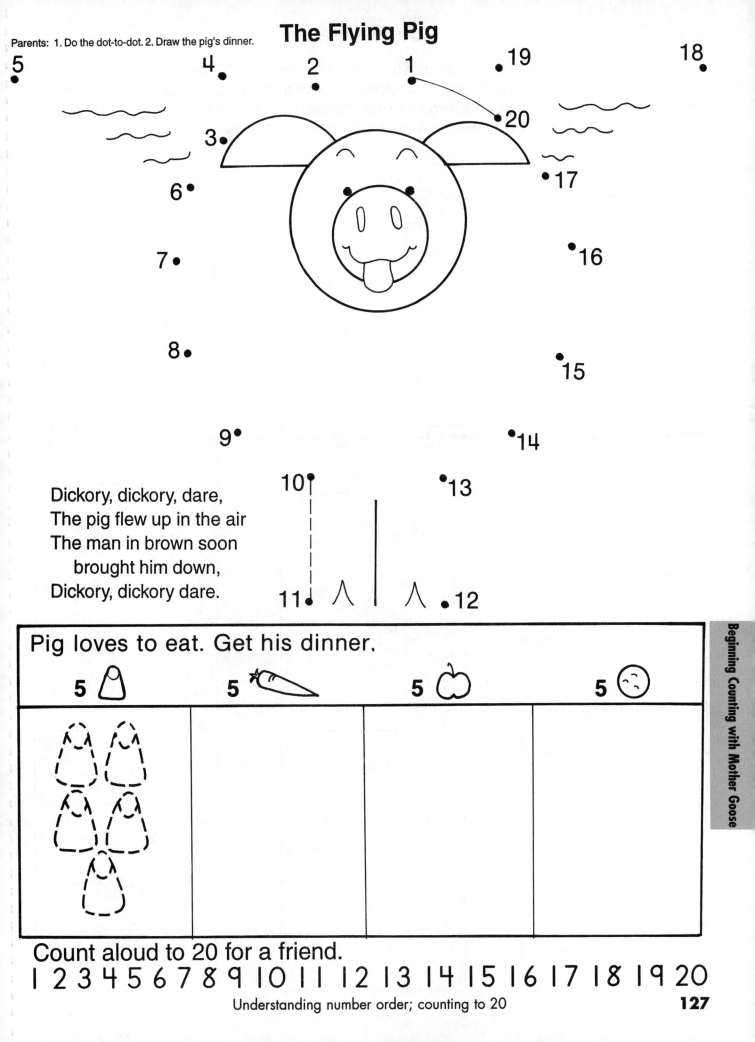

5 4 2 1 19 18

3

6

7

8

9

10   13

Dickory, dickory, dare,
The pig flew up in the air
The man in brown soon
    brought him down,
Dickory, dickory dare.

11   12

20

17

16

15

14

Pig loves to eat. Get his dinner.

5 △	5 🥕	5 🍎	5 ☺

Count aloud to 20 for a friend.
1 2 3 4 5 6 7 8 9 10 11 12 13 14 15 16 17 18 19 20

Understanding number order; counting to 20

127

Beginning Counting with Mother Goose

Answer Key

Please take time to go over the work your child has completed. Ask your child to explain what he/she has done. Praise both success and effort. If mistakes have been made, explain what the answer should have been and how to find it. Let your child know that mistakes are a part of learning. The time you spend with your child helps let him/her know you feel learning is important.

page 99

page 100

page 101

page 102

page 103

page 104

page 105

page 106

page 107

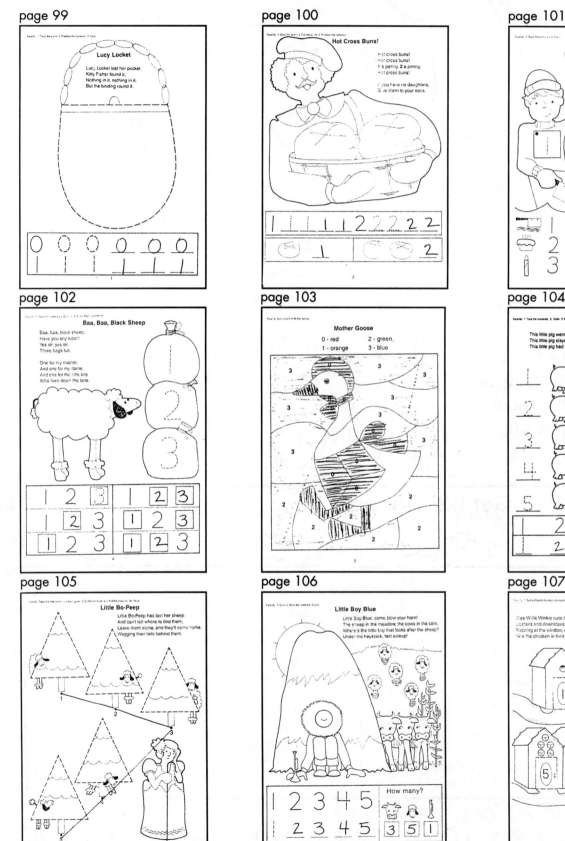

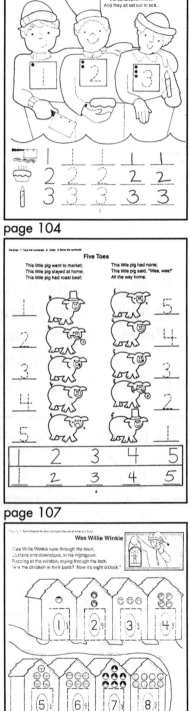

page 108

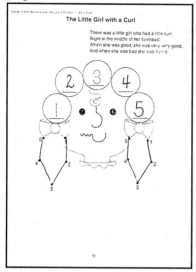

page 109

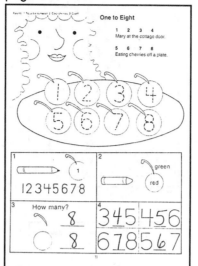

page 110

page 111

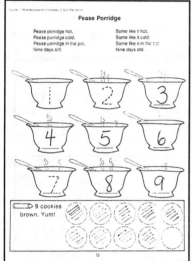

page 112

page 113

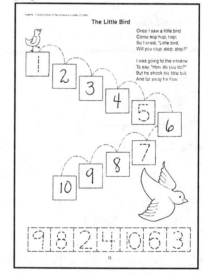

page 114

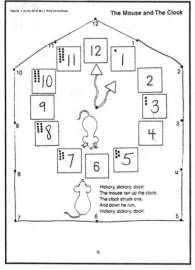

page 115

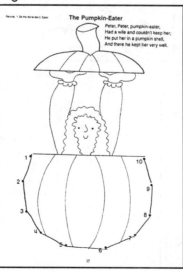

page 116

Answers

page 117

page 118

page 119

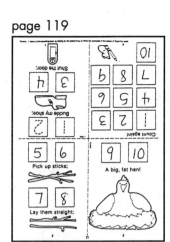

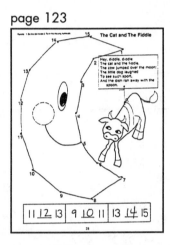

page 121

page 122

page 123

page 124

page 125

page 126

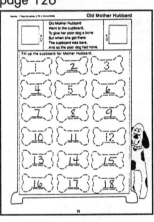

page 127

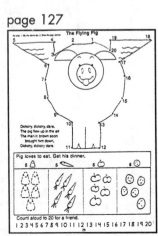

Motor Skills Checklist

Parents: Don't have your child begin cutting or writing tasks before he/she is ready. This will only frustrate your child. Encourage big muscle activities such as painting with large brushes and scribbling with fat crayons and pencils first. Remember, children develop at different rates. Be patient with your child. These skills will all come in time.

Checking Large Motor Skills:
Most of these motions should be done outdoors. You can observe your child at play and check off the ones he/she does successfully, or take your child aside and ask him/her to show you the movement.

- [ ] run
- [ ] skip
- [ ] hop on one foot
- [ ] jump on two feet
- [ ] walk along a line (drawn in the dirt)
- [ ] catch a thrown object (beanbag, soft ball, or small pillow)
- [ ] throw an object toward a specific spot (beanbag or soft ball)
- [ ] stand on one foot for a few seconds

Checking Small Motor Skills:

- [ ] string beads (or macaroni) on a shoelace
- [ ] tie his/her own shoes
- [ ] button a jacket or sweater
- [ ] make a simple picture with:
      a crayon
      a pencil
- [ ] cut with scissors:
      straight line
      curved line

Parents: Place a strip of rope on the ground in the shapes shown in the picture below. Have your child move along the rope and hop back and forth over it.

Fun With a Rope

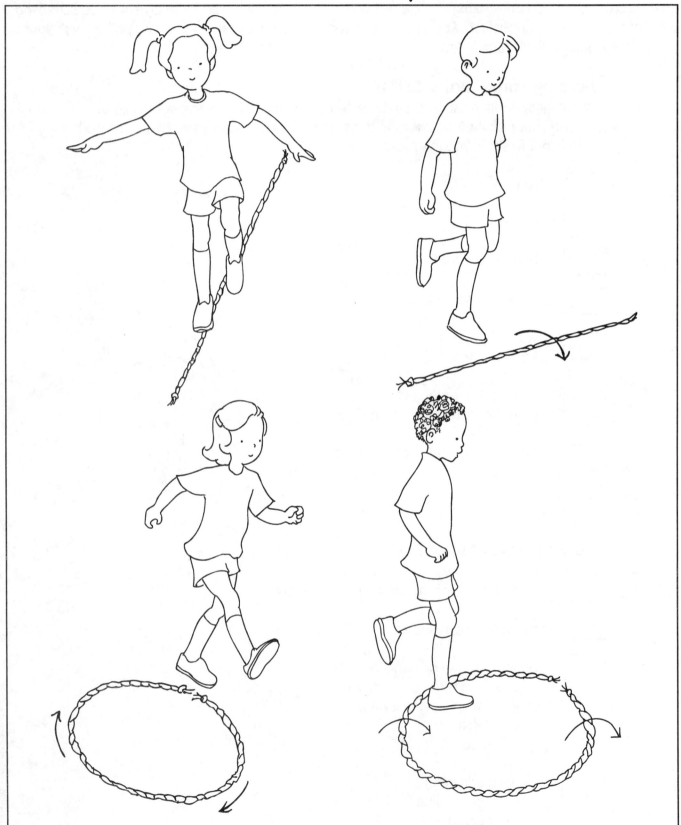

Practicing large motor skills

Be an Animal

Practicing large motor skills

Motor Skills

Parent: Have your child show you in pantomime how to use the objects shown below.

Act it Out

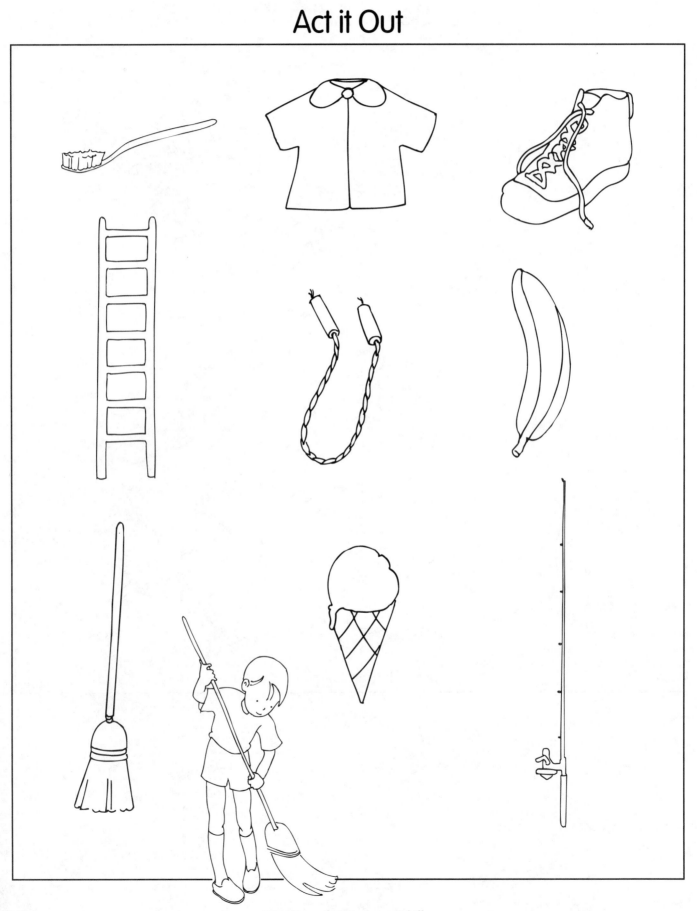

Practicing large motor skills

Parents: Provide a tray of sand or cornmeal for your child to use in this activity. He/She is to try to draw the shapes shown on this page in the sand. If he/she has trouble, you draw it and have your child trace it.

In the Sandbox

Draw:

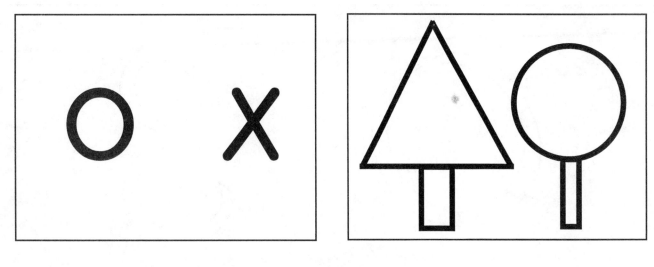

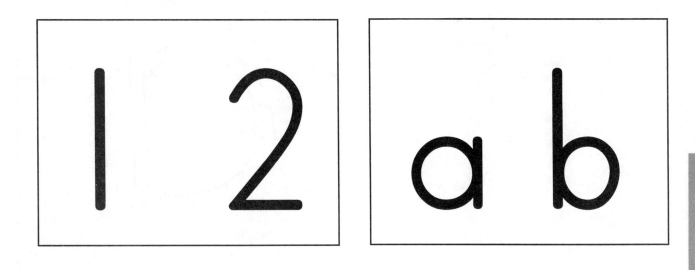

Motor Skills

Parents: Your child will need clay or Playdough to do this activity. He/She is to roll the clay in thin "snakes" and to lay the clay in the shapes shown on the page.

Fun with Clay

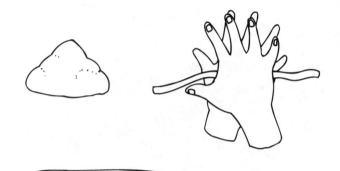

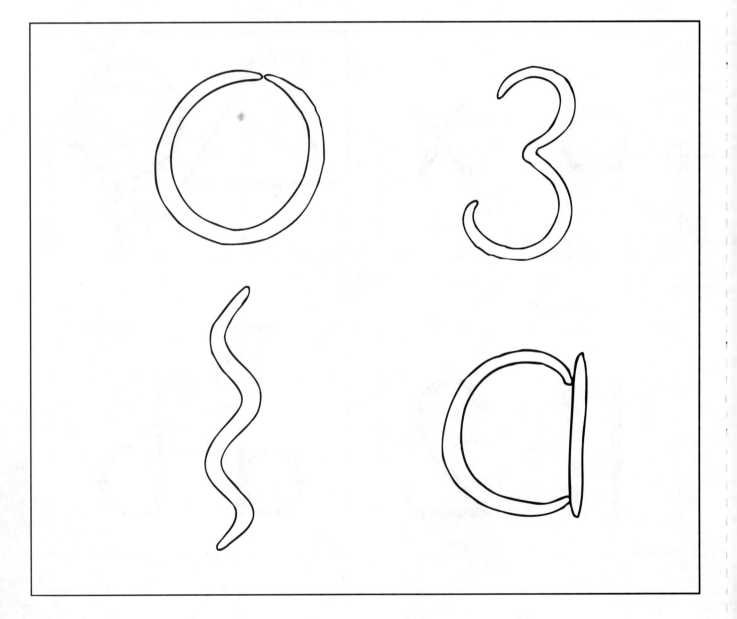

　　　　Practicing finger/hand skills

Parents: Your child will need a fat paintbrush, a bucket of water, and a wall or sidewalk on which to "paint" to do this activity. He/She is to paint the shapes and letters shown on this page using the water and brush.

Paint Water Pictures

Practicing finger/hand skills

Parents: Your child will need a sturdy shoe lace and a bowl with some cereal with holes to do this activity. You could also provide thread spools, rubber washers, macaroni, or buttons with large holes. Tie a large knot in one end of the lace before your child begins. Help him/her tie a large knot in the other end of the completed lace so the items will not fall off.

Lace It Up

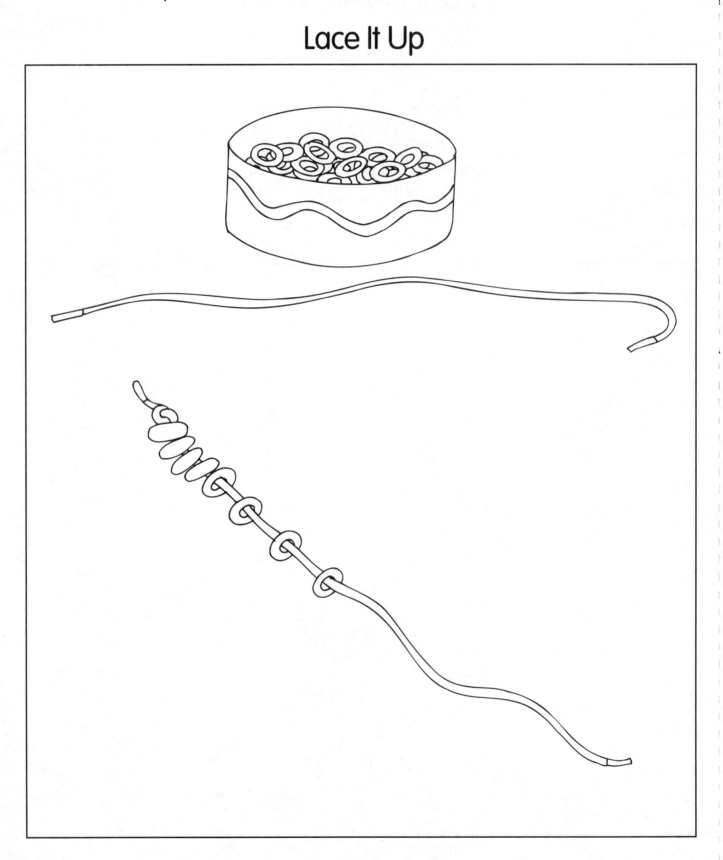

Practicing finger/hand skills

Parent: Have your child trace the path with his/her finger first, then with a crayon.

Here We Go

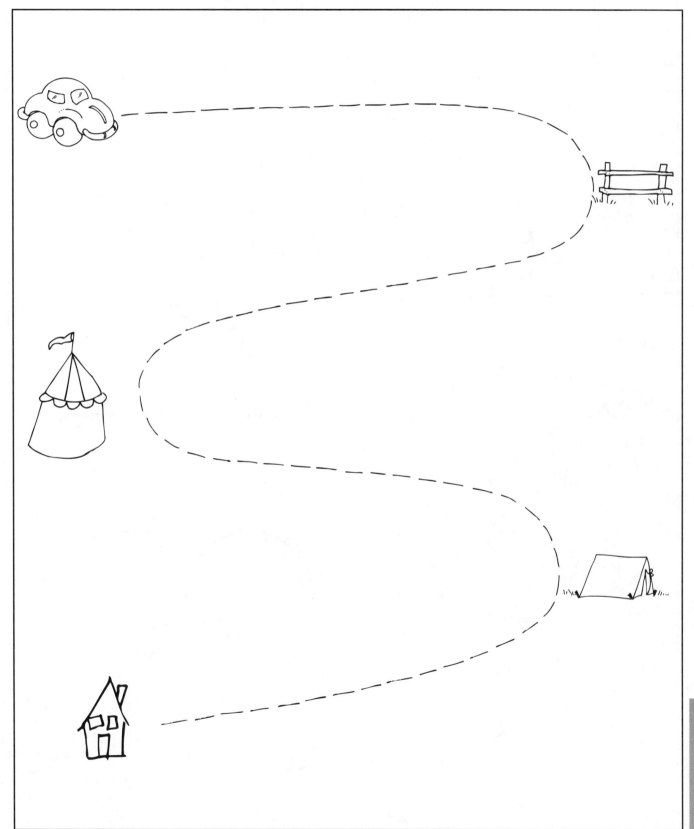

Motor Skills

Animal Trails

Parents: Have your child trace the path with his/her finger first, then with a crayon.

Creepy Crawlers

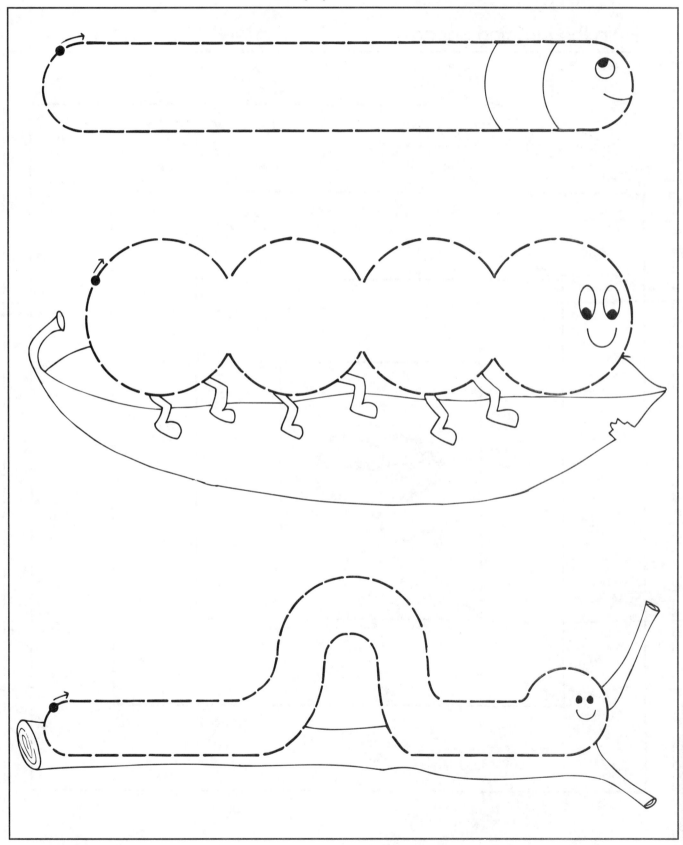

Motor Skills

Parents: Have your child trace the path with his/her finger first, then with a crayon.

The Bird's Nest

Help the bird find her nest.

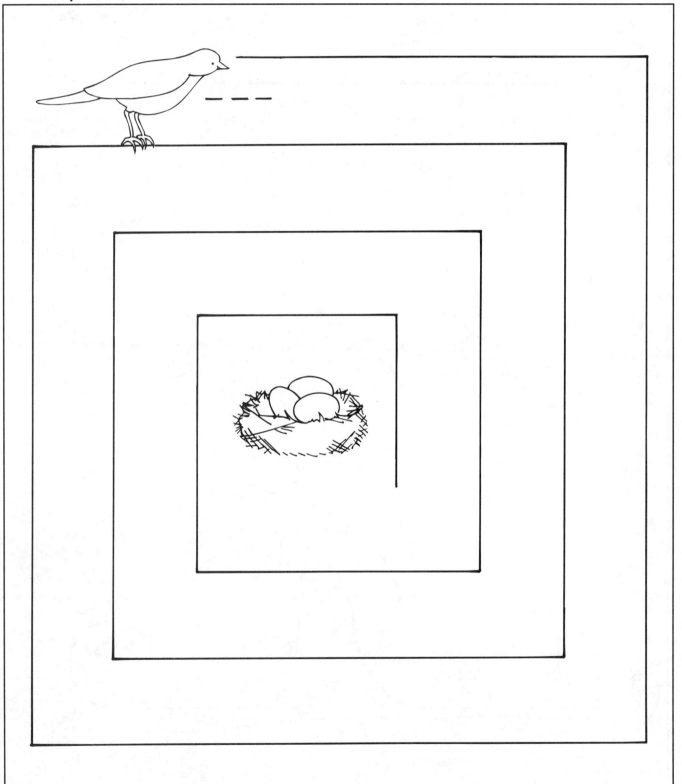

Kitty Toy

Help the kitten find her toy mouse.

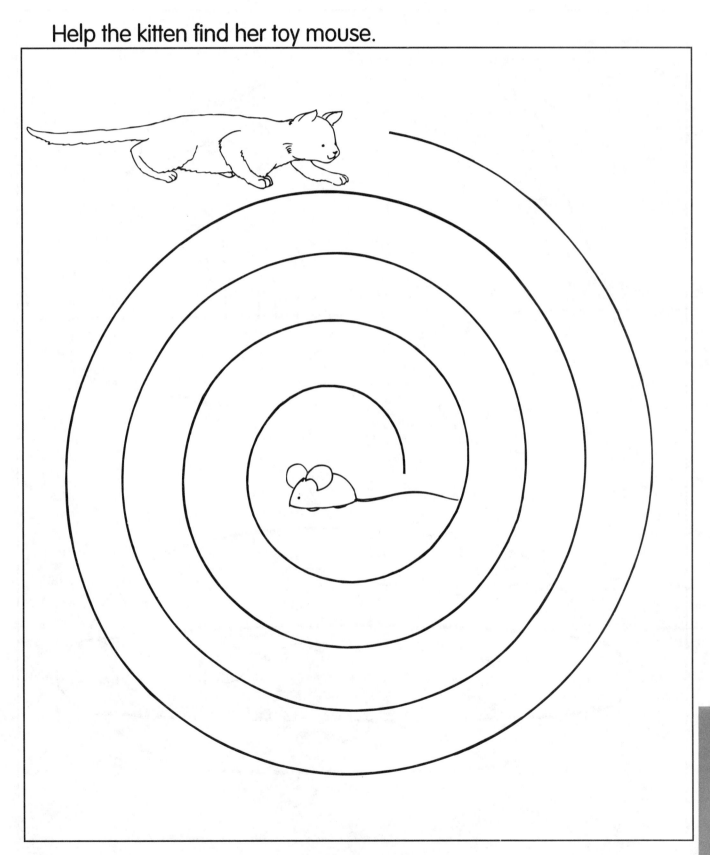

Motor Skills

Parents: Have your child trace the path with his/her finger first, then with a crayon.

Snack Time

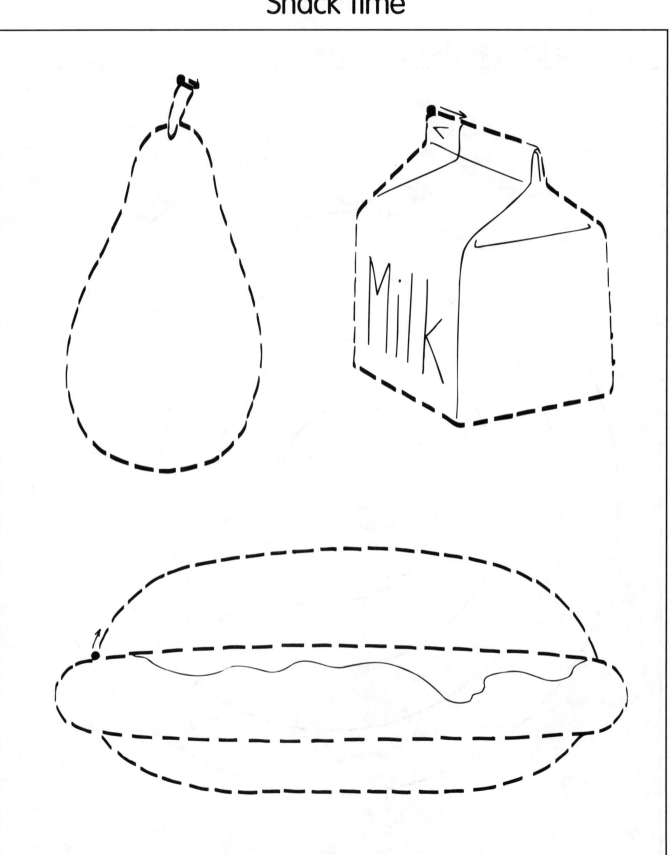

Tracing

Parents: Have your child trace the path with his/her finger first, then with a crayon.

Trace the Shape

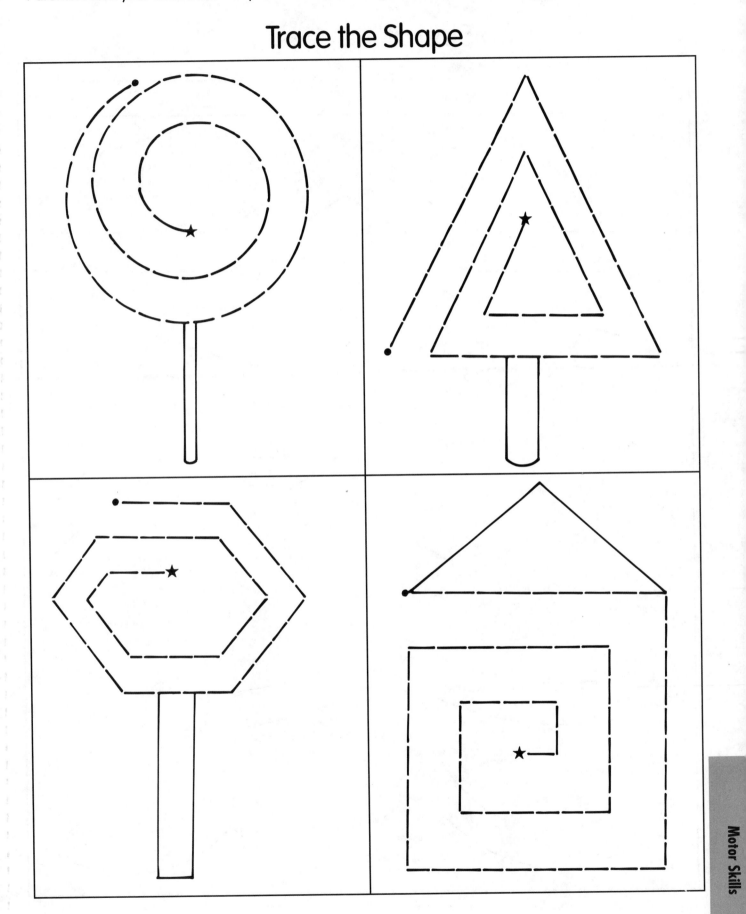

Parents: Have your child trace the path with his/her finger first, then with a crayon.

Start at the 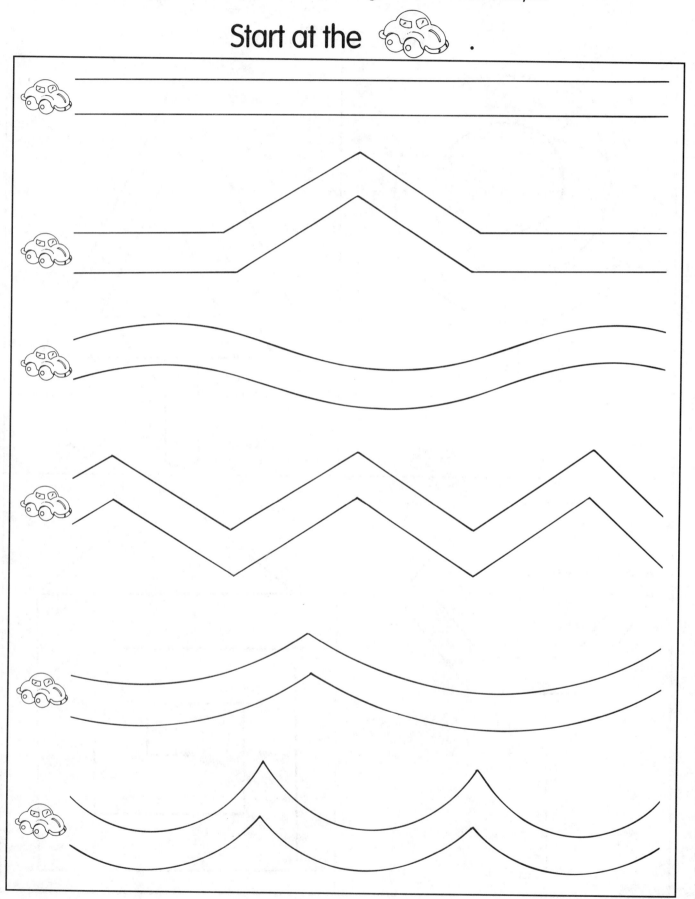 .

Tracing

Write

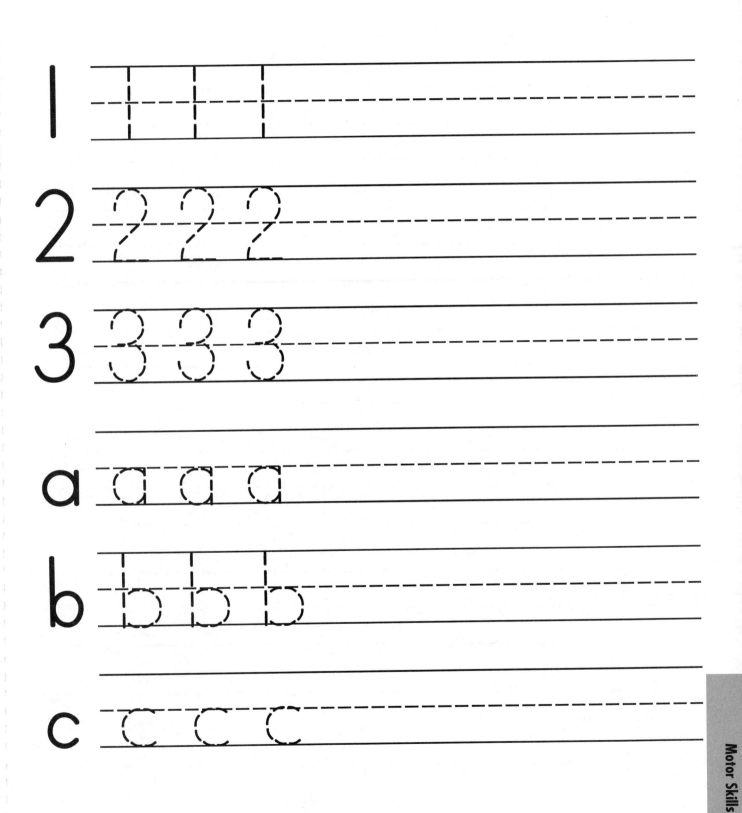

Motor Skills

Write Your Name

Writing my name

Parents: Your child will need a pair of scissors to cut along the lines.

Scissor Practice

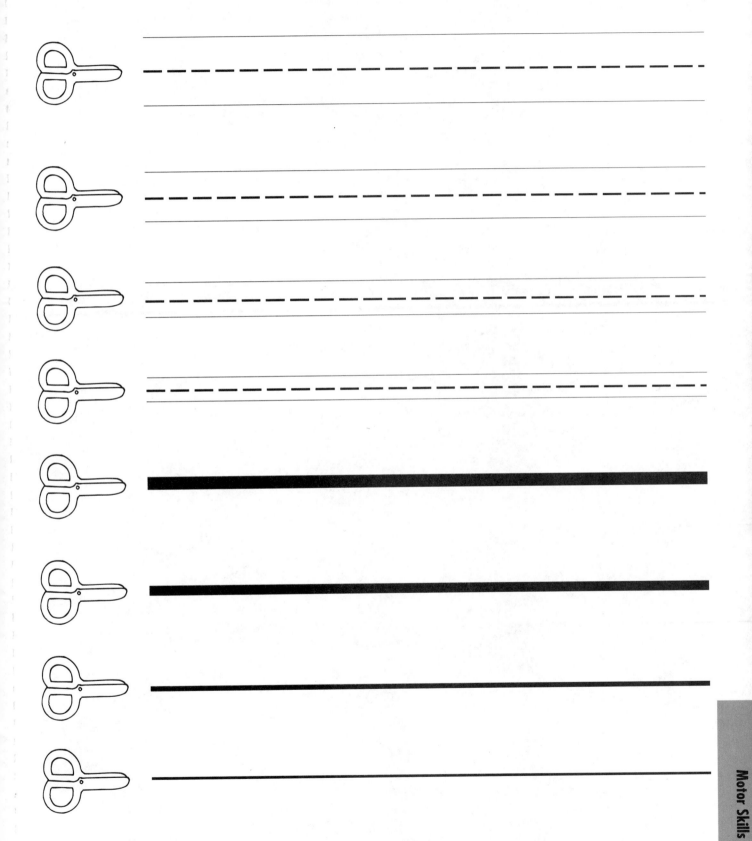

Squares and Triangles

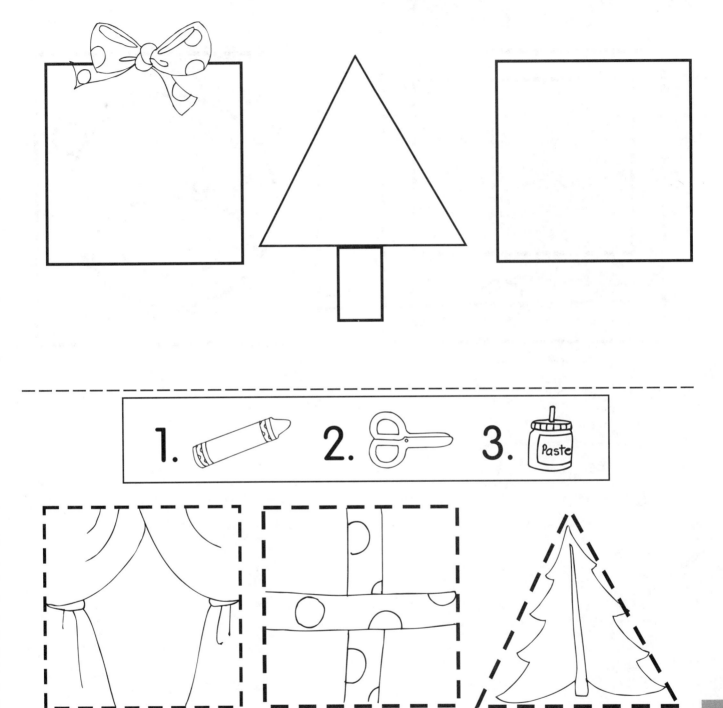

Using scissors; matching shapes

Motor Skills

Parents: Have your child trace the path with his/her finger first, then with a crayon.

Trace the Shapes

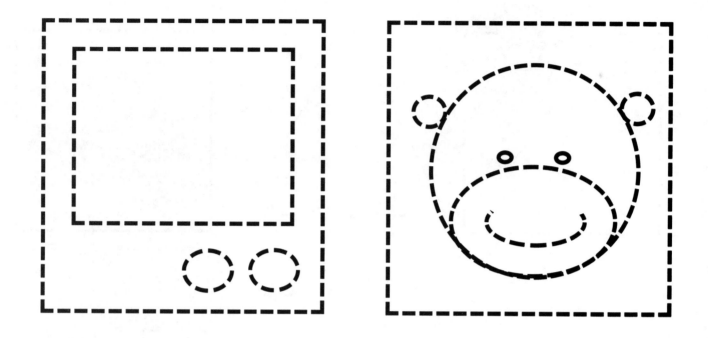

Circles

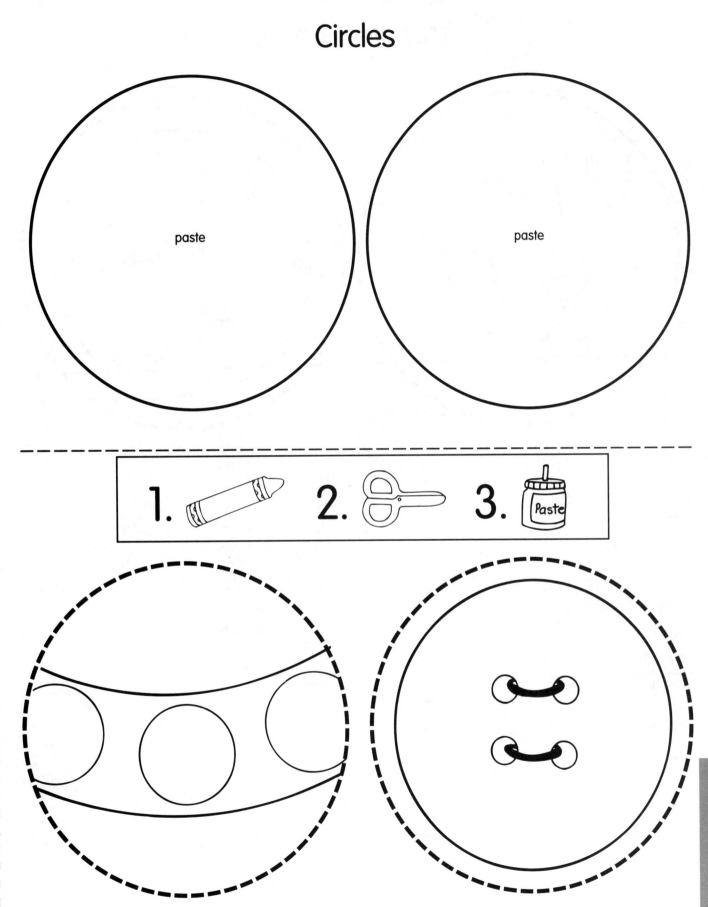

Using scissors; matching shapes

Motor Skills

Trace the Shapes

Tracing

The Squirrel

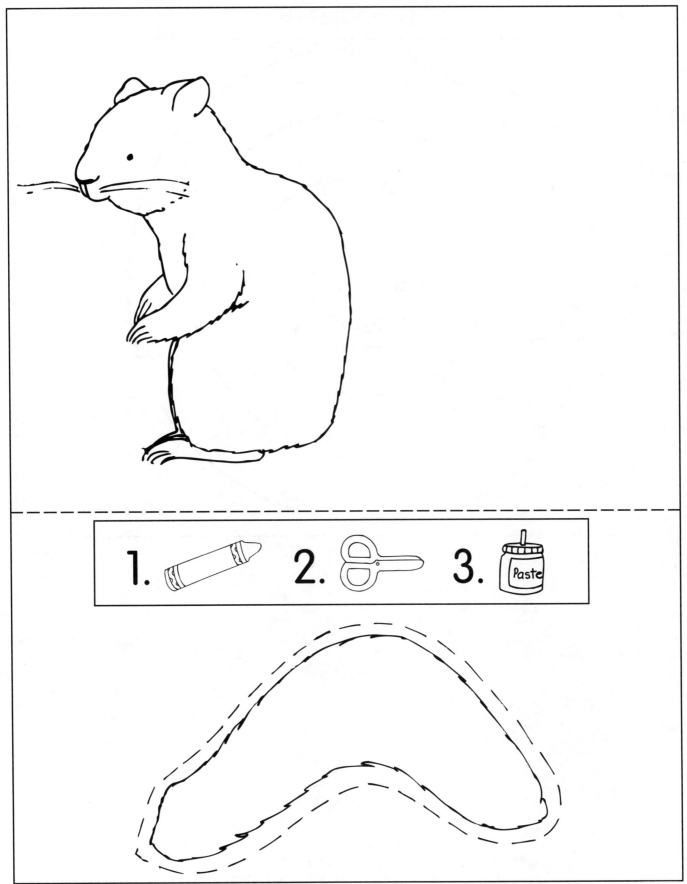

1. 2. 3. Paste

Motor Skills

Parents: Your child will need crayons and scissors for this page. Cut along the dotted line starting at the star.

Snake

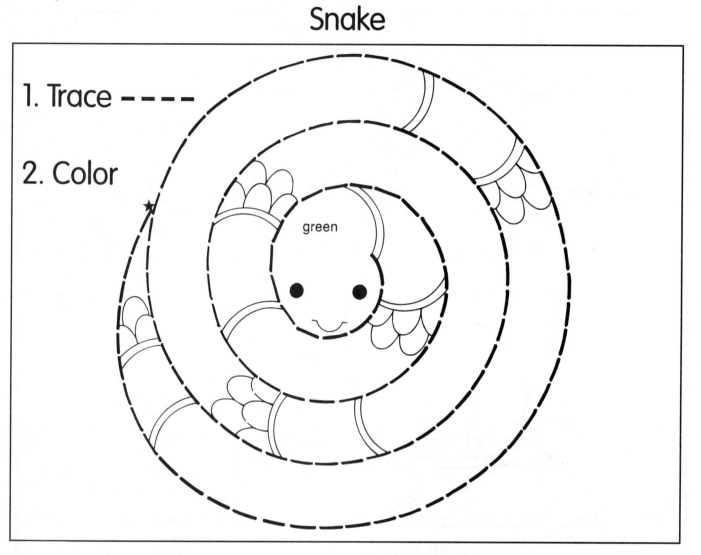

1. Trace - - - - -

2. Color

green

My Bird Cage

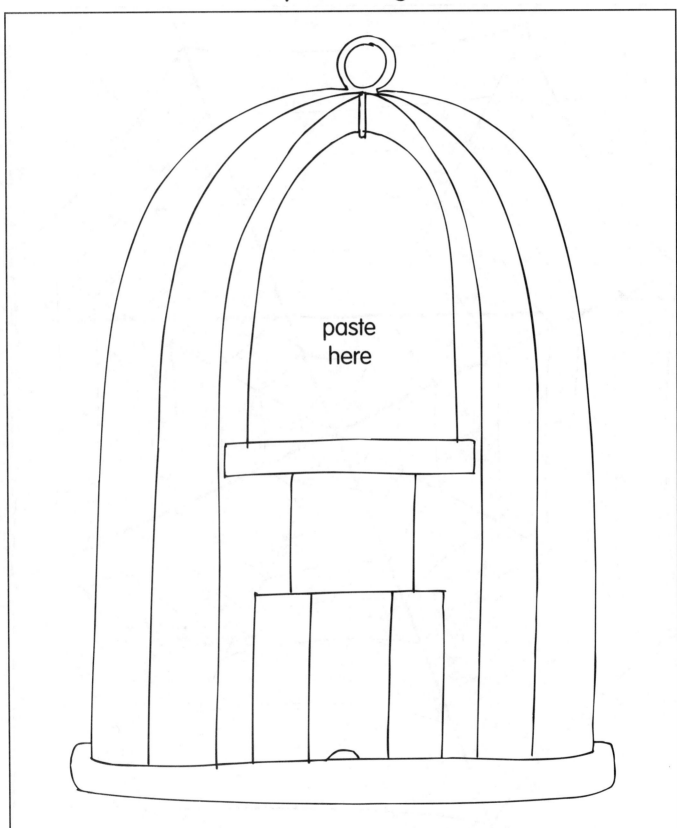

paste
here

Motor Skills

A Spider's Web

Using scissors

Parents: Your child will need scissors, paste and the fish on page 161 to do this page.

A Fish Bowl

Flower Garden

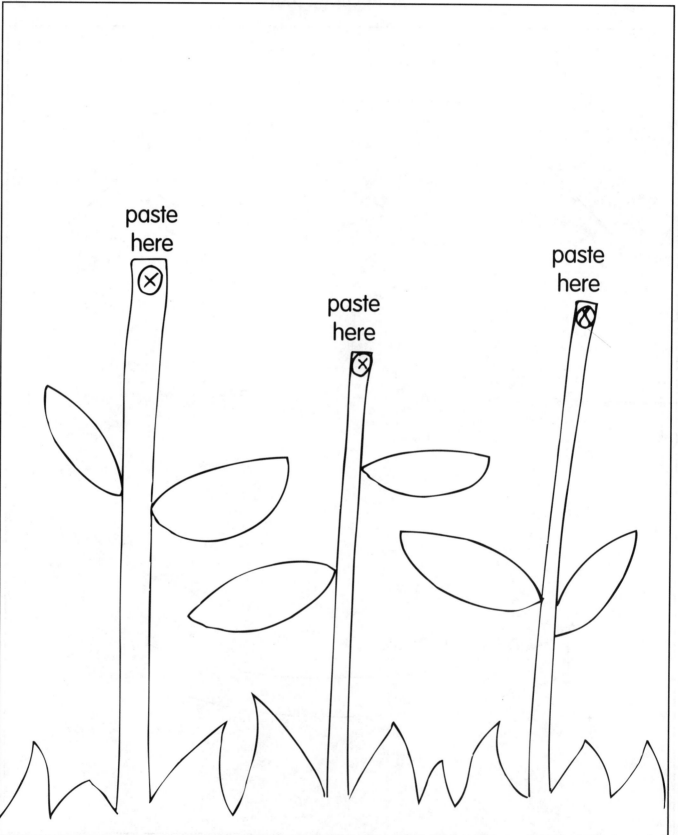

Using scissors

Cutouts for pages 157-160

Motor Skills

Answer Key

Please take time to go over the work your child has completed. Ask your child to explain what he/she has done. Praise both success and effort. If mistakes have been made, explain what the answer should have been and how to find it. Let your child know that mistakes are a part of learning. The time you spend with your child helps let him/her know you feel learning is important.

page 151

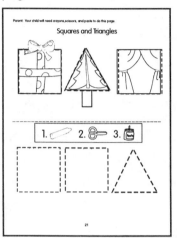

page 153

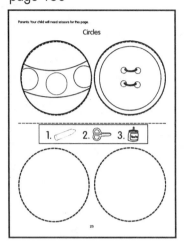

page 155

page 157

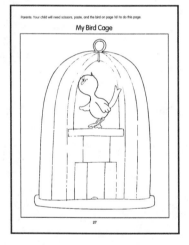

page 158

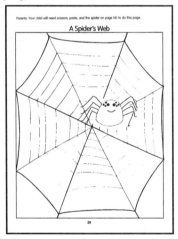

page 159

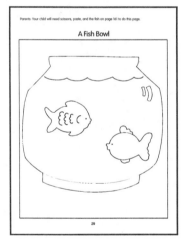

page 160

Motor Skills

Circle the ones that are the same.

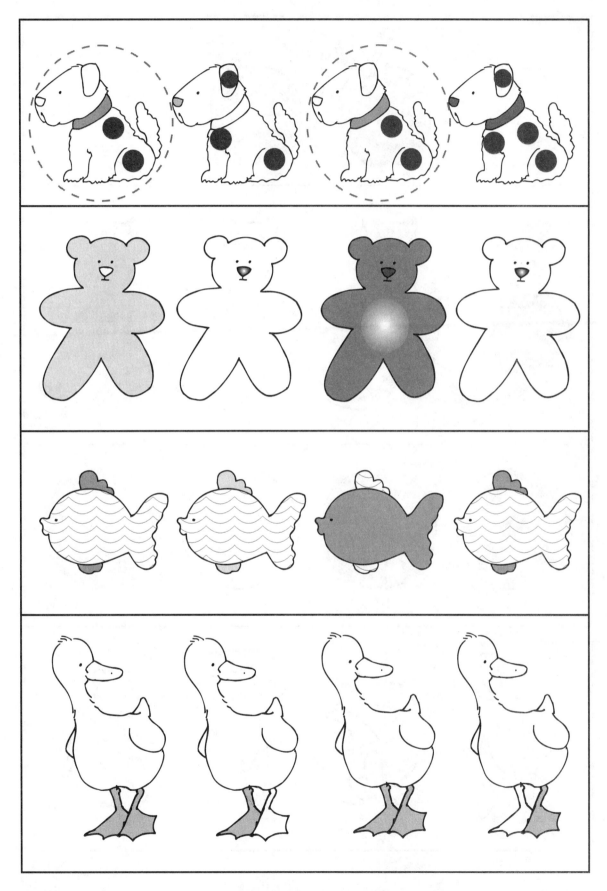

Classifying objects and pictures

Which ones are the same?

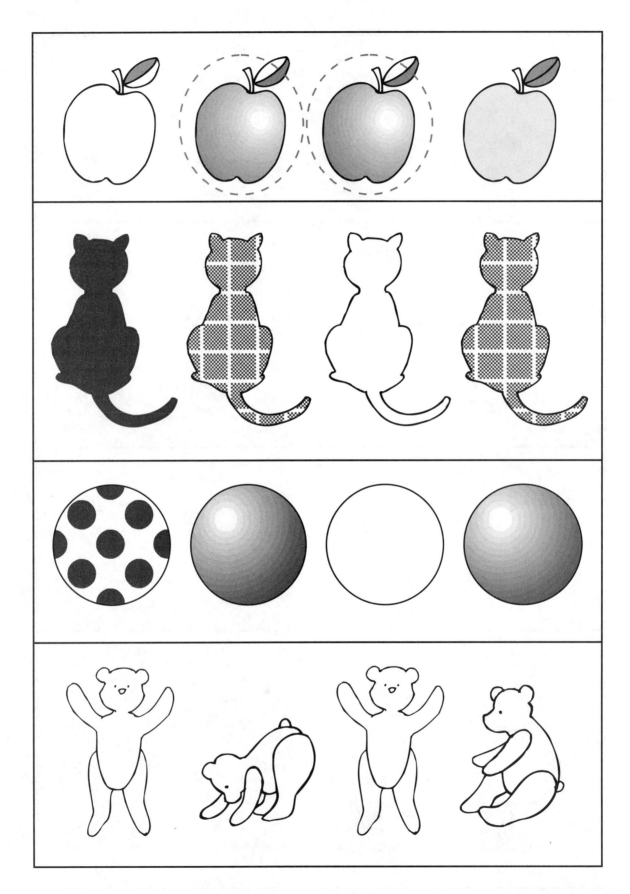

　　　　　　Classifying objects and pictures

Which one is different?

Classifying objects and pictures

Cats and Dogs

yellow

brown

Following directions

Match.

Put it away!

Classifying objects and pictures

Where will you see me?

land   sea   air

Classifying objects and pictures

Who lives here?

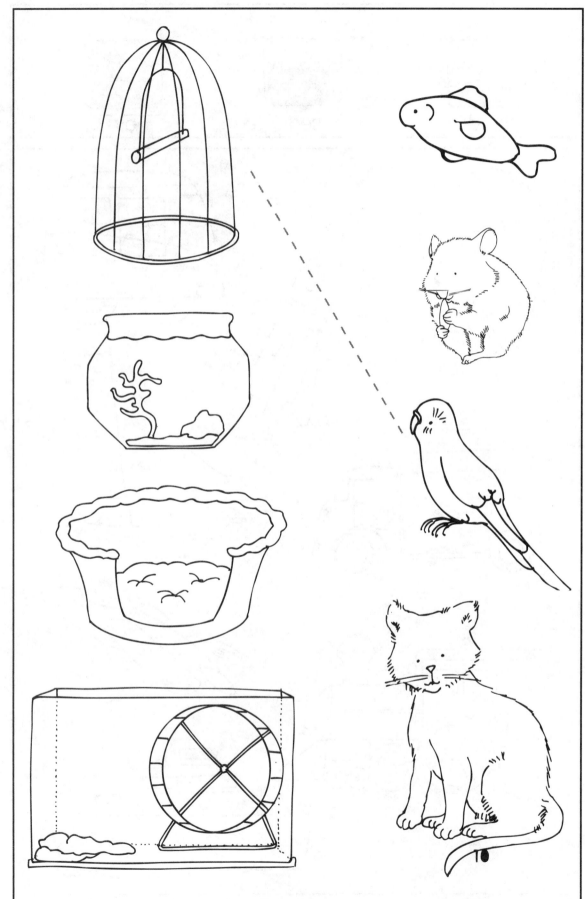

Classifying objects and pictures

Find my baby.

What goes together?

zoo   farm   pet

Classifying objects and pictures

Which tools will I use?

Think & Do

Where will you find it?

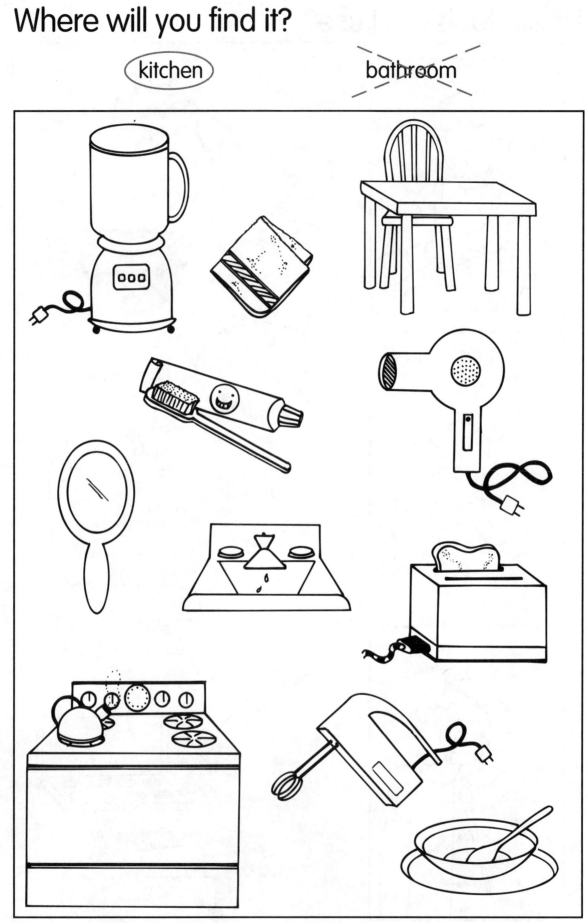

Color all of the machines.

What goes together?

What goes together?

red   green   blue

Classifying objects and pictures

What goes together?

Classifying objects and pictures

Color the shapes.

big - red   little - blue

Distinguishing big from little

Match.

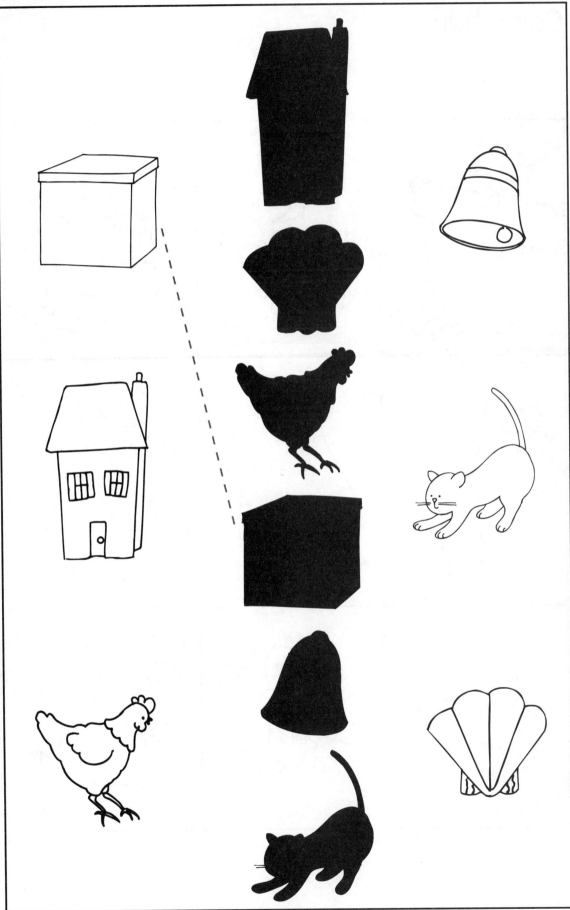

Matching shapes

Find the animals.
Color them.

Classifying objects and pictures

Real?   Toy?

Classifying objects and pictures

183

Find the animals.
Color them.

Classifying objects and pictures

Note: Your child will need paste and a piece of paper for pasting this page in order.

Can you run fast?

Sequencing

185

Can you jump rope?

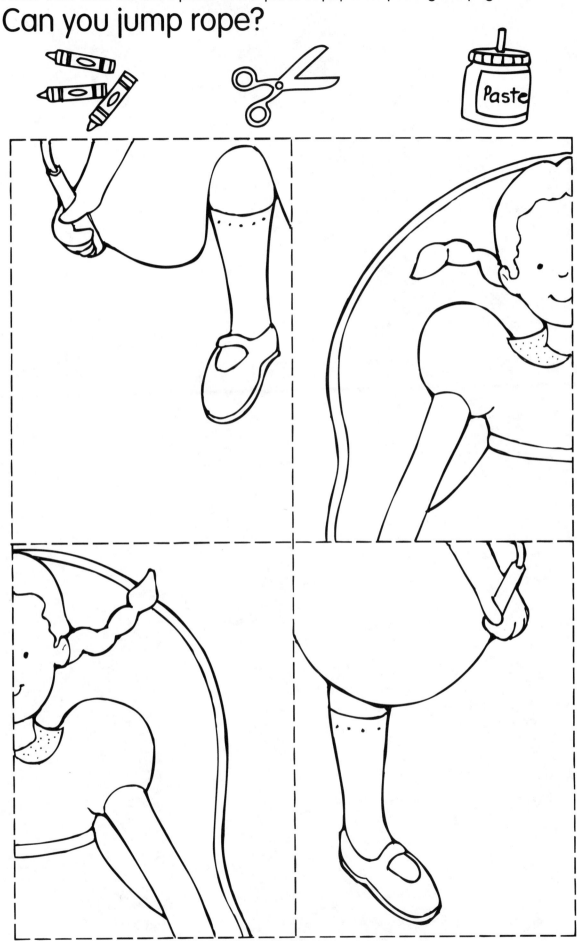

Sequencing

Note: Your child will need paste and a piece of paper for pasting this page in order.

A robin makes a nest for her eggs.

Put in order.

1	2	3	4

Sequencing

Answer Key

Please take time to go over the work your child has completed. Ask your child to explain what he/she has done. Praise both success and effort. If mistakes have been made, explain what the answer should have been and how to find it. Let your child know that mistakes are a part of learning. The time you spend with your child helps let him/her know you feel learning is important.

page 165

page 166
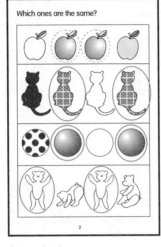

page 167

page 168

page 169
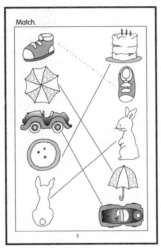

page 170
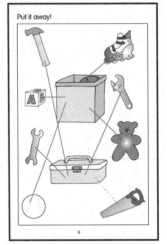

page 171

page 172
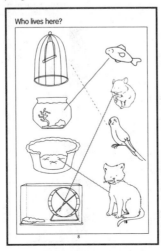

page 173
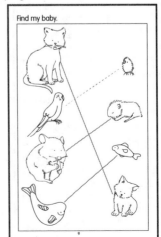

page 174

What goes together?

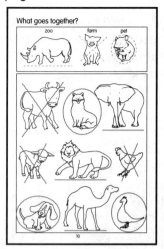

page 175

Which tools will I use?

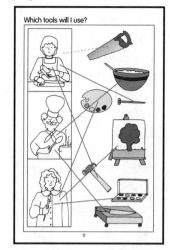

page 176

Where will you find it?

page 177

What goes together?

page 178

What goes together?

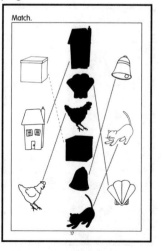

page 179

What goes together?

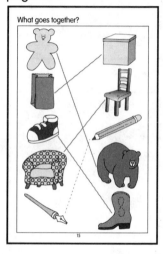

page 180

Color the shapes.

page 181

Match.

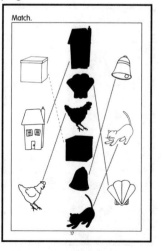

page 182

Find the animals.
Color them.

page 183

19

page 184

Find the animals.
Color them.

20

page 185

Note: Your child will need paste and a piece of paper for pasting this page in order.
Can you run fast?

21

page 187

Note: Your child will need paste and a piece of paper for pasting this page in order.
Can you jump rope?

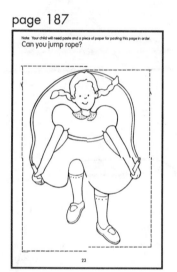

23

page 189

Note: Your child will need paste and a piece of paper for pasting this page in order.
A robin makes a nest for her eggs.

25

Answers

193

Trace the lines.
Connect the dots.

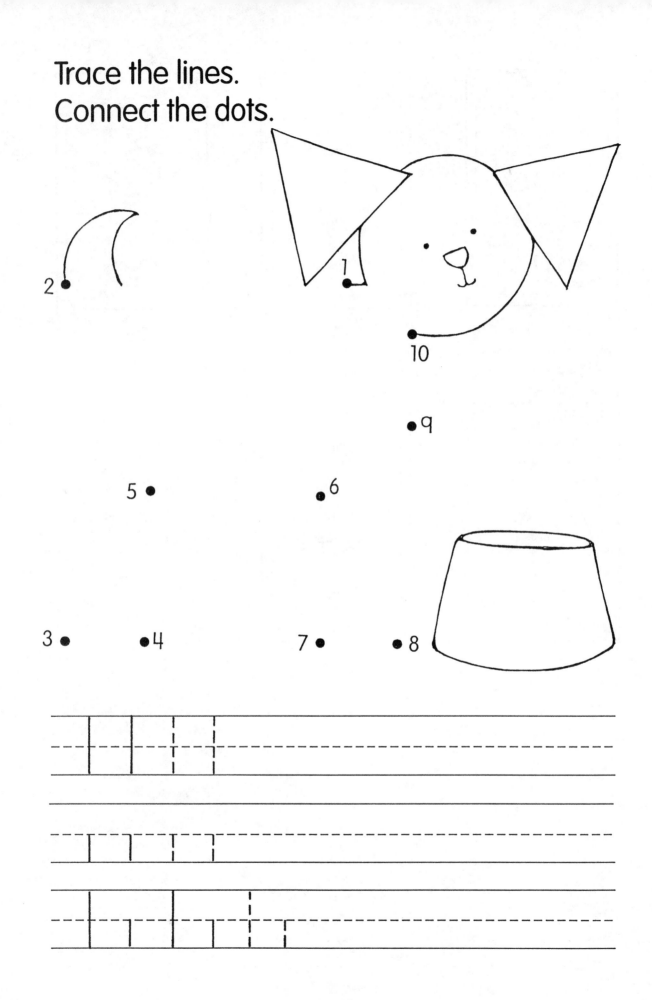

Trace the circles.

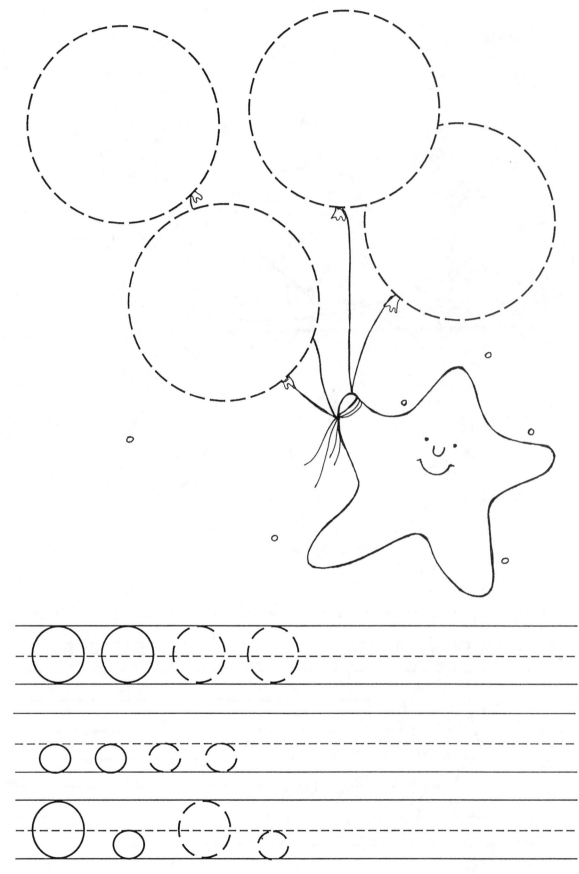

Trace the lines.

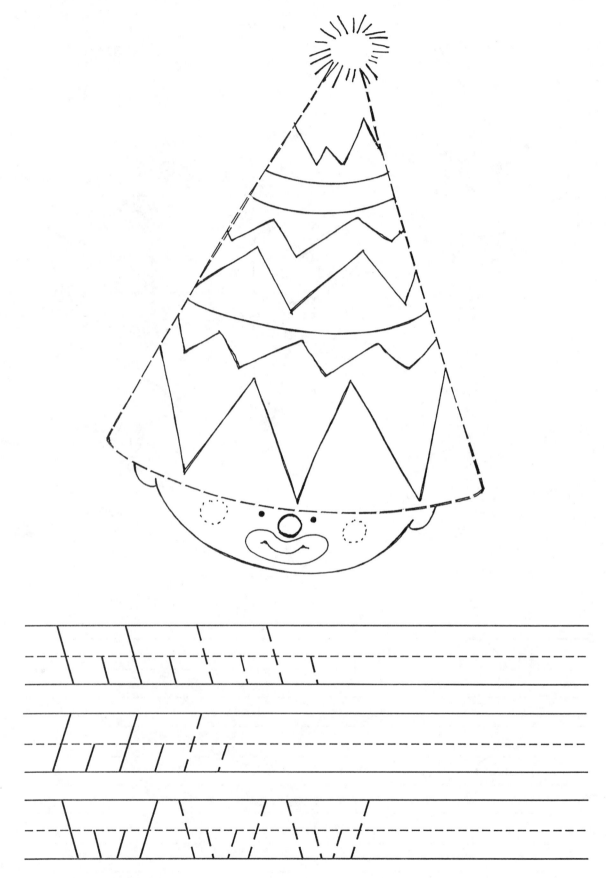

Tracing

Connect the dots.
Color the apple.

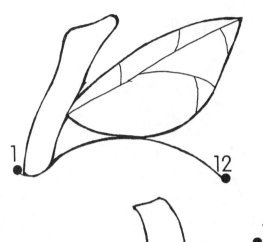

2 •

3 •

4 •

5 •

6 •

7 •

8 •

9 •

10 •

11 •

12 •

1 •

Trace and write.

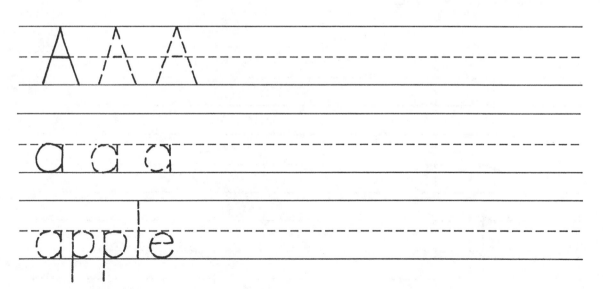

A A A

a a a

apple

Trace the ball.
Color the ball.

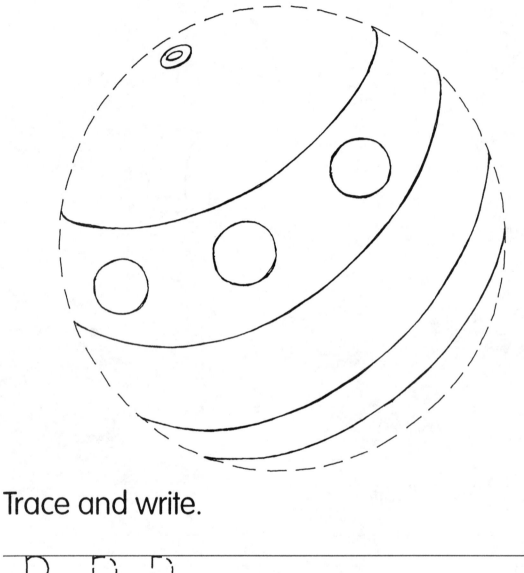

Trace and write.

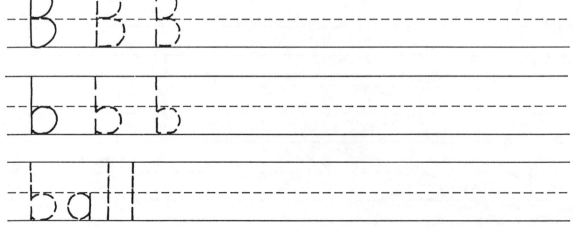

B B B

b b b

ball

Put a  on the clown.

Trace and write.

C C C

c c c

clown

Trace the duck.
Color it.

Trace and write.

D D D

d d d

duck

Tracing and writing letters

Connect the dots.
Color the elephant.

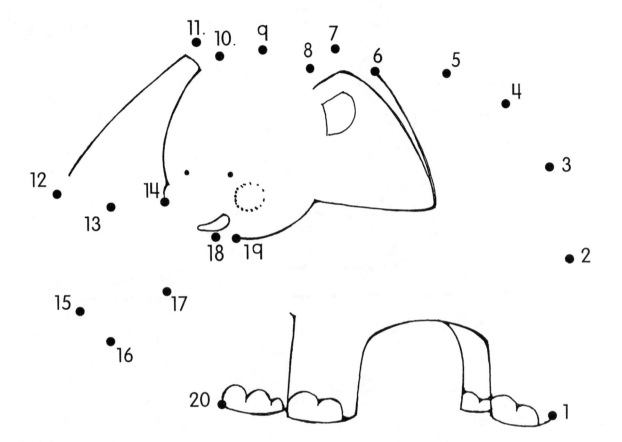

Trace and write.

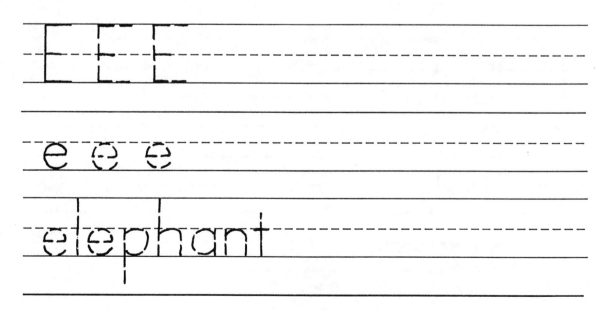

Connect the dots.
Color the frog.

Trace and write.

Trace the grapes.
Color them.

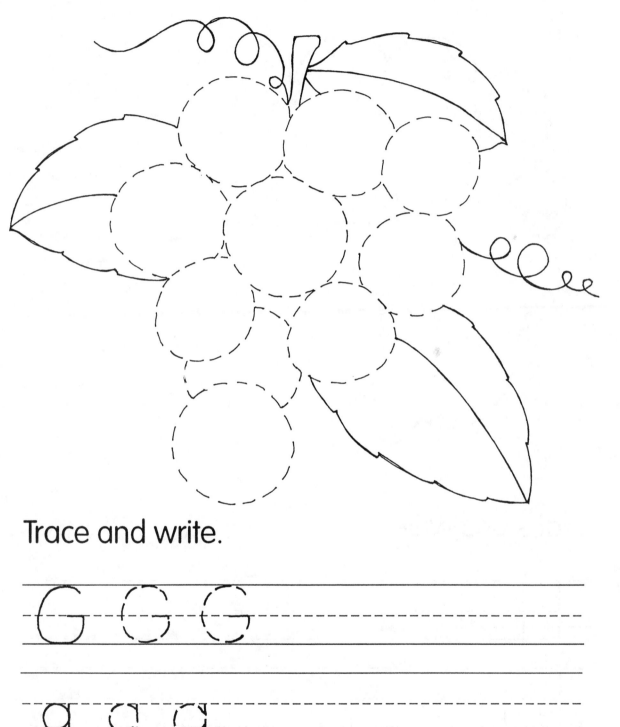

Trace and write.

G G G

g g g

grapes

Connect the dots.
Color the heart.

Be My
Valentine

Trace and write.

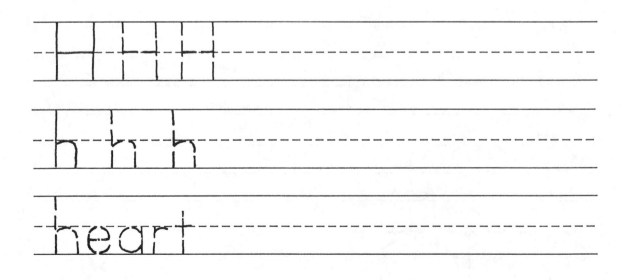

Connect the dots.
Put ice cream in the cone.

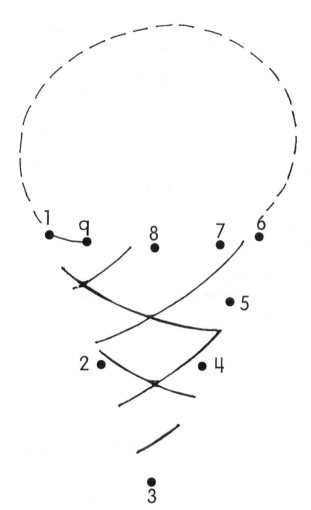

Trace and write.

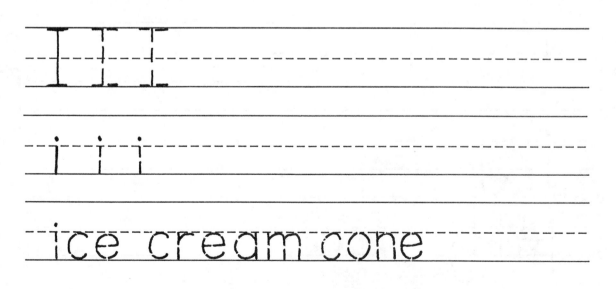

Trace the jar.
Color the jelly.

Trace and write.

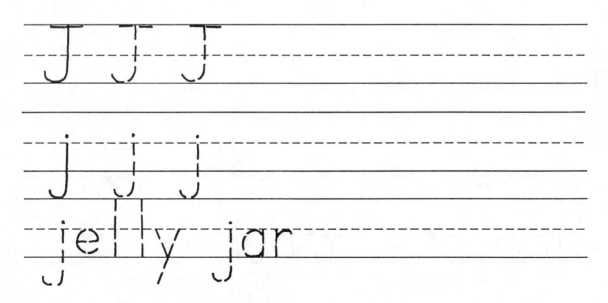

J J J

j j j

jelly jar

Tracing and writing letters

Connect the dots.
Color the kite.

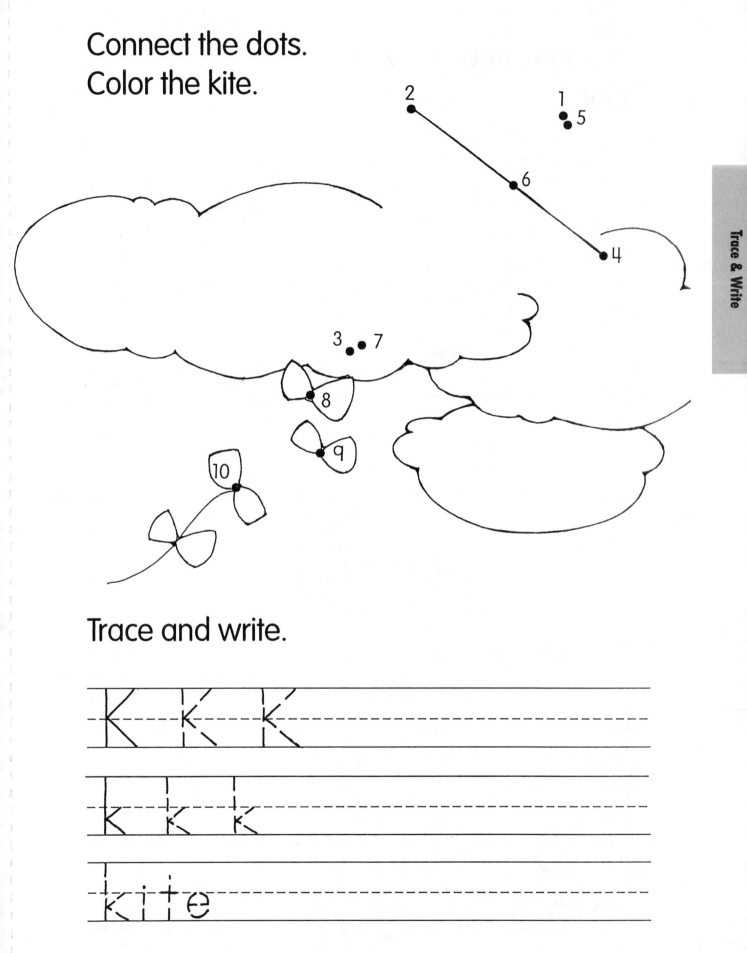

Trace and write.

K K K

K K K

kite

Trace the lamb.
Color it.

Trace and write.

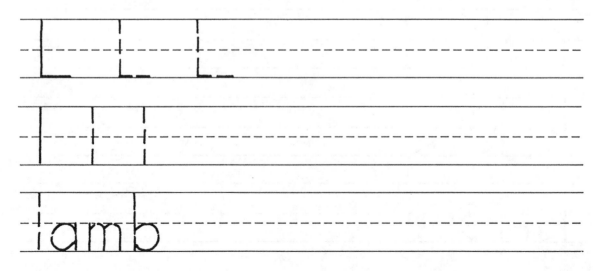

Tracing and writing letters

Connect the dots.
Color the 🐭 and the 🧀.

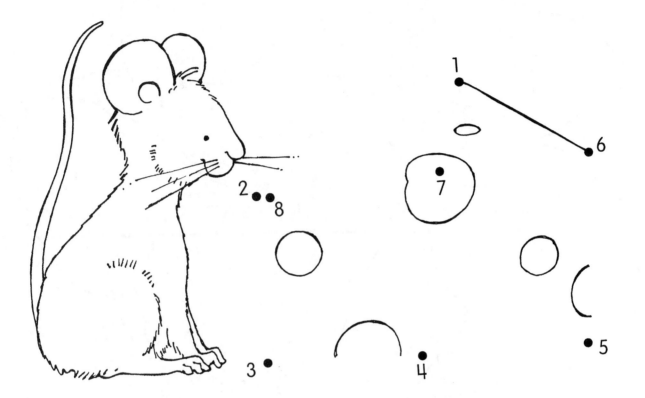

Trace and write.

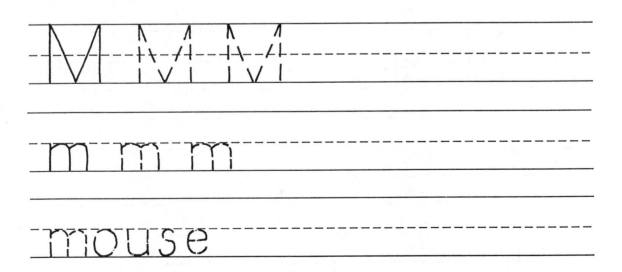

M M M

m m m

mouse

Trace the nuts.
Color them.

Trace and write.

N N N

n n n

nuts

Trace the 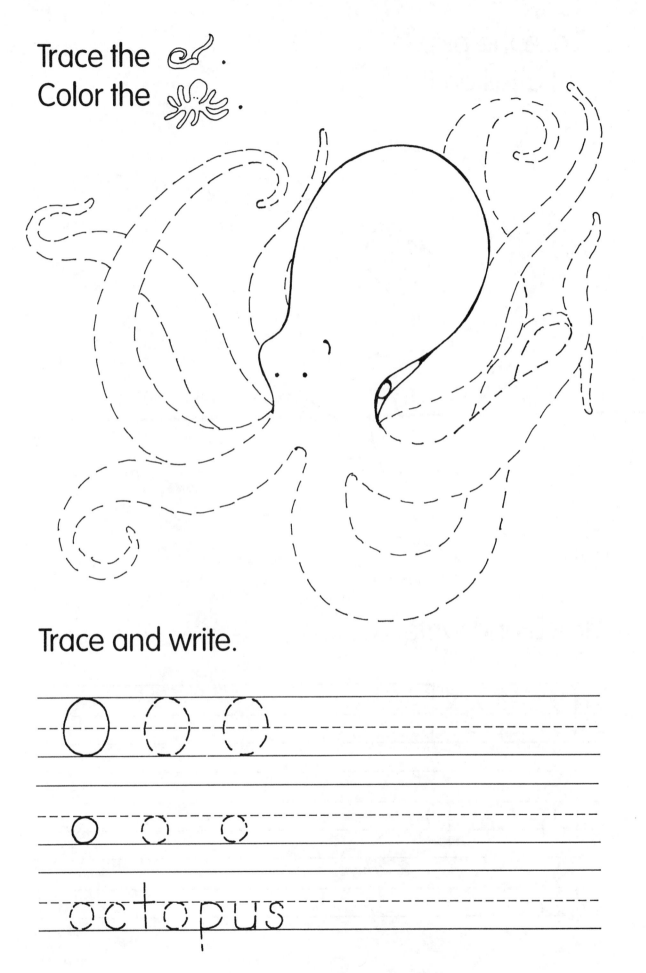.
Color the .

Trace and write.

octopus

Trace the pig.
Put a tail on it.

Trace and write.

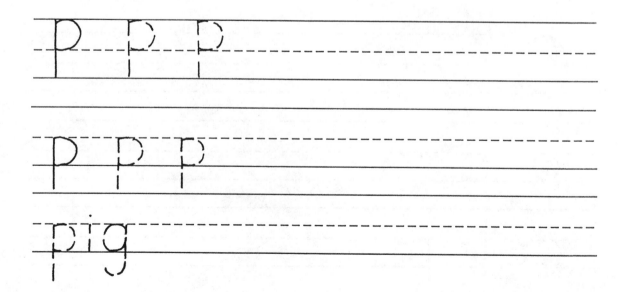

Tracing and writing letters

Connect the dots.
Color the quilt.

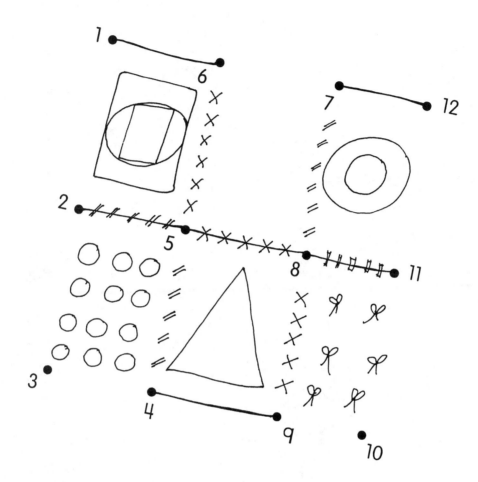

Trace and write.

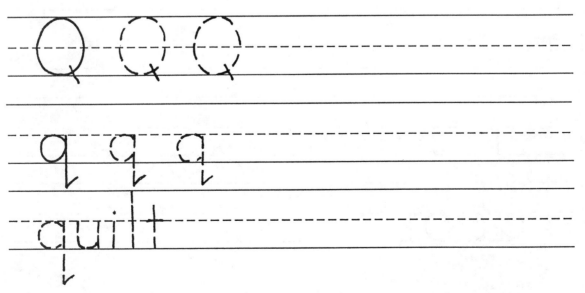

Connect the dots.
Color the 🥕 and 🐰 .

1
2
8
3
7
4
6
5

Trace and write.

R R R

r r r

rabbit

Connect the dots.
Color the sun.

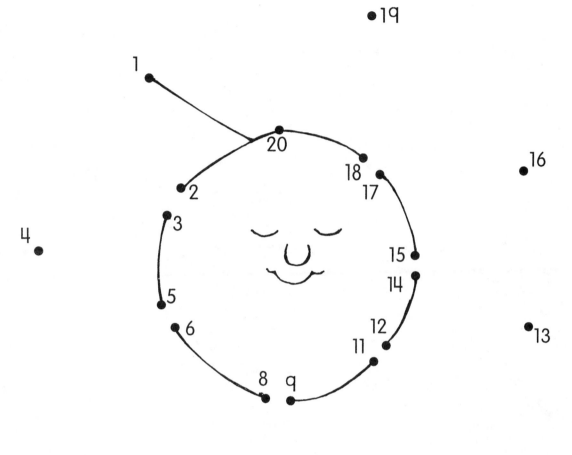

Trace and write.

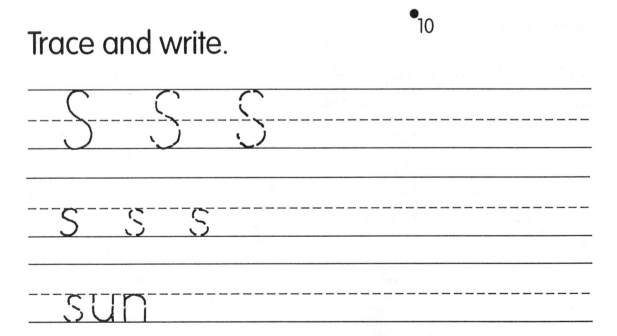

Trace the top.
Color it.

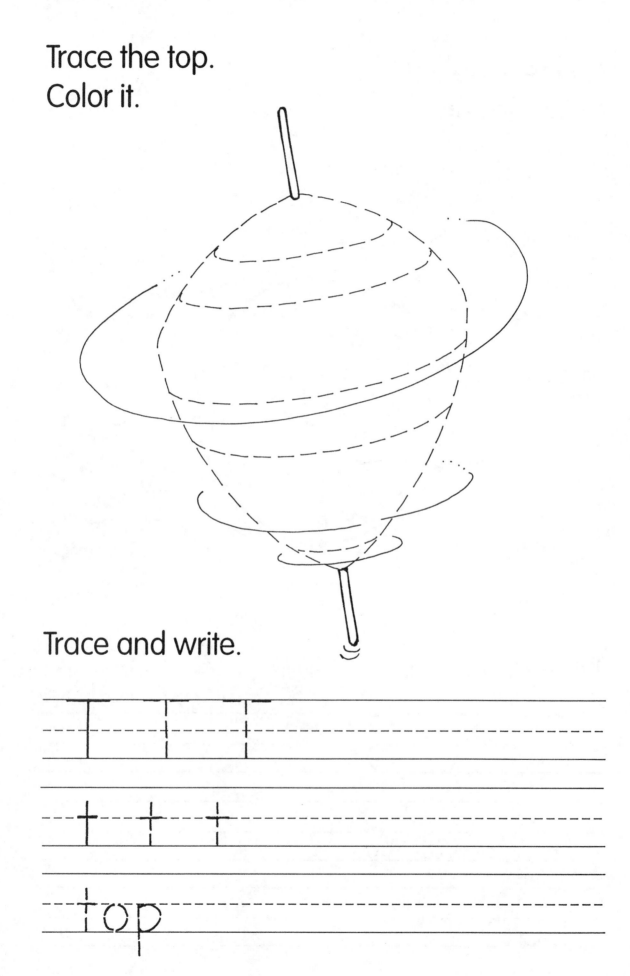

Trace and write.

T T T

t t t

top

Trace the .
Make .

Trace and write.

U U U

u u u

umbrella

Connect the dots.
Put 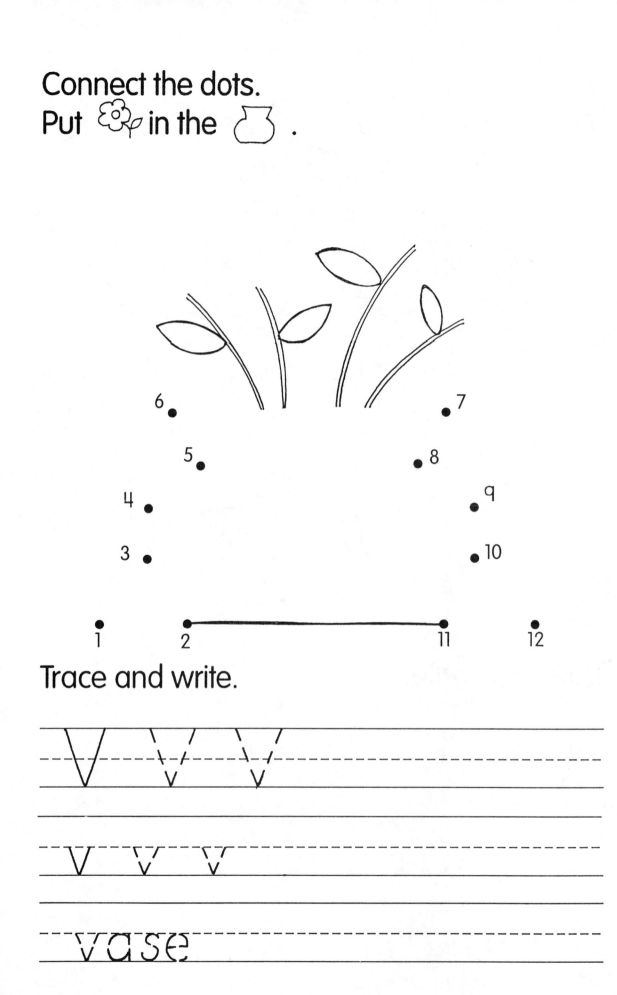 in the .

Trace and write.

V V V

V V V

vase

Tracing and writing letters

Connect the dots.
Put a 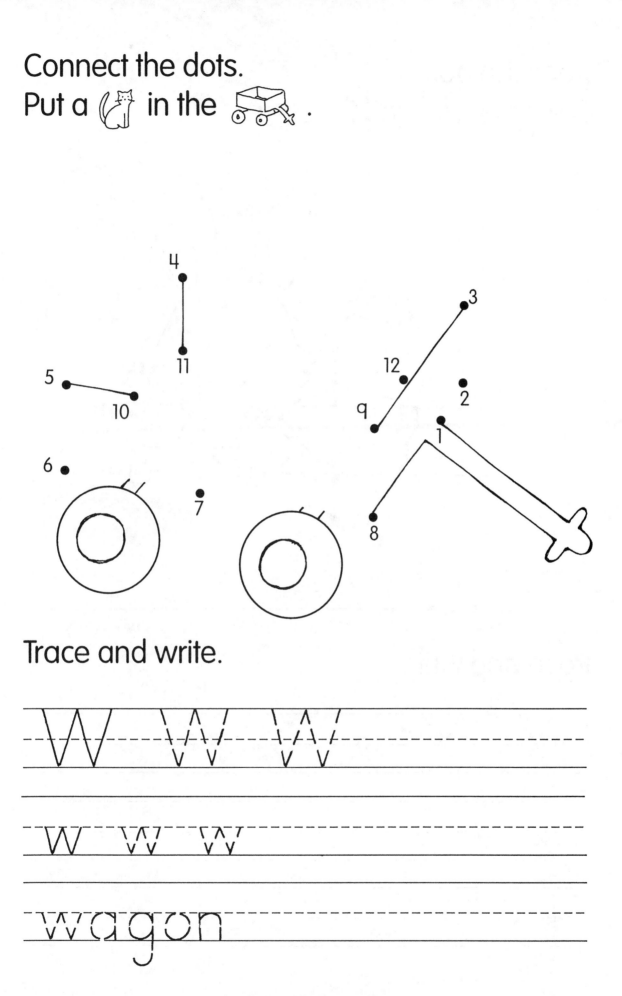 in the 🛒 .

Connect the dots. Put a cat in the wagon.

Trace and write.

W W W

w w w

wagon

Trace the box.
Color the  and the ⬚ .

Trace and write.

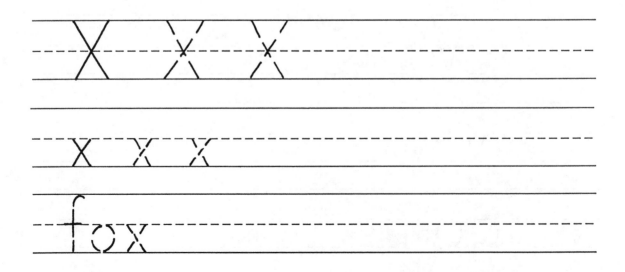

Tracing and writing letters

Connect the dots.
Color the yo-yo.

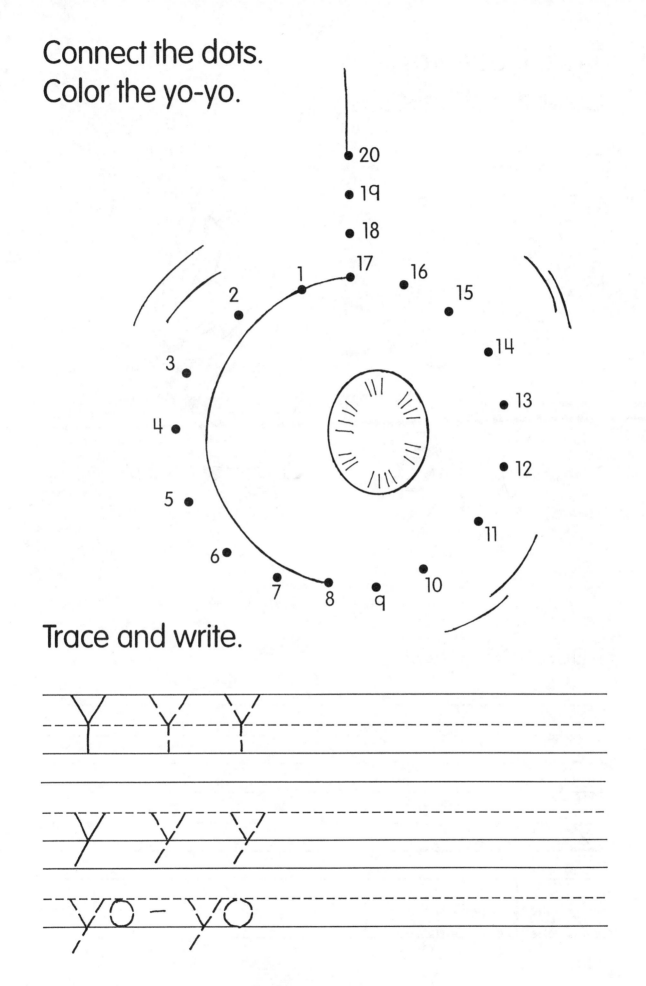

Trace and write.

Y Y Y

Y Y Y

yo - yo

Trace the zebra.
Color the stripes.

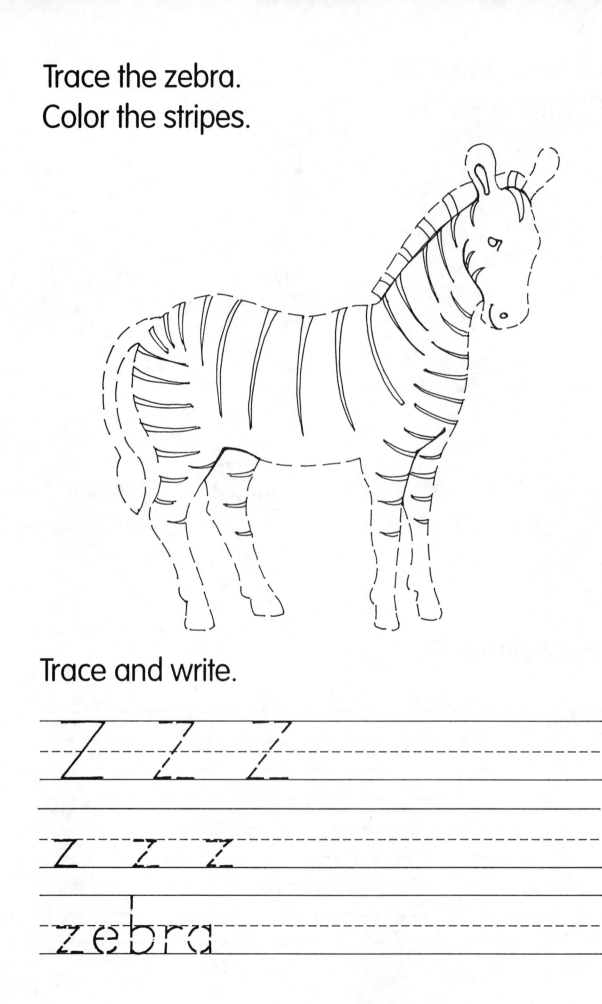

Trace and write.

Z Z Z

z z z

zebra

Tracing and writing letters

Answer Key

Please take time to go over the work your child has completed. Ask your child to explain what he/she has done. Praise both success and effort. If mistakes have been made, explain what the answer should have been and how to find it. Let your child know that mistakes are a part of learning. The time you spend with your child helps let him/her know you feel learning is important.

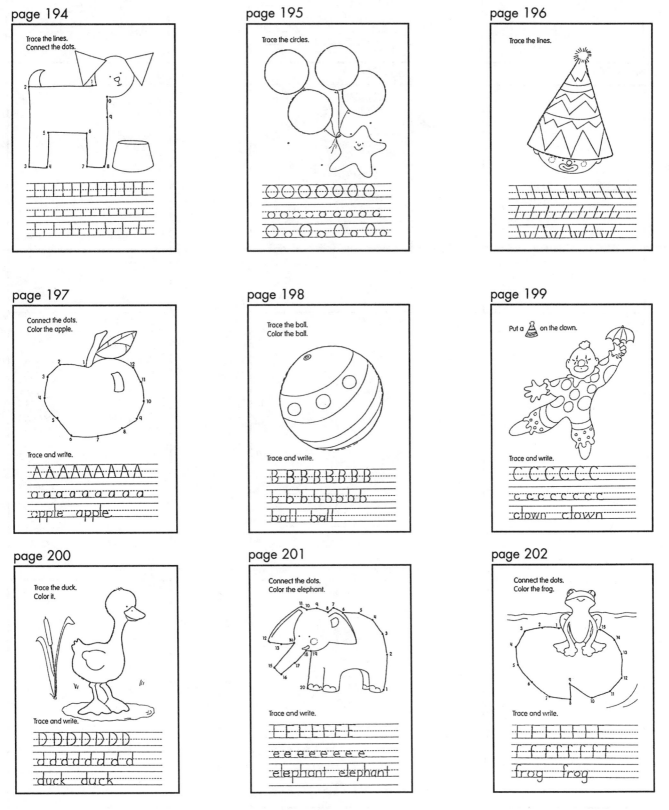

Trace the grapes.
Color them.

Trace and write.

G G G G G G

g g g g g g g

grapes   grapes

Connect the dots.
Color the heart.

Be My
Valentine

Trace and write.

H H H H H H Hh

h h h h h h h

heart   heart

Connect the dots.
Put ice cream in the cone.

Trace and write.

I I I I I I I

i i i i i i i i i

ice cream cone

Trace the jar.
Color the jelly.

Trace and write.

J J J J J J J

j j j j j j j

jelly jar   jelly jar

Connect the dots.
Color the kite.

Trace and write.

K K K K K K

k k k k k k k

kite   kite

Trace the lamb.
Color it.

Trace and write.

L L L L L L

l l l l l l

lamb   lamb

Connect the dots.
Color the 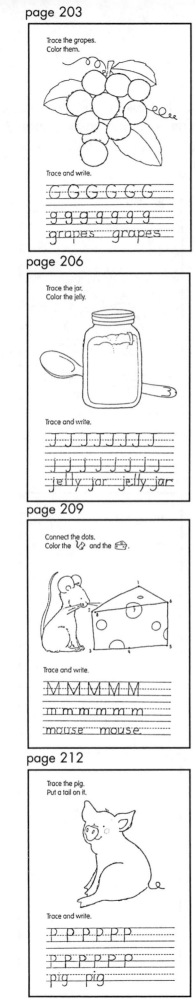 and the .

Trace and write.

M M M M M

m m m m m m

mouse   mouse

Trace the nuts.
Color them.

Trace and write.

N N N N N N

n n n n n n

nuts   nuts

Trace the .
Color the 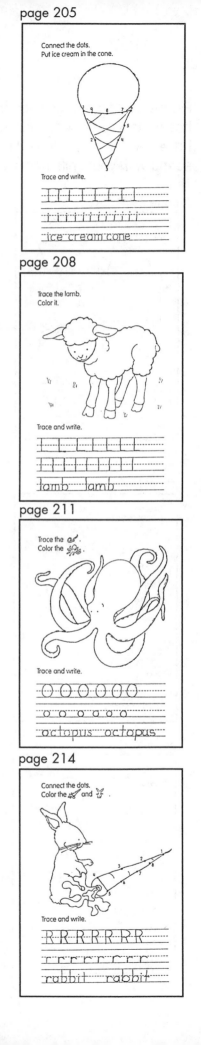 .

Trace and write.

O O O O O O

o o o o o o

octopus   octopus

Trace the pig.
Put a tail on it.

Trace and write.

P P P P P P

p p p p p p

pig   pig

Connect the dots.
Color the quilt.

Trace and write.

Q Q Q Q Q Q

q q q q q q q

quilt   quilt

Connect the dots.
Color the 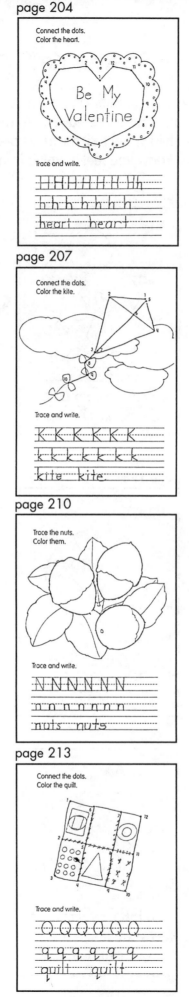 and .

Trace and write.

R R R R R R R

r r r r r r r

rabbit   rabbit

page 215

Connect the dots.
Color the sun.

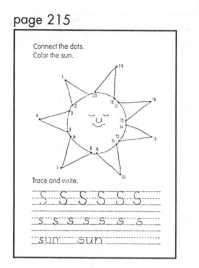

Trace and write.

S S S S S S
s s s s s s
sun sun

page 216

Trace the top.
Color it.

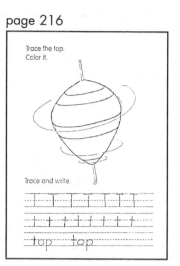

Trace and write.

T T T T T T
t t t t t t t
top top

page 217

Trace the
Make

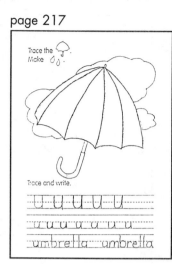

Trace and write.

U U U U U U
u u u u u u
umbrella umbrella

page 218

Connect the dots.
Put in the .

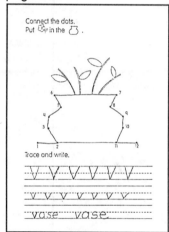

Trace and write.

V V V V V V
v v v v v v
vase vase

page 219

Connect the dots.
Put a in the .

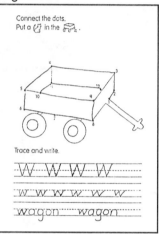

Trace and write.

W W W W
w w w w w w
wagon wagon

page 220

Trace the box.
Color the  and the

Trace and write.

X X X X X
x x x x x x x
fox fox

page 221

Connect the dots.
Color the yo-yo.

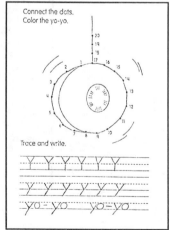

Trace and write.

Y Y Y Y Y Y
y y y y y y y
yo-yo yo-yo

page 222

Trace the zebra.
Color the stripes.

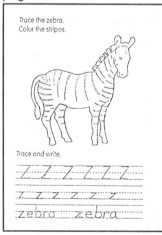

Trace and write.

Z Z Z Z Z Z
z z z z z z
zebra zebra

Trace and color.

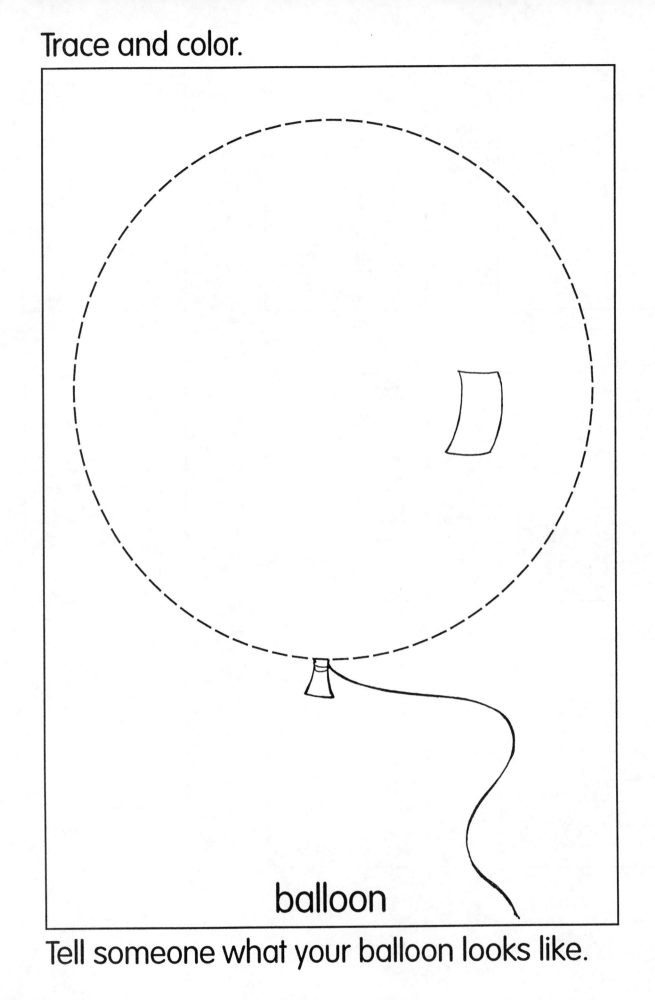

balloon

Tell someone what your balloon looks like.

Tracing; talking about a picture

Trace and color.

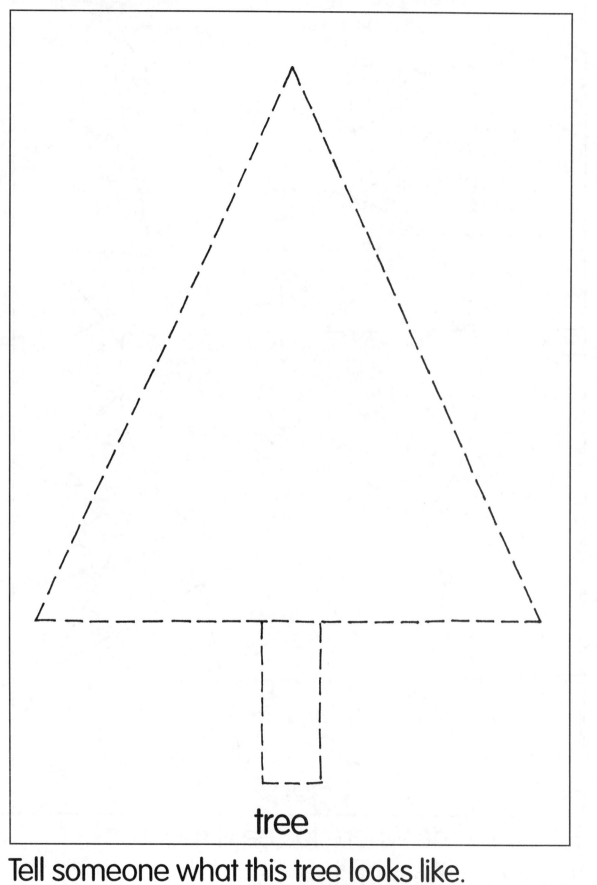

tree

Tell someone what this tree looks like.

Draw & Talk

Trace and color.

sun

Tell someone where to see a real sun.
What can the sun do?

Tracing; talking about a picture

Trace and color.

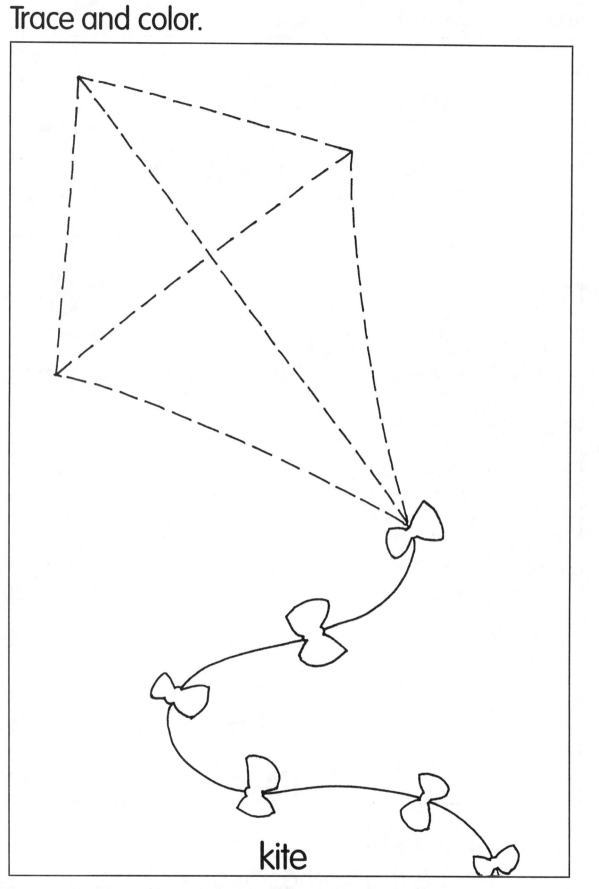

kite

Tell someone how to play with a kite.

Draw & Talk

Trace and color.

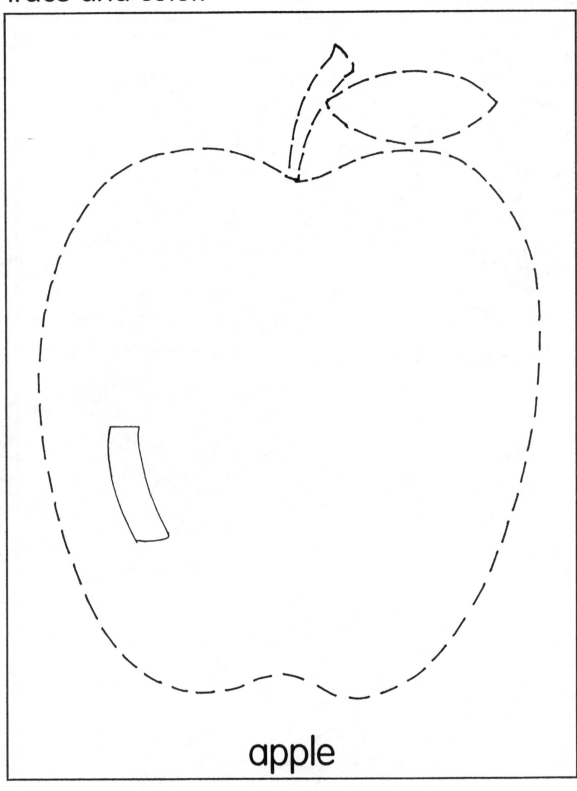

apple

An apple is a fruit.
Tell someone the names of other kinds
of fruit.

Tracing; talking about a picture

Trace and color.

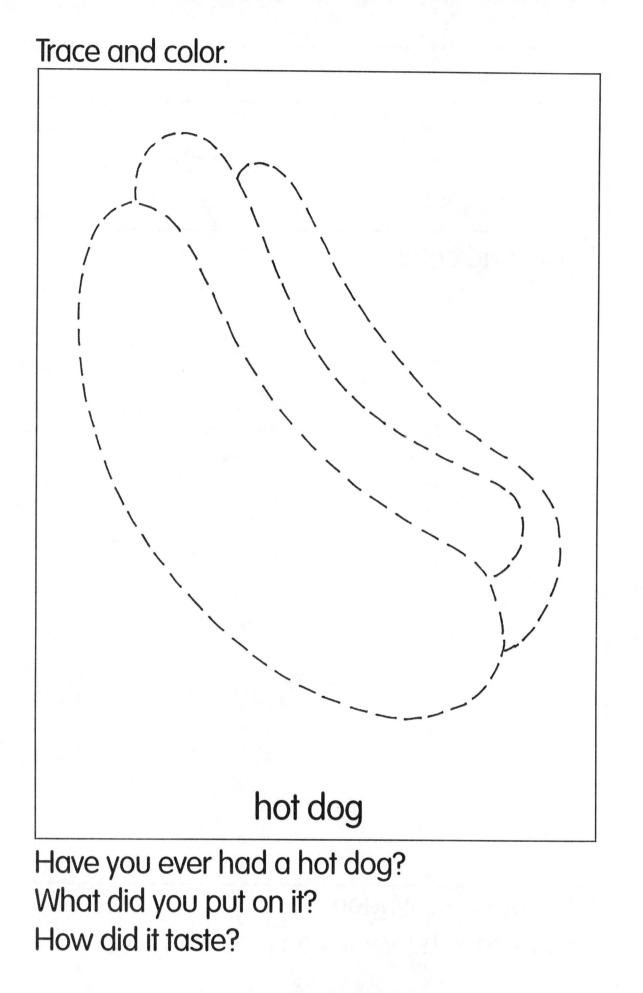

hot dog

Have you ever had a hot dog?
What did you put on it?
How did it taste?

Draw and color.

Put a toy in the wagon.

Tell someone how you can play with a wagon.

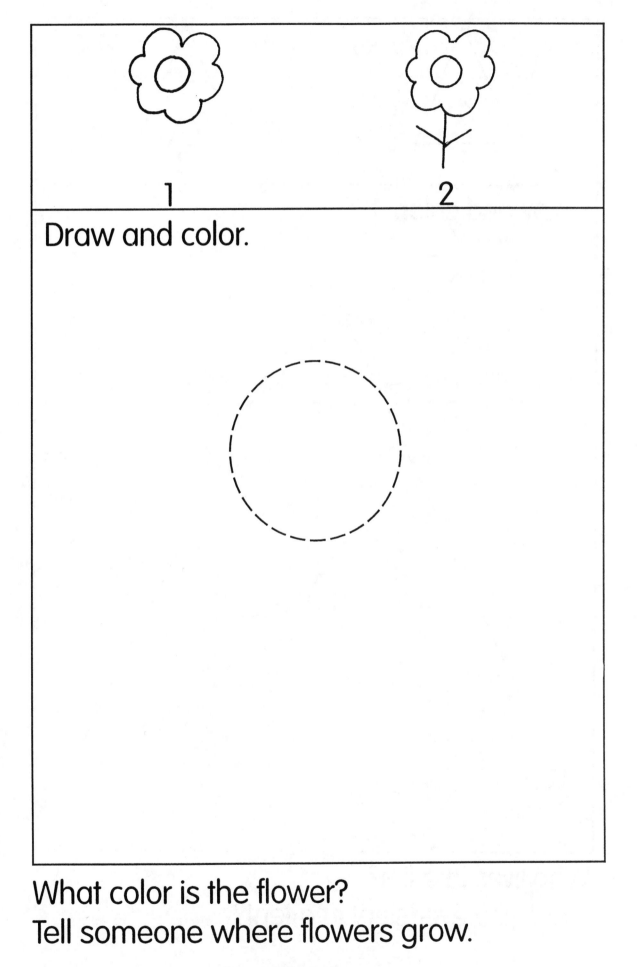

Draw and color.

What color is the flower?
Tell someone where flowers grow.

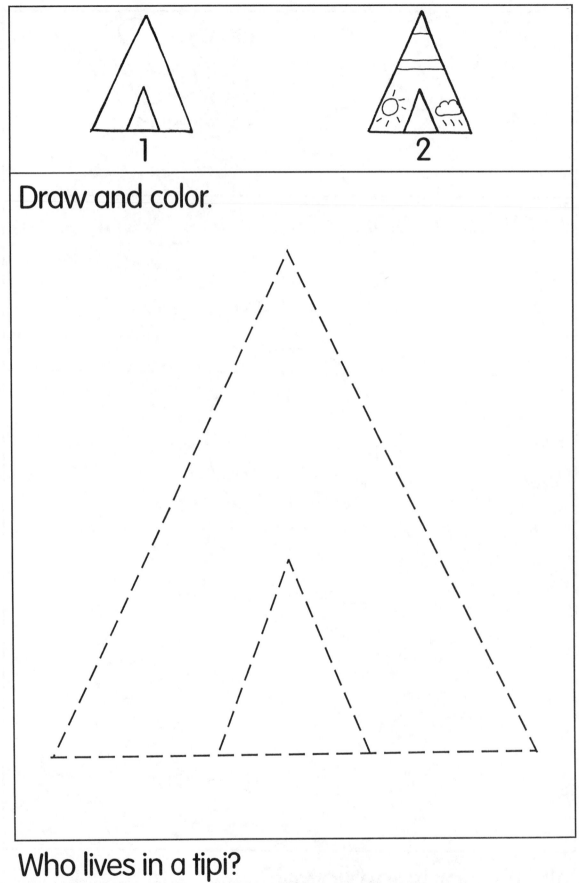

Draw and color.

Who lives in a tipi?

Have you ever slept in a tent?

Tracing; talking about a picture

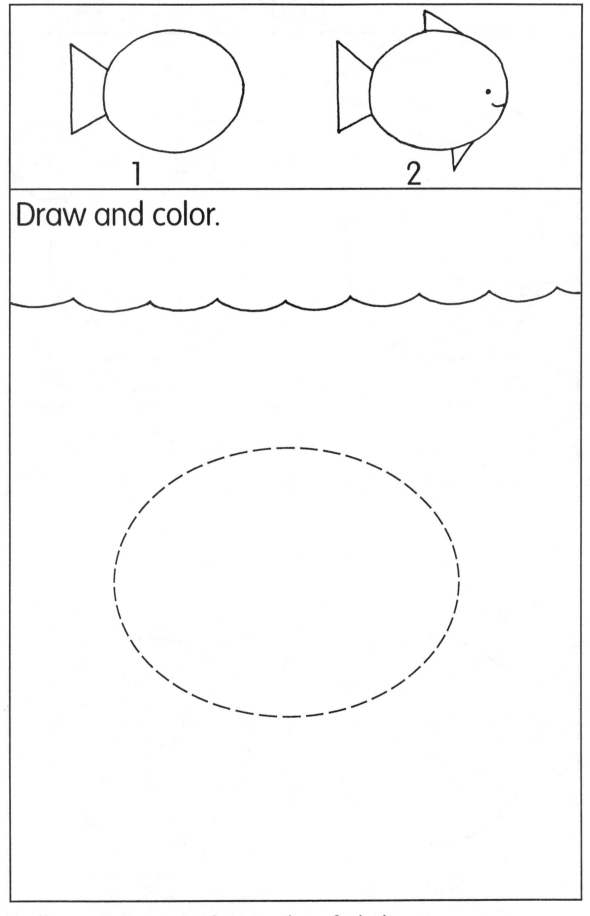

Draw and color.

Tell someone where this fish lives.

Draw & Talk

Bear

1

2

3

4

Drawing; talking about the drawing

Draw and color the 🐻 .

Tell someone three things you know about bears.

Drawing; talking about the drawing

Mouse

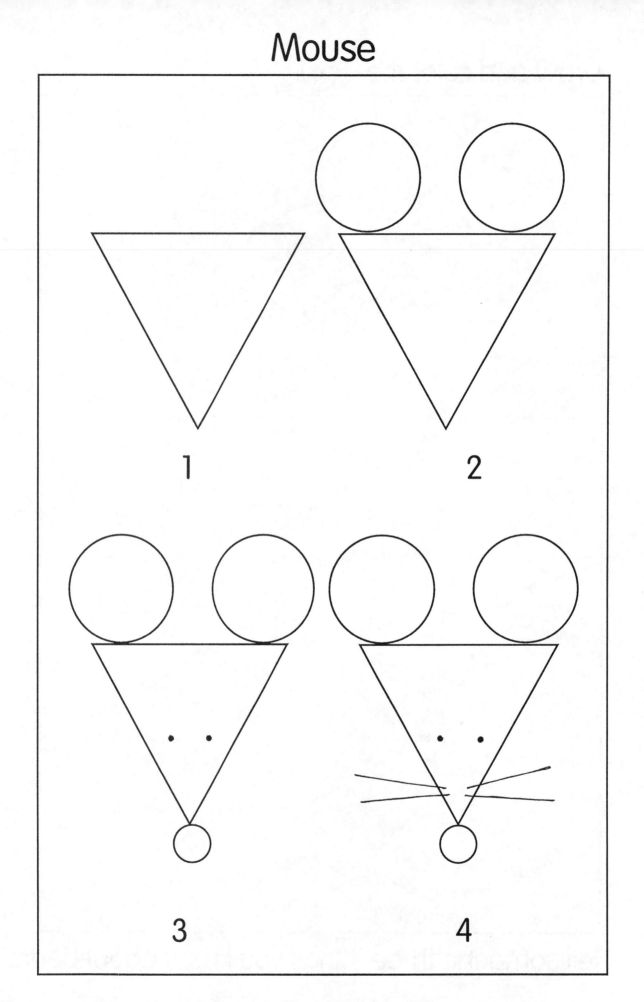

1

2

3

4

Drawing; talking about the drawing

Draw and color the 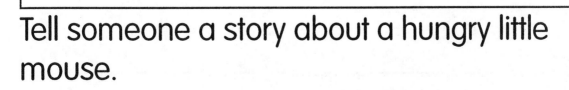 .

Tell someone a story about a hungry little mouse.

Draw & Talk

House

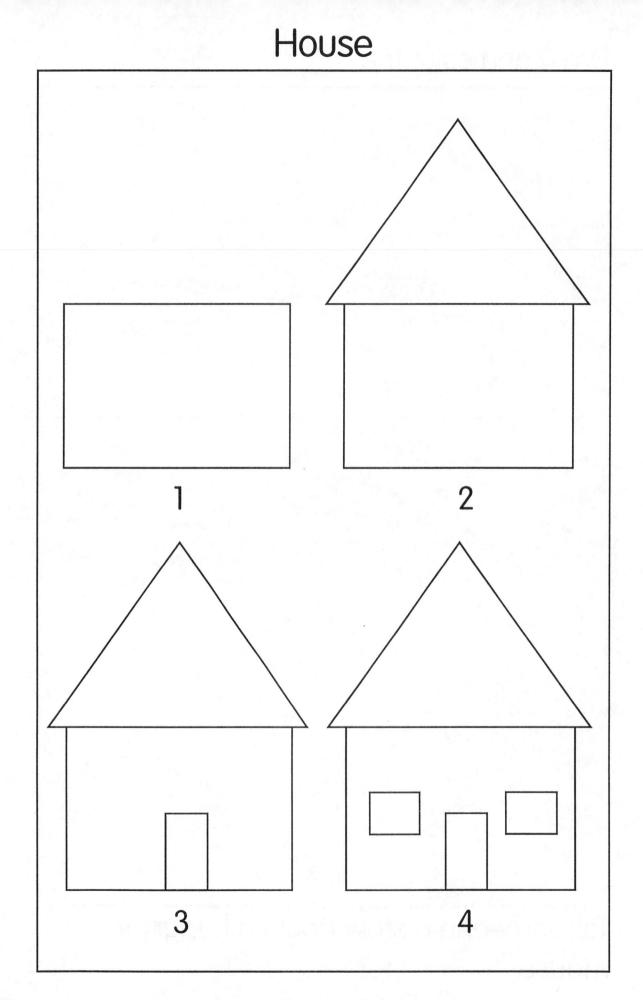

Drawing; talking about the drawing

Draw and color the 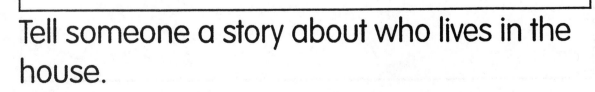 .

Tell someone a story about who lives in the house.

Duck

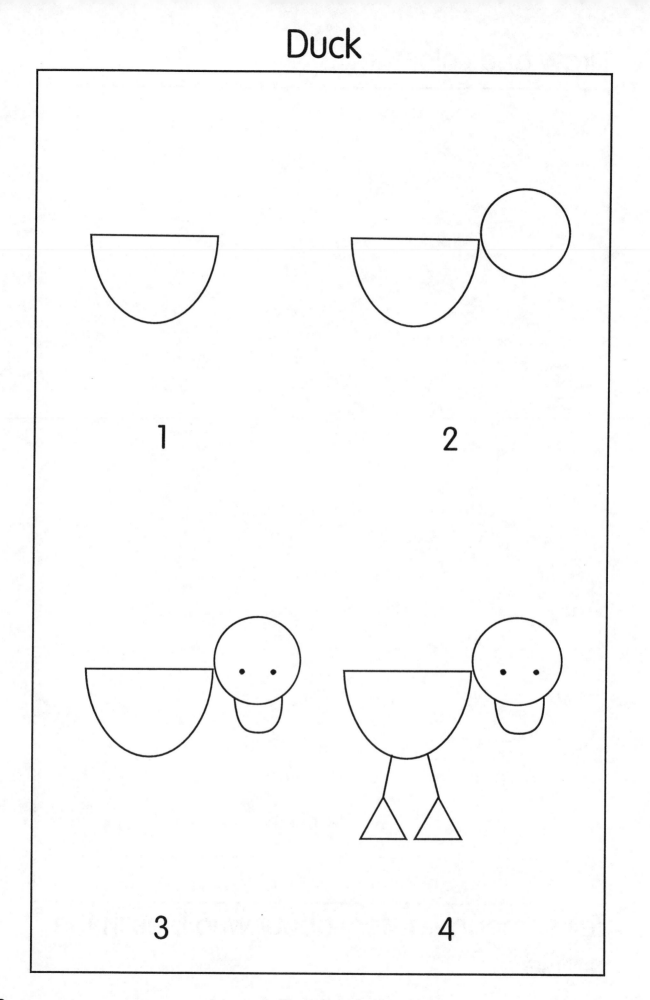

1

2

3

4

Drawing; talking about the drawing

Draw and color the   .

A duck says "Quack."
Make some animal sounds and tell which
animals make them.

Car

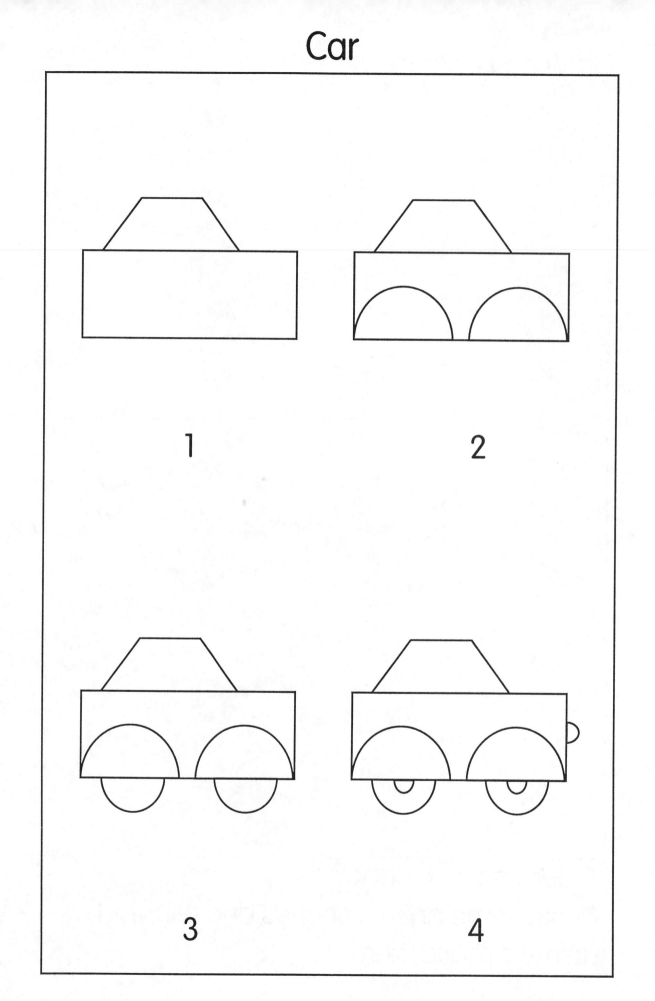

1

2

3

4

Drawing; talking about the drawing

Draw and color the 🚗 .

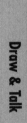

Tell someone where you would like to go in this car.

Lion

1

2

3

4

Drawing; talking about the drawing

Draw and color the 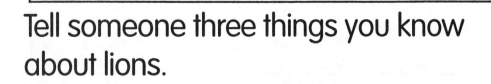 .

Tell someone three things you know
about lions.

Draw & Talk

Clown

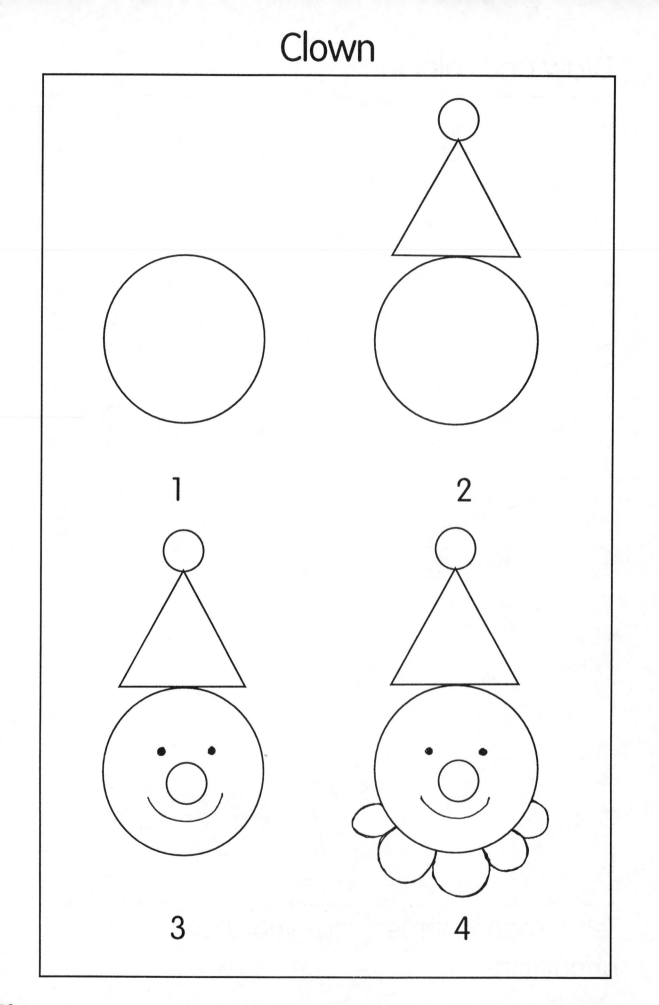

1

2

3

4

Drawing; talking about the drawing

Draw and color the .

Clowns make people laugh.
Tell someone something to make them laugh.

Birthday Cake

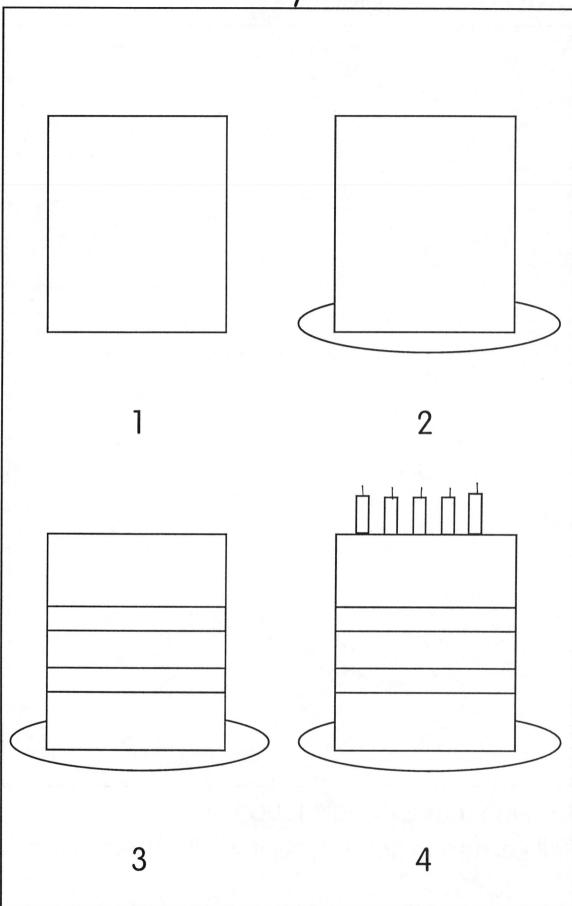

1

2

3

4

Drawing; talking about the drawing

Draw and color the .

Tell someone how many candles would be on your birthday cake.

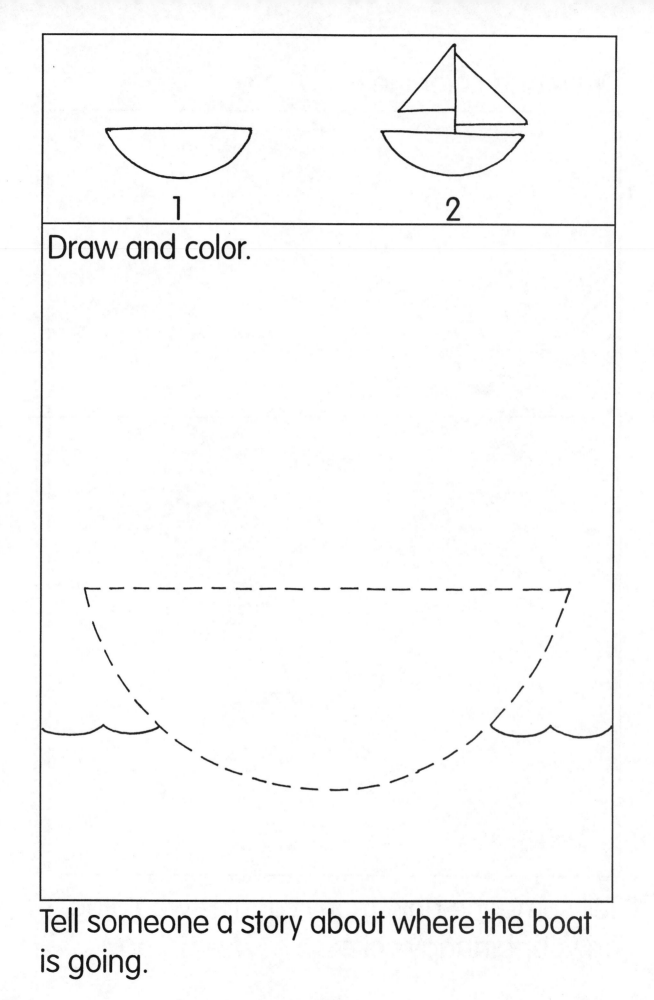

Draw and color.

Tell someone a story about where the boat is going.

Tracing; talking about a picture

This is me.

Tell someone about what you do best of all.

This is my family.

Tell someone the names of everyone in the picture.

Drawing; talking about the drawing

This is my pet.

Tell someone how you take care of your pet.

This is my house.

Tell someone about your favorite room.

Drawing; talking about the drawing

Color the balloon red.

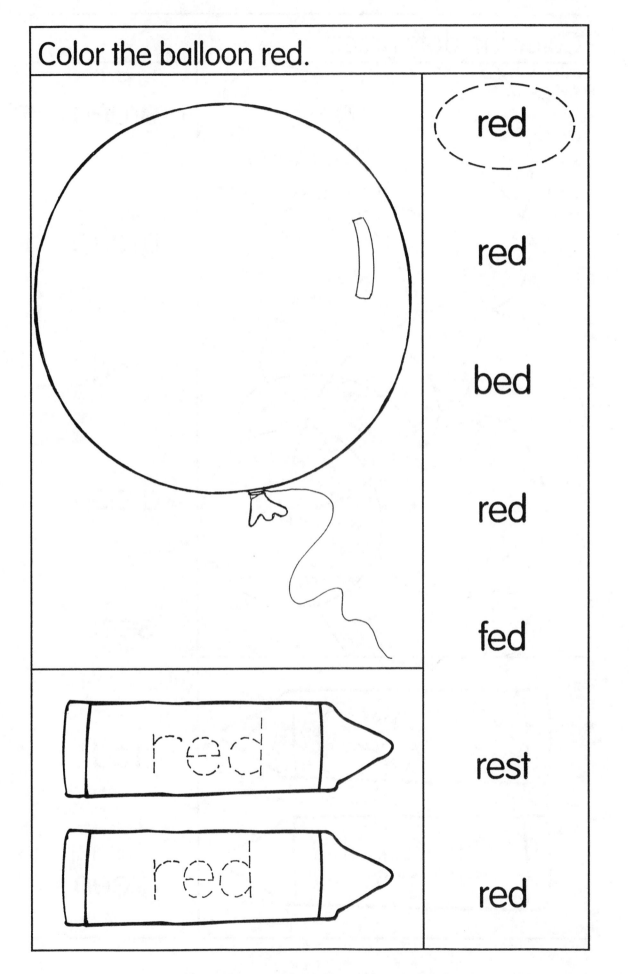

red

red

bed

red

fed

rest

red

Colors & Shapes

Color the dots green.

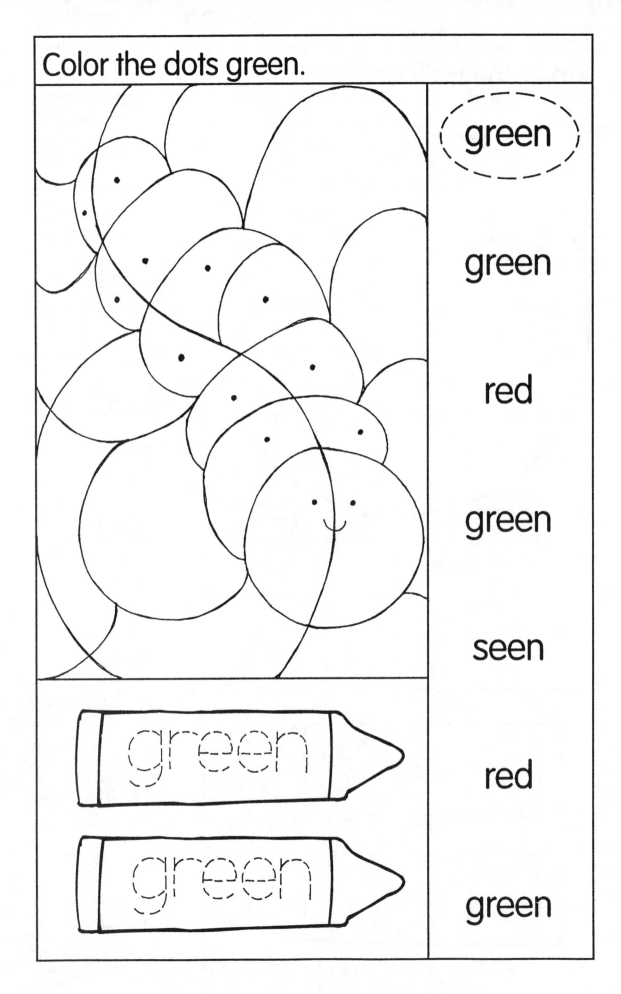

green

green

red

green

seen

red

green

Recognizing and tracing a color word

Make a basket for the girl.

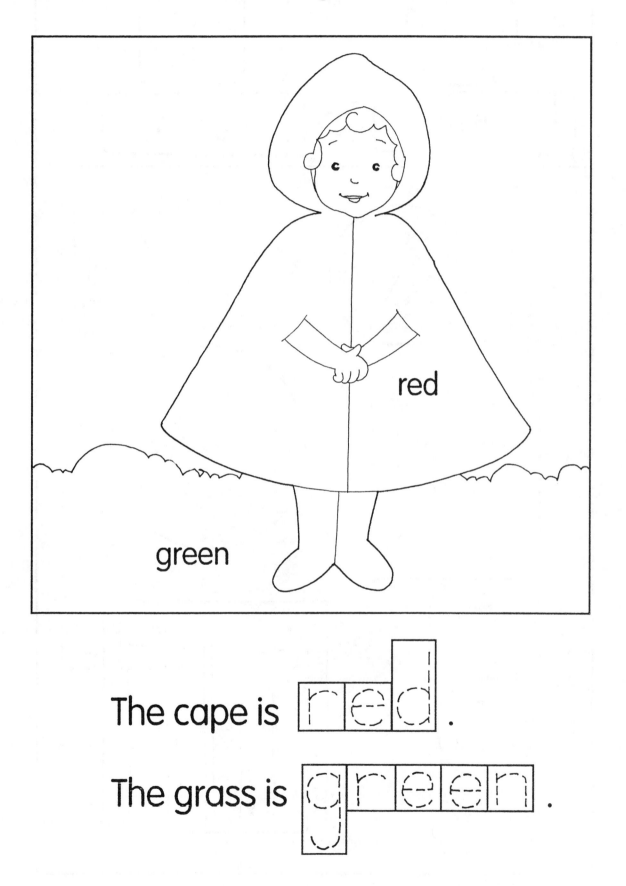

The cape is red.

The grass is green.

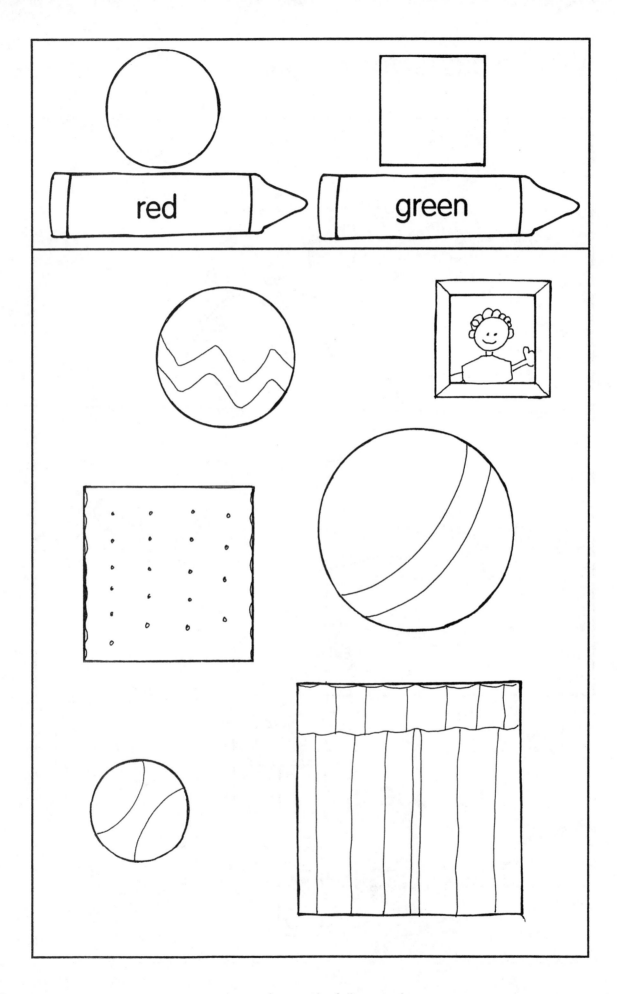

Recognizing color words; following directions

Color the dots yellow.

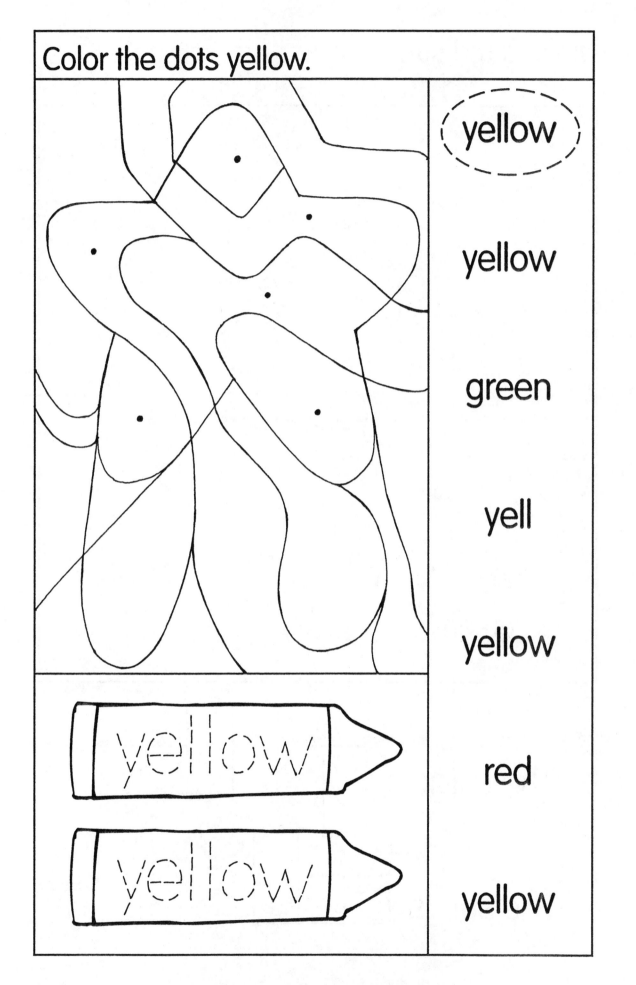

yellow

yellow

green

yell

yellow

red

yellow

Colors & Shapes

Make a red sun.

yellow

green

The chick is **yellow**.

The sun is **red**.

Recognizing and tracing color words

Color the bird blue.

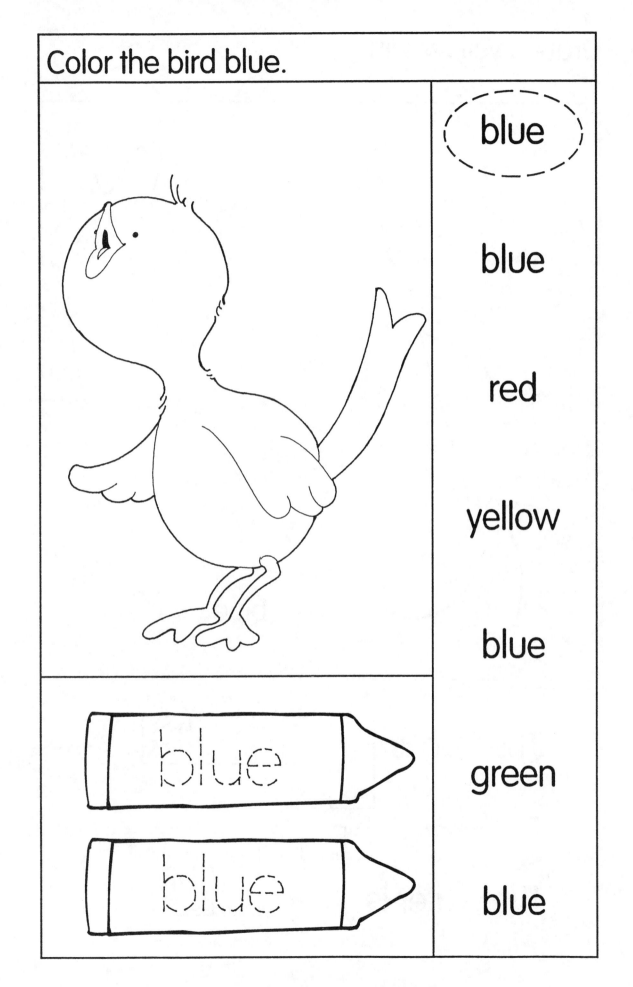

blue

blue

red

yellow

blue

green

blue

Colors & Shapes

Draw a yellow sun.

The frog is green.

The water is blue.

Tracing color words; following directions

Color the butterfly orange.

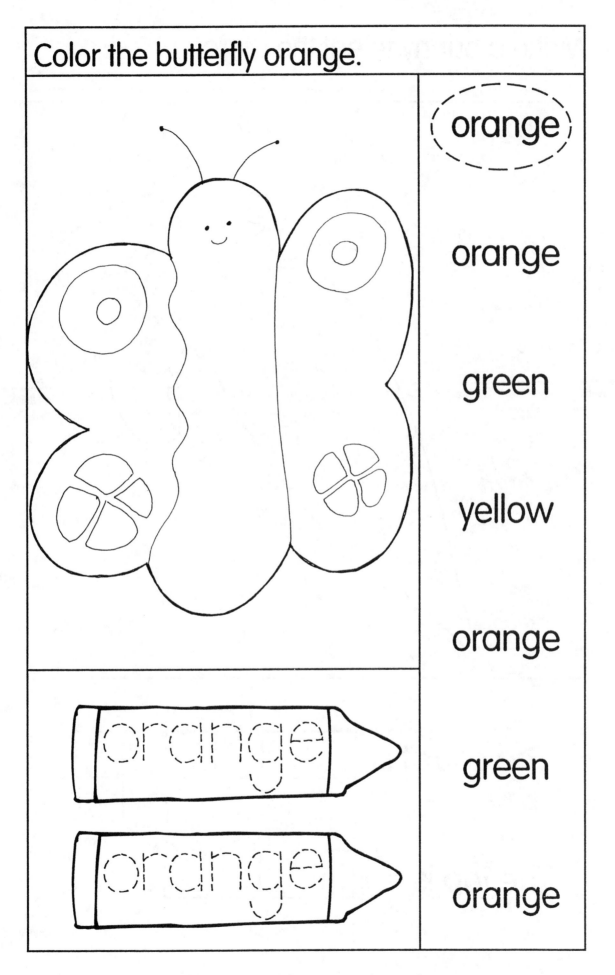

orange

orange

green

yellow

orange

green

orange

Colors & Shapes

Make a bunny to eat the carrot.

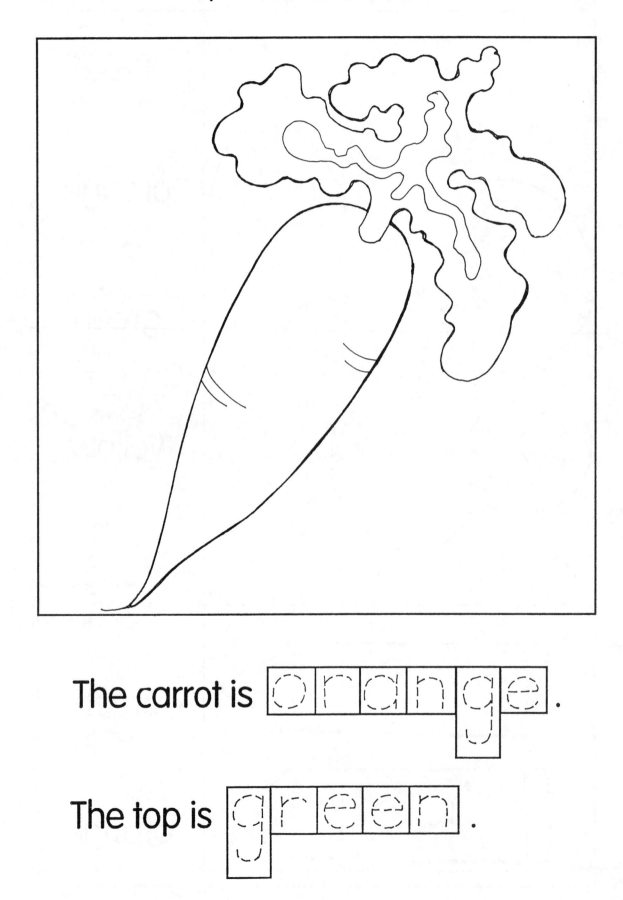

The carrot is orange.

The top is green.

Tracing color words; following directions

Circles

Trace the circles.

Color them.

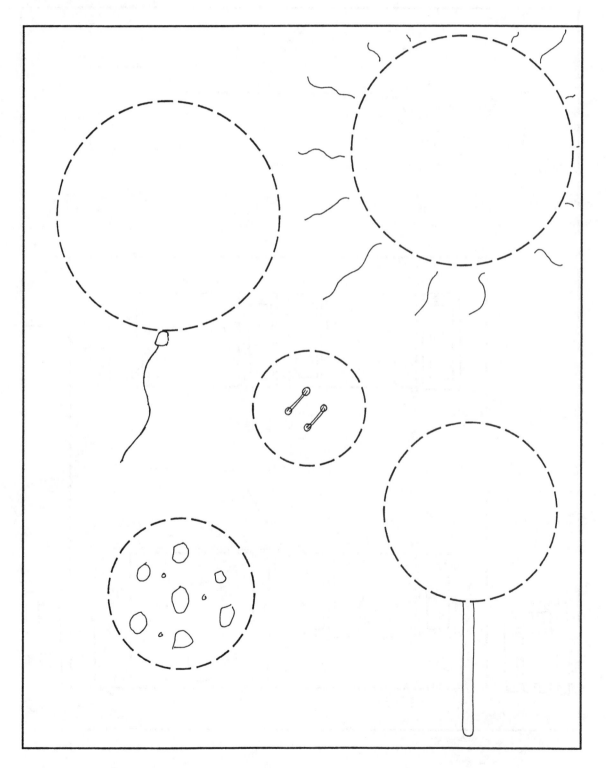

Colors & Shapes

Squares

Trace the squares.

Color them.

Tracing shapes

Color the dots black.

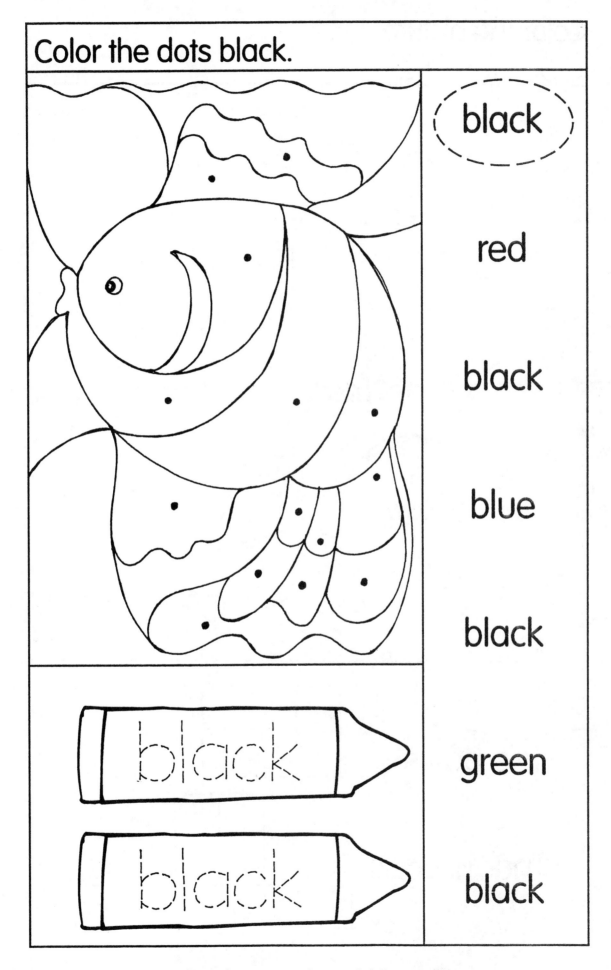

black

red

black

blue

black

green

black

Colors & Shapes

Color the picture.

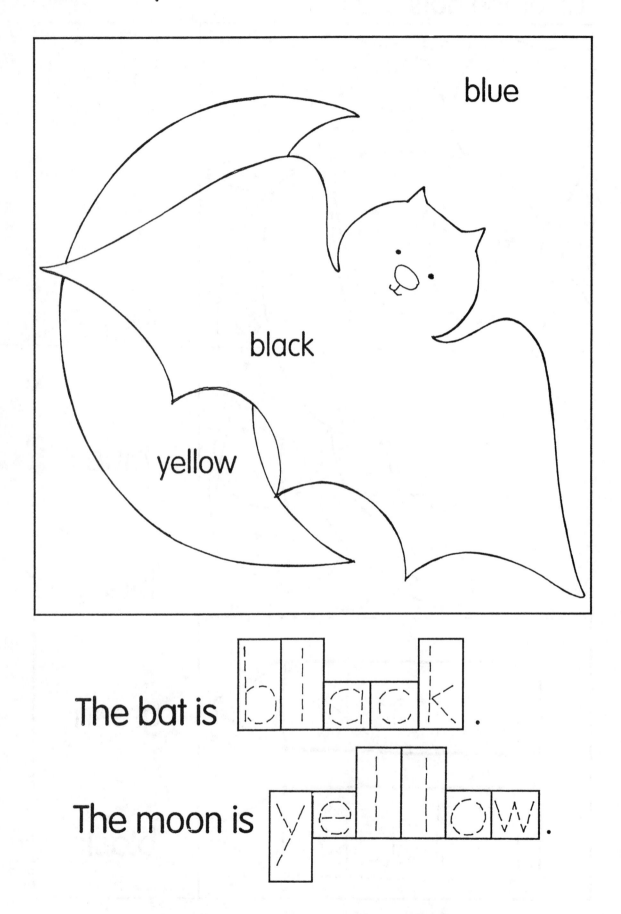

blue

black

yellow

The bat is black.

The moon is yellow.

Tracing color words; following directions

Find the circles and squares.

red

yellow

Recognizing shapes

271

Color the dots brown.
Color the triangles red.

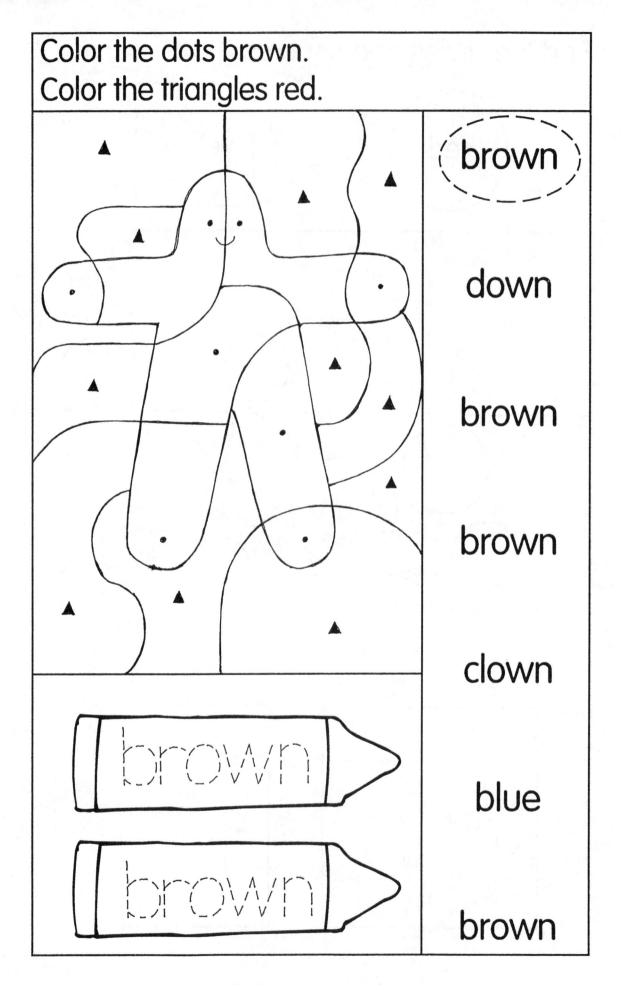

brown

down

brown

brown

clown

blue

brown

Recognizing and tracing a color word; following directions

Make a blue coat on the bear.

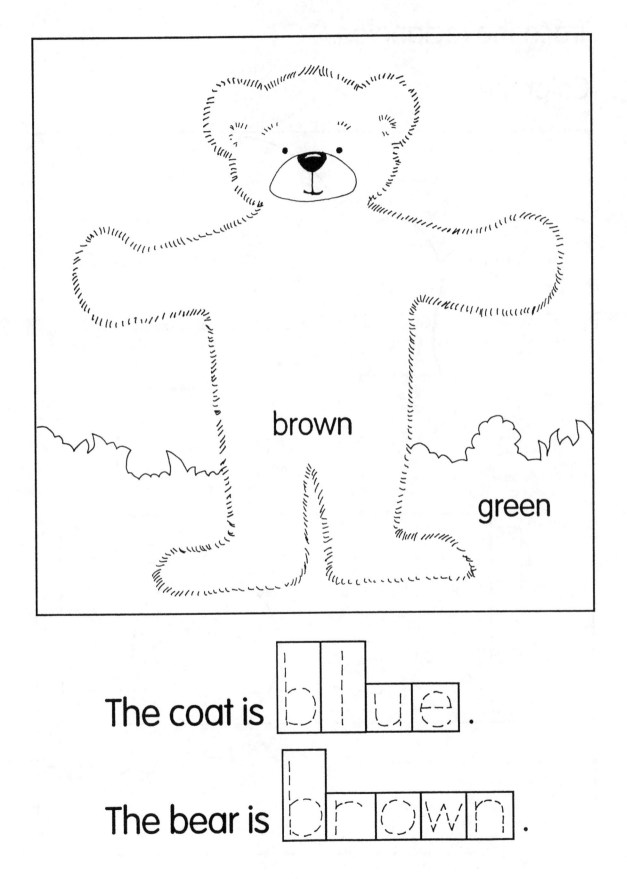

brown

green

The coat is blue.

The bear is brown.

Colors & Shapes

Rectangles

Trace the rectangles.

Color them.

Tracing shapes

Triangles

Trace the triangles.

Color them.

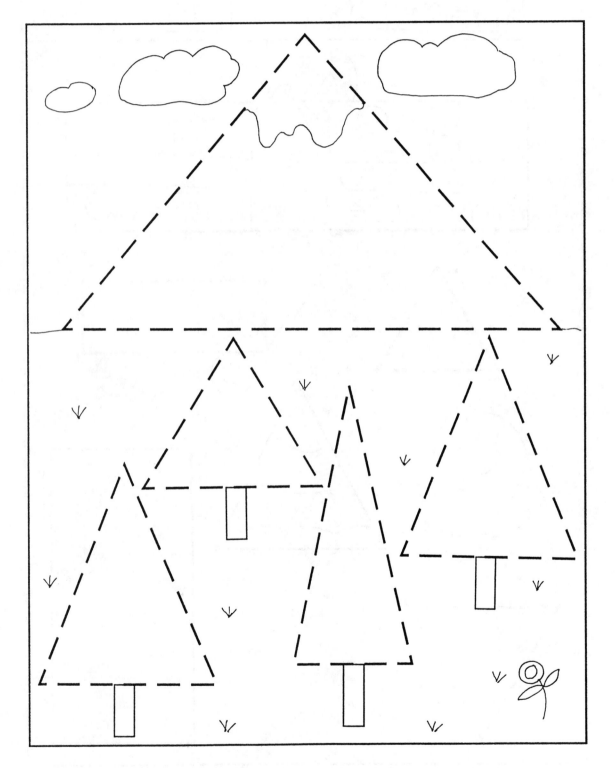

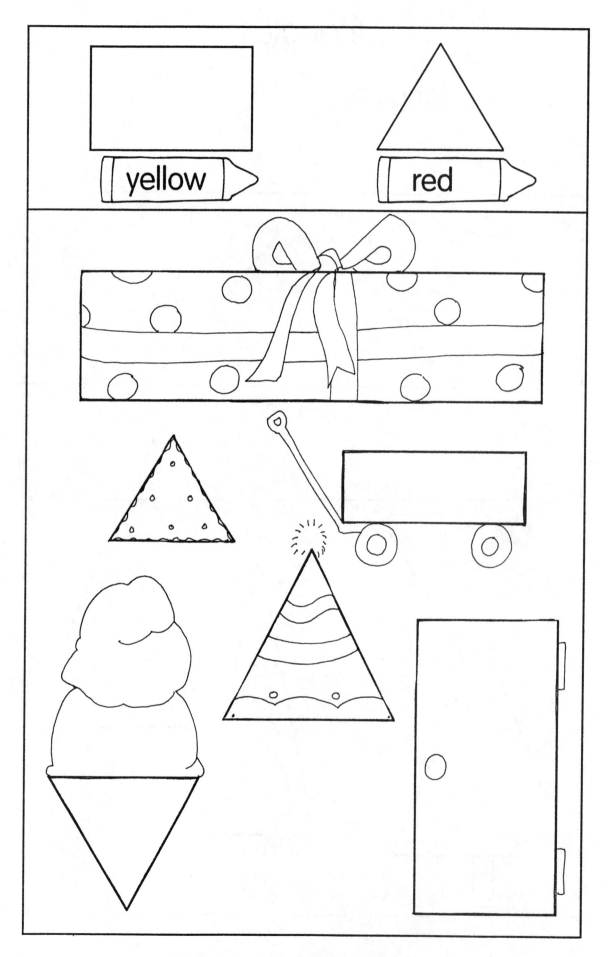

yellow

red

Recognizing shapes; following directions

Color the grapes purple.

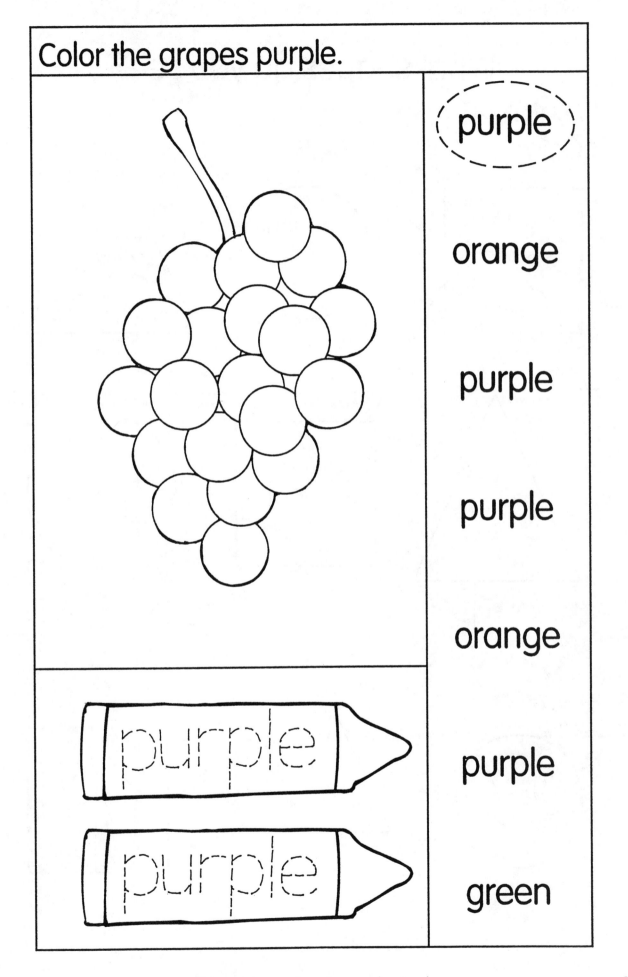

purple

orange

purple

purple

orange

purple

green

Colors & Shapes

What shapes do you see?

Match.
Color.

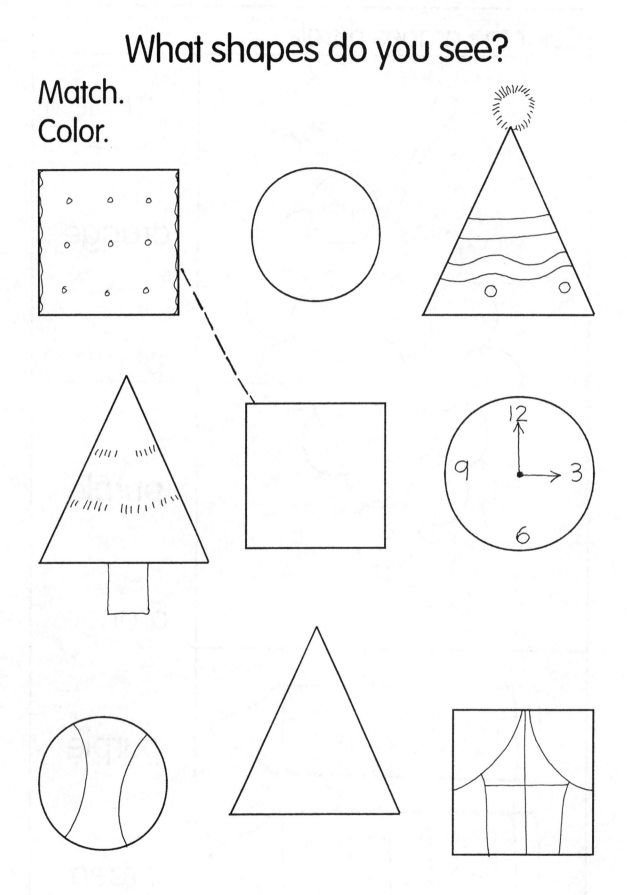

Matching shapes

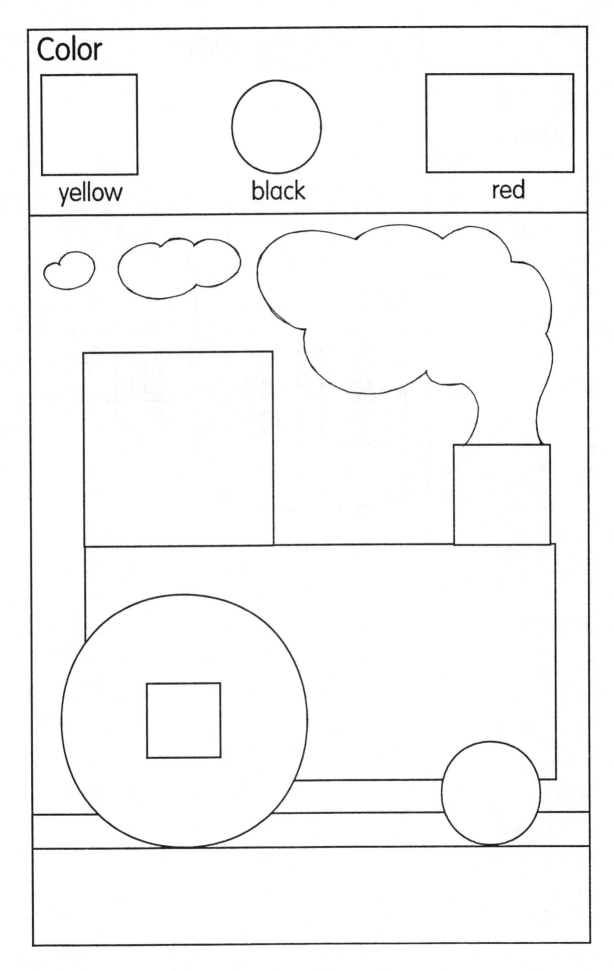

Color

yellow   black   red

Connect the Dots

Start at 1.
Color.

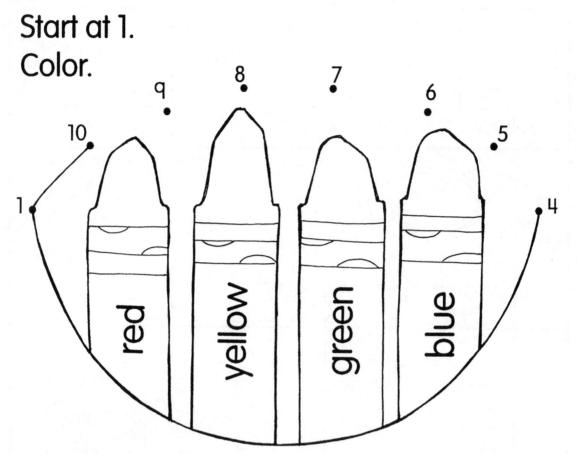

red

yellow

green

blue

Recognizing color words

Color the dots blue.
The clouds are white.

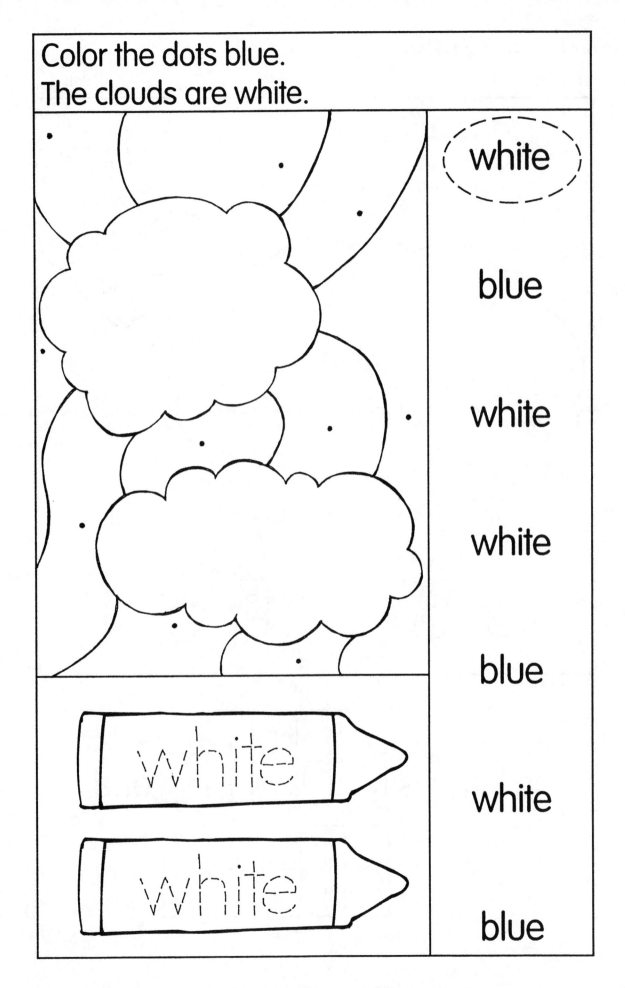

white

blue

white

white

blue

white

blue

Recognizing and tracing a color word; following directions

Colors & Shapes

Color the lamb.

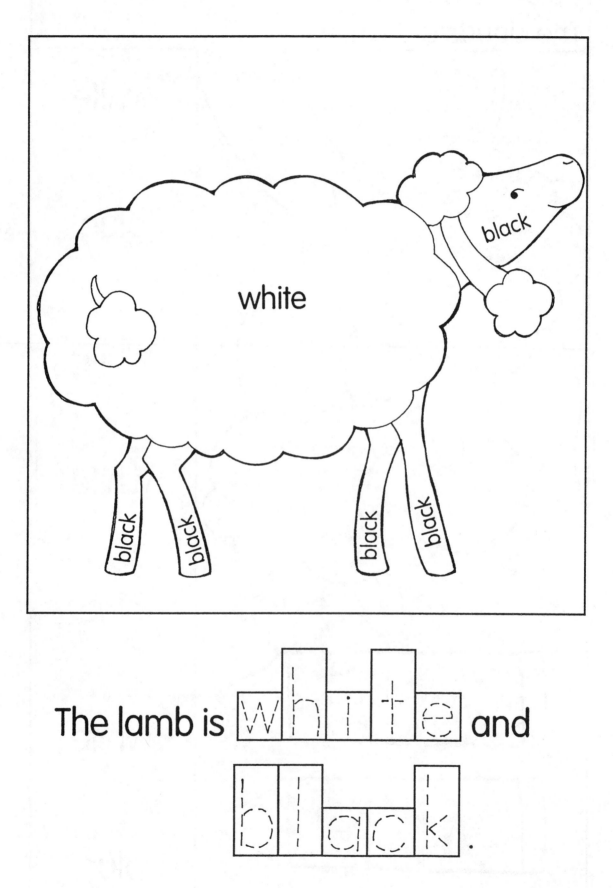

The lamb is white and black.

Tracing color words; following directions

green yellow blue

Colors & Shapes

Trace and color.

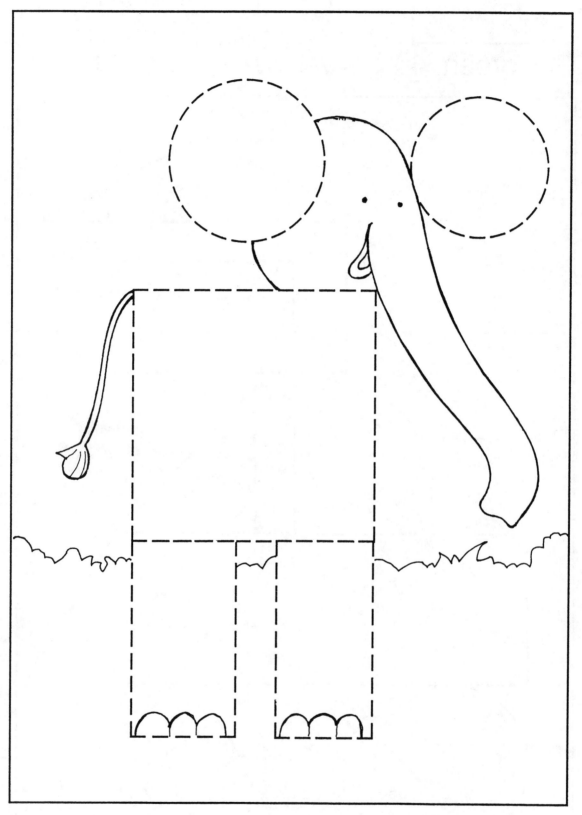

Tracing shapes

Connect the dots.
Color the shapes.

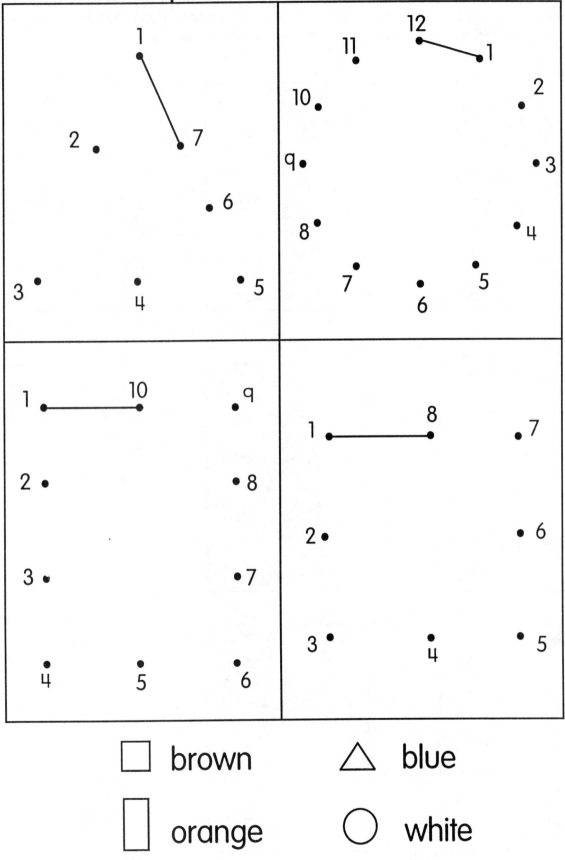

⬜ brown   △ blue

▯ orange   ◯ white

Colors & Shapes

Answer Key

Please take time to go over the work your child has completed. Ask your child to explain what he/she has done. Praise both success and effort. If mistakes have been made, explain what the answer should have been and how to find it. Let your child know that mistakes are a part of learning. The time you spend with your child helps let him/her know you feel learning is important.

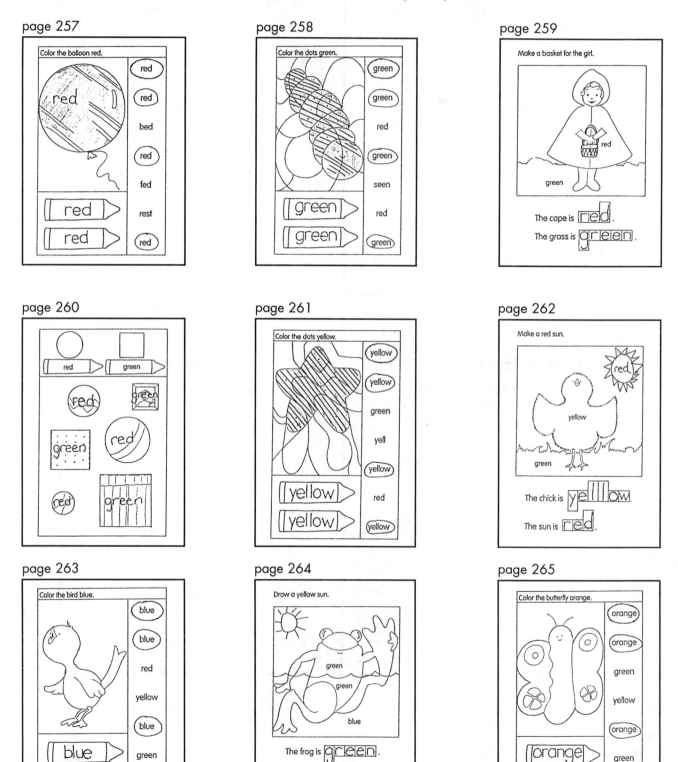

page 257

page 258

page 259

page 260

page 261

page 262

page 263

page 264

page 265

page 266

Make a bunny to eat the carrot.

The carrot is orange.

The top is green.

page 267

Circles

Trace the circles.

Color them.

page 268

Squares

Trace the squares.

Color them.

page 269

Color the dots black.

black

red

black

blue

black

black

green

black

black

page 270

Color the picture.

blue

black

yellow

The bat is black.

The moon is yellow.

page 271

Find the circles and squares.

red

yellow

red

red

red

red

red

red

red

red

red

yellow

yellow

page 272

Color the dots brown.

Color the triangles red.

brown

down

brown

brown

clown

brown

blue

brown

brown

page 273

Make a blue coat on the bear.

brown

green

The coat is blue.

The bear is brown.

page 274

Rectangles

Trace the rectangles.

Color them.

page 275

Triangles

Trace the triangles.

Color them.

page 276

yellow

red

page 277

Color the grapes purple.

purple

orange

purple

purple

orange

purple

purple

green

Answers

Colors & Shapes

page 278

What shapes do you see?
Match.
Color.

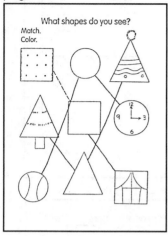

page 279

Color

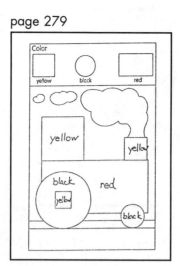

page 280

Connect the Dots

Start at 1.
Color.

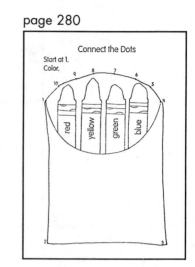

page 281

Color the dots blue.
The clouds are white.

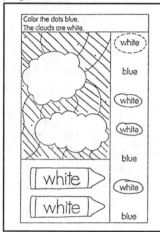

page 282

Color the lamb.

The lamb is white and black.

page 283

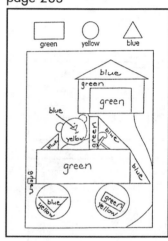

page 284

Trace and color.

page 285

Connect the dots.
Color the shapes.

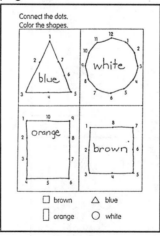

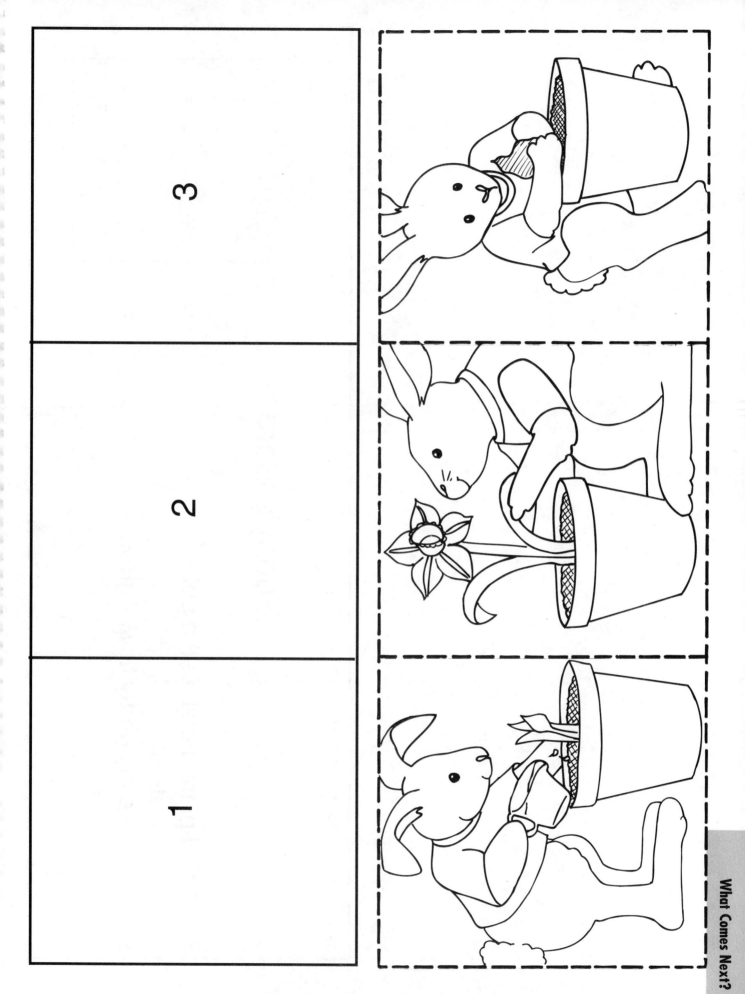

What Comes Next?

Bunny's Garden

I plant a bulb in the pot.
I water it.
See my pretty flower grow.

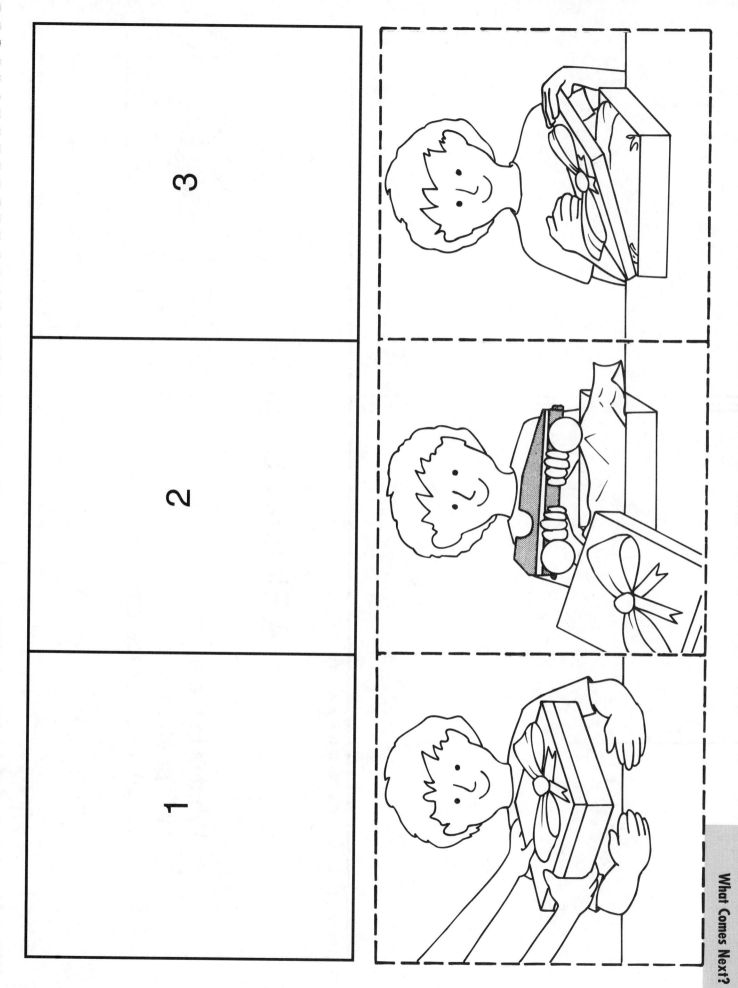

Putting pictures in correct order

Parent: Please share this little story with your child.

A Birthday Surprise

What is in the box?
I will peek inside.
Wow! I got a race car.

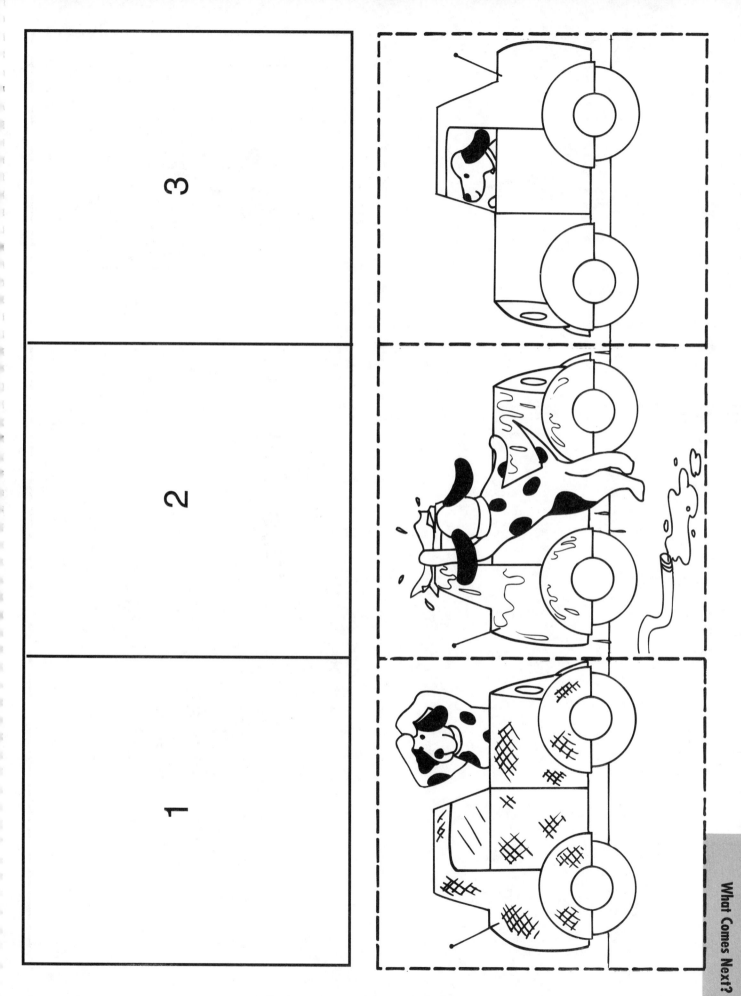

1	2	3

What Comes Next?

Wash Day

This car is a dirty mess.
I will wash it.
Let's ride in my clean car.

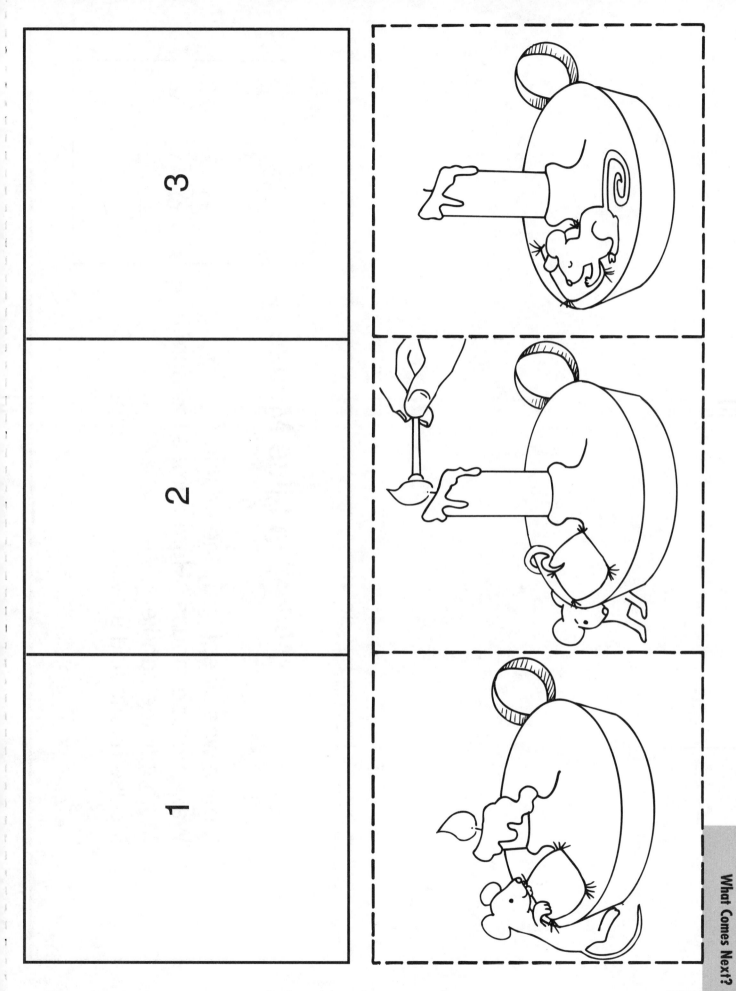

Putting pictures in correct order

295

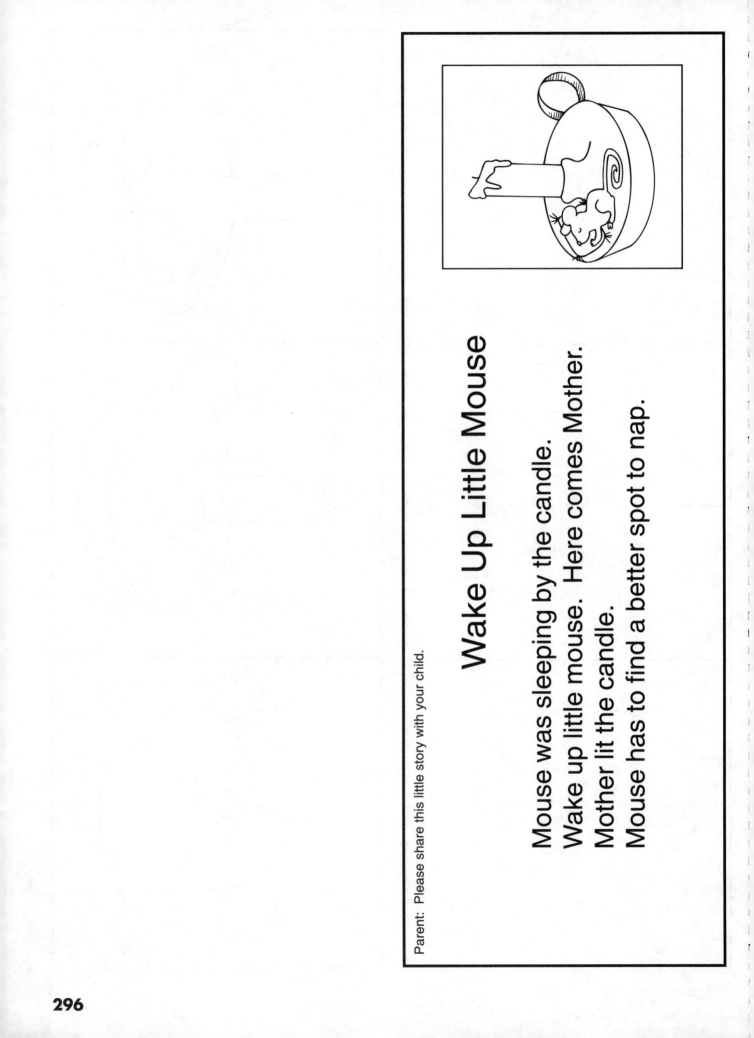

Wake Up Little Mouse

Mouse was sleeping by the candle.
Wake up little mouse. Here comes Mother.
Mother lit the candle.
Mouse has to find a better spot to nap.

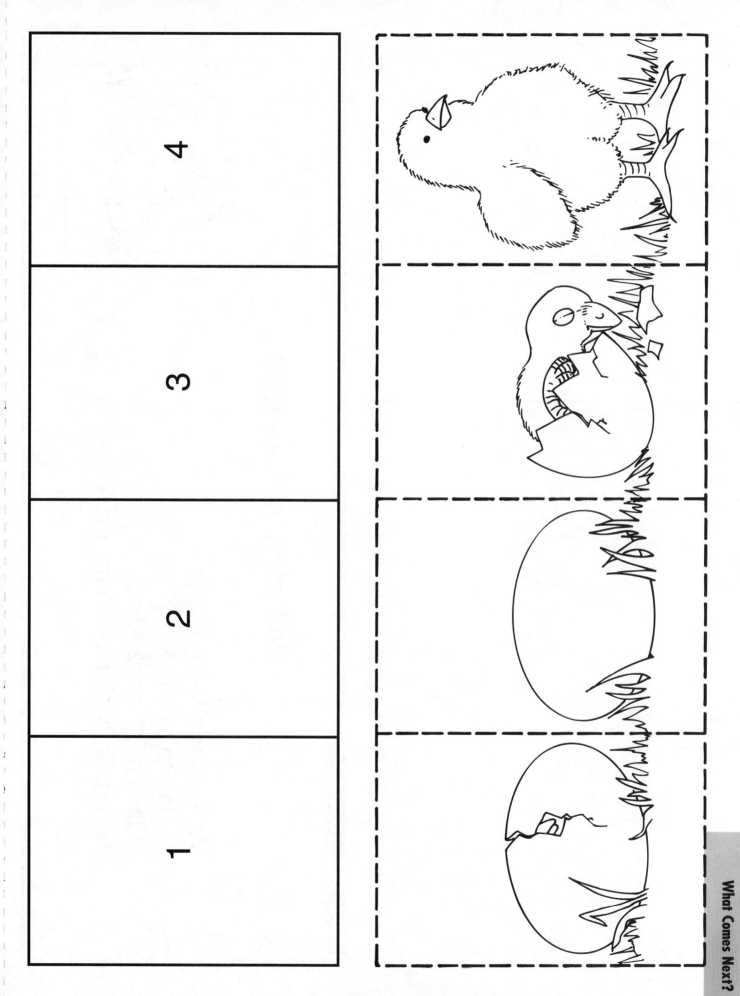

| 1 | 2 | 3 | 4 |

What Comes Next?

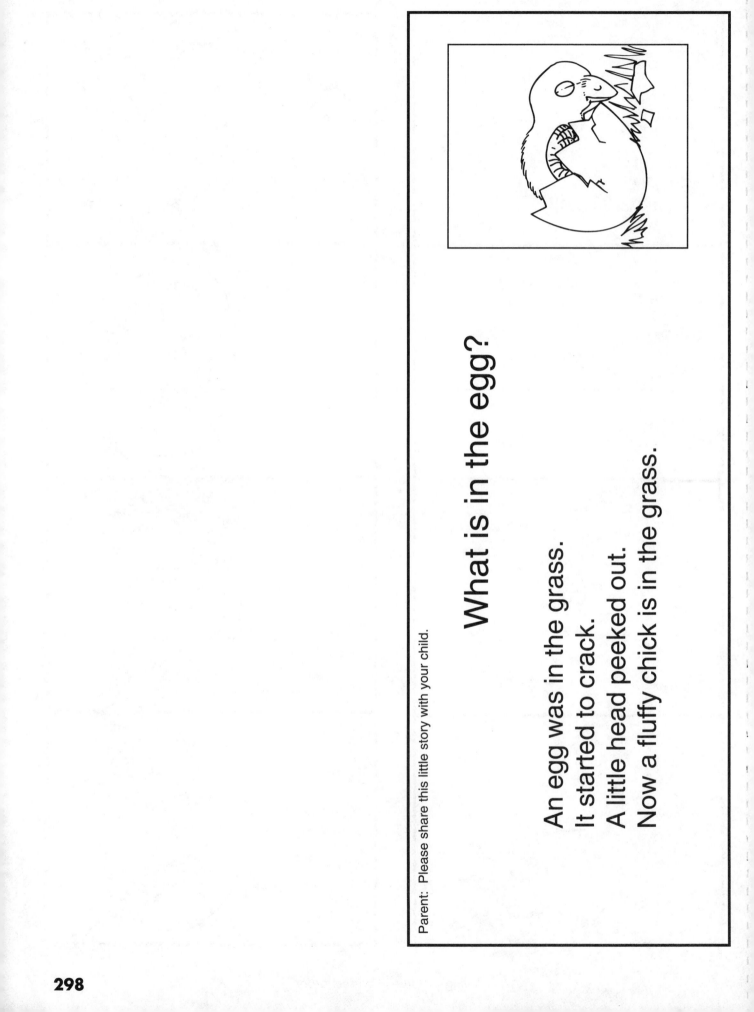

What is in the egg?

An egg was in the grass.
It started to crack.
A little head peeked out.
Now a fluffy chick is in the grass.

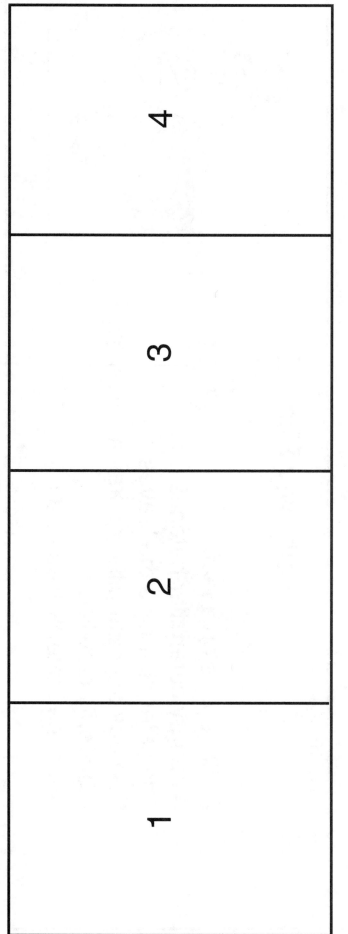

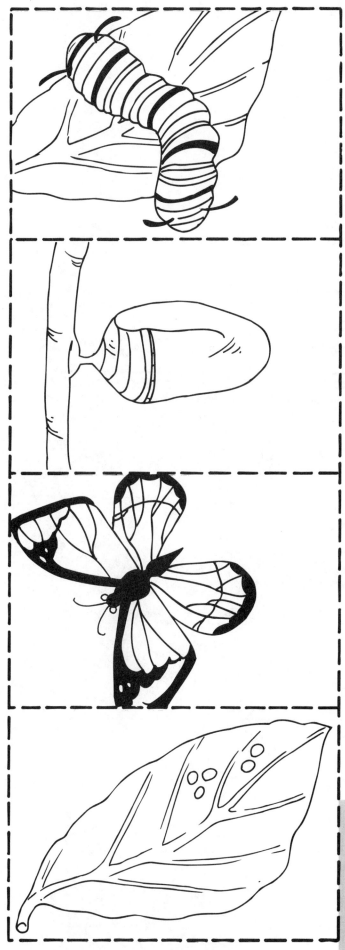

Parent: Please share this little story with your child.

Butterfly Flies By

A little egg is on a leaf.
A hungry caterpillar hatches out.
The caterpillar eats the leaves.
One day the caterpillar makes a chrysalis.
A butterfly crawls out.
Soon the butterfly flies away.

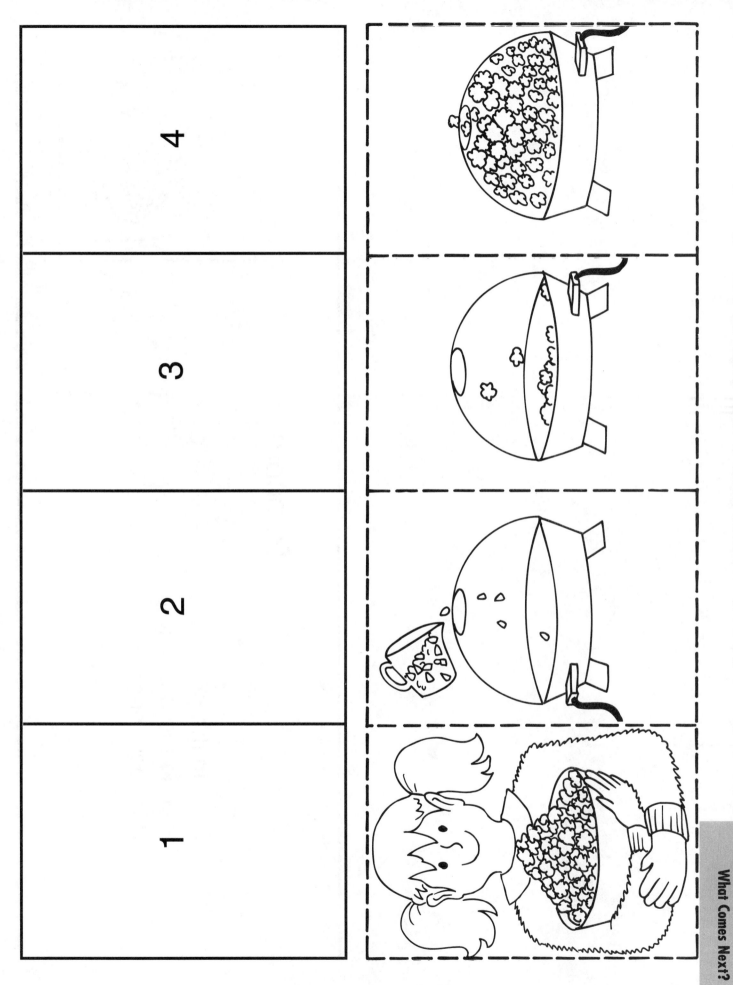

Putting pictures in correct order

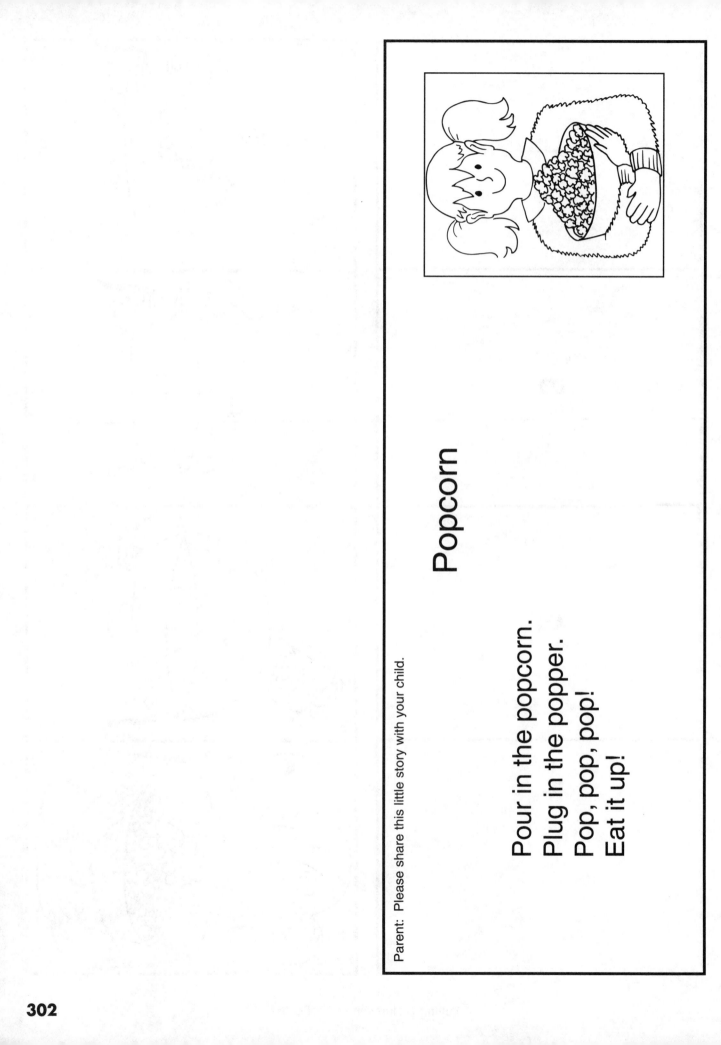

Parent: Please share this little story with your child.

Popcorn

Pour in the popcorn.
Plug in the popper.
Pop, pop, pop!
Eat it up!

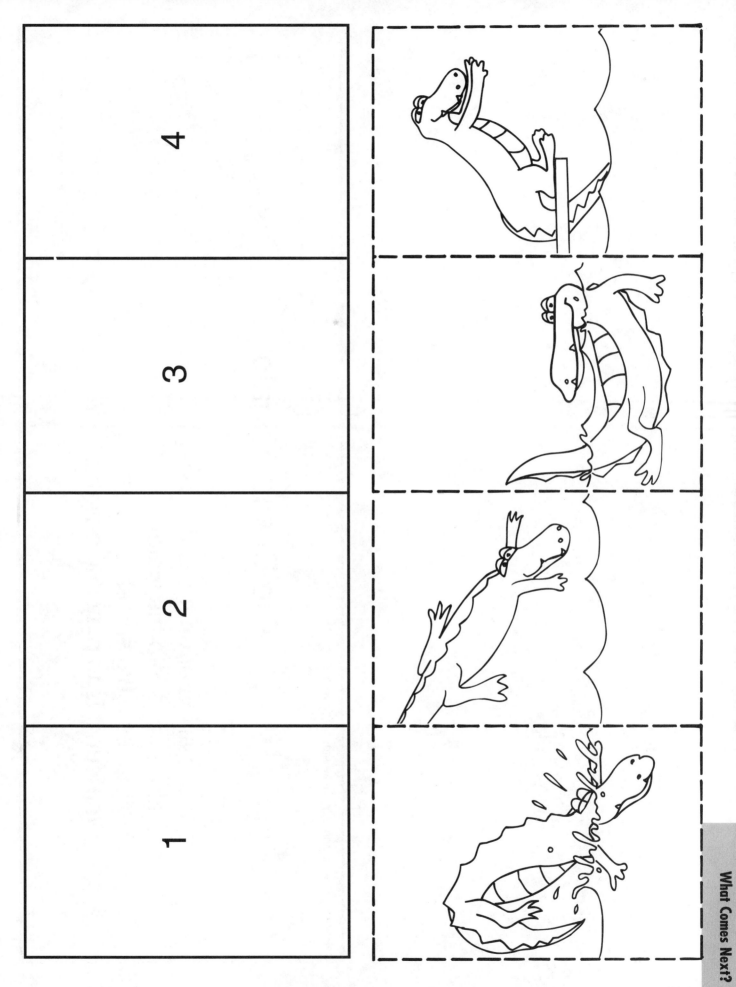

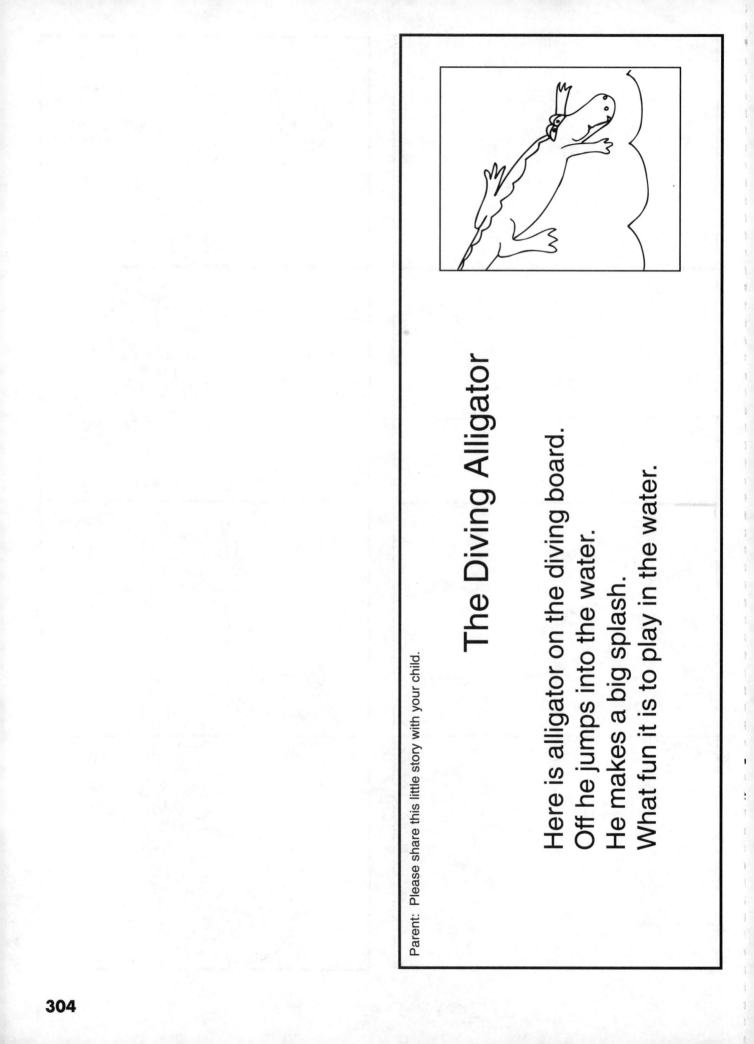

The Diving Alligator

Here is alligator on the diving board.
Off he jumps into the water.
He makes a big splash.
What fun it is to play in the water.

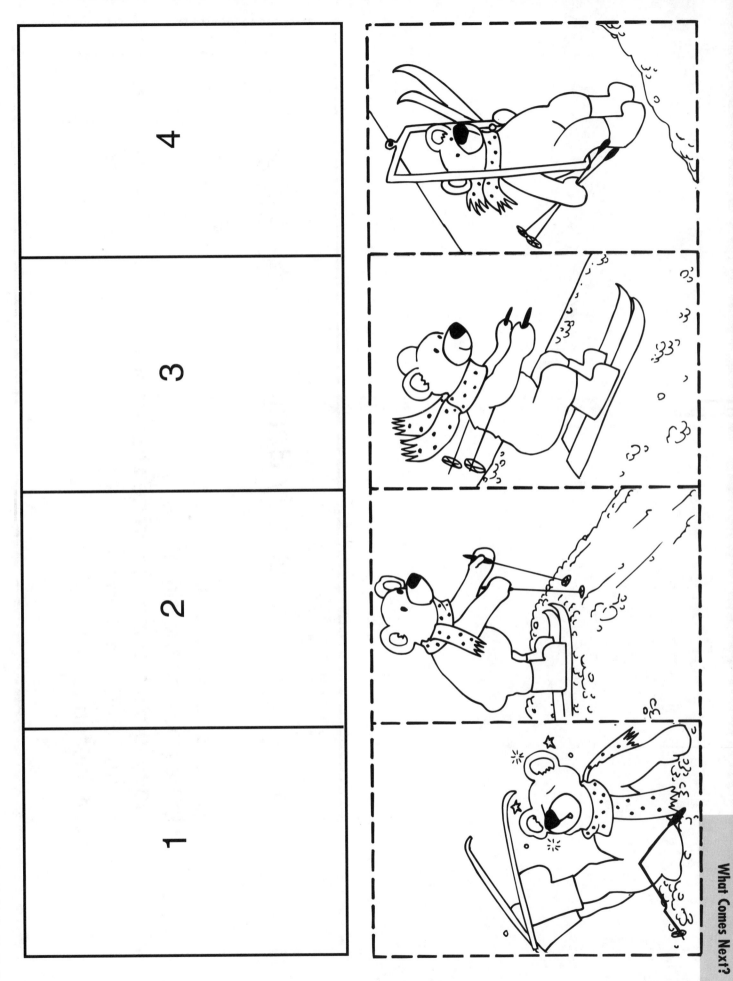

Putting pictures in correct order

What Comes Next?

Parent: Please share this little story with your child.

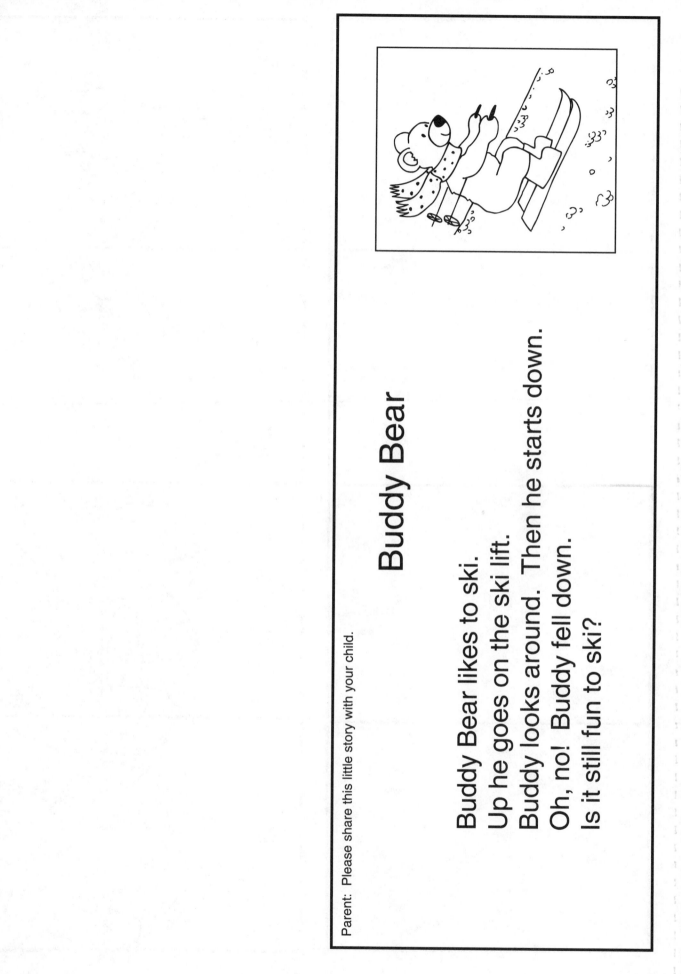

Buddy Bear

Buddy Bear likes to ski.
Up he goes on the ski lift.
Buddy looks around. Then he starts down.
Oh, no! Buddy fell down.
Is it still fun to ski?

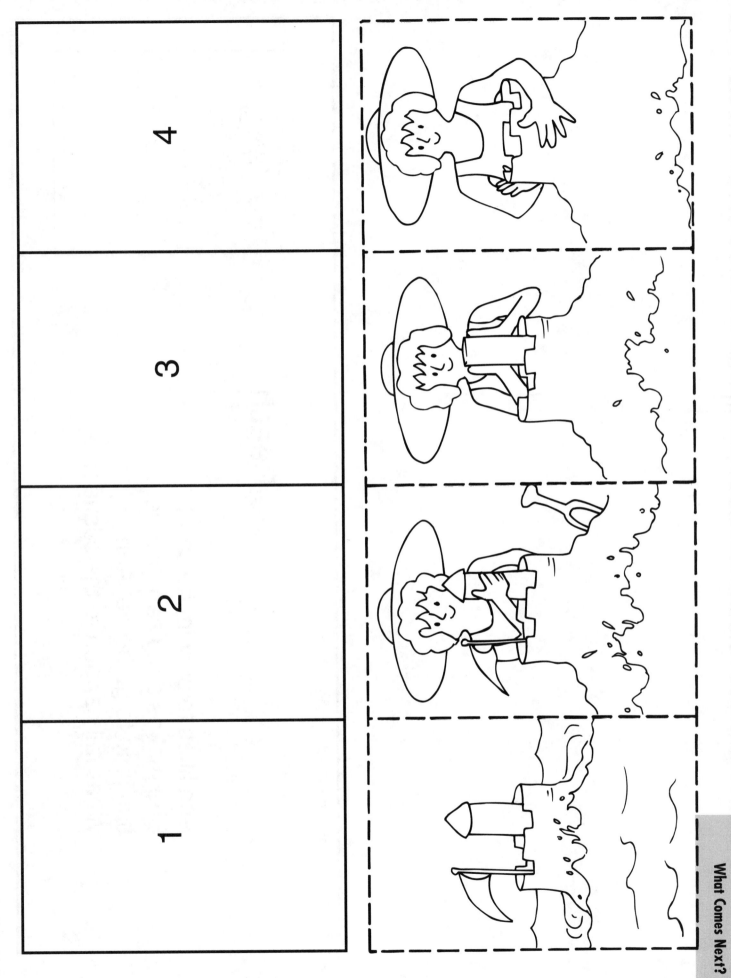

| 1 | 2 | 3 | 4 |

Parent: Please share this little story with your child.

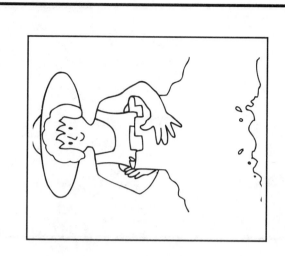

At the Beach

Ann likes to play in the sand.

She makes a big sand castle.

It is time to go home, Ann.

What will happen to the castle now?

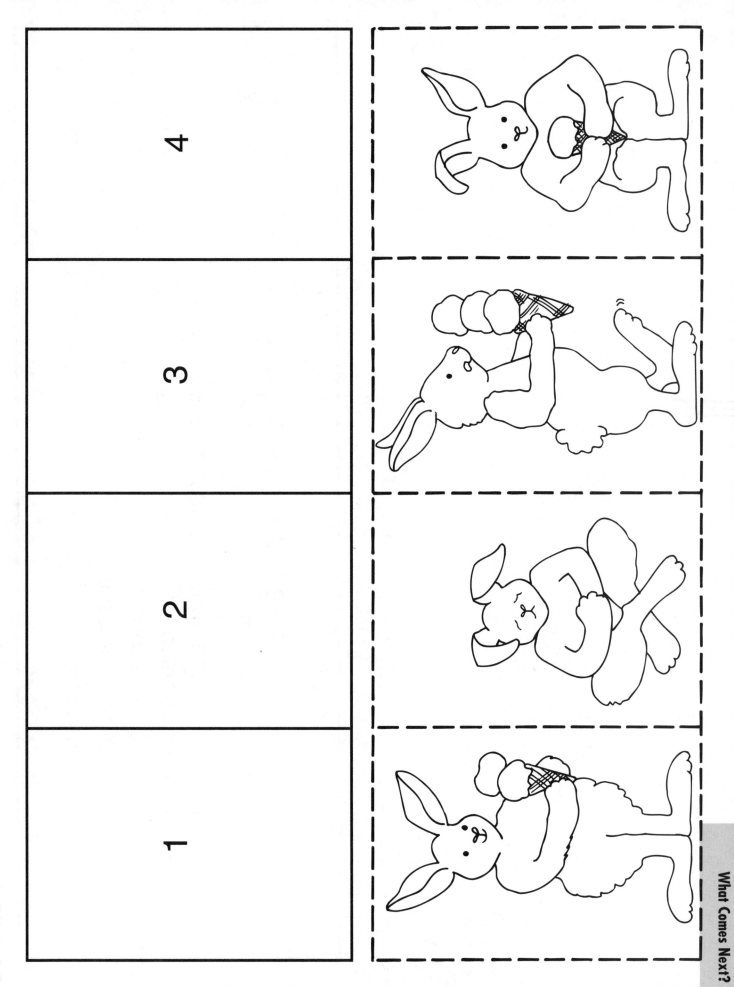

4	3	2	1

Putting pictures in correct order

309

Parent: Please share this little story with your child.

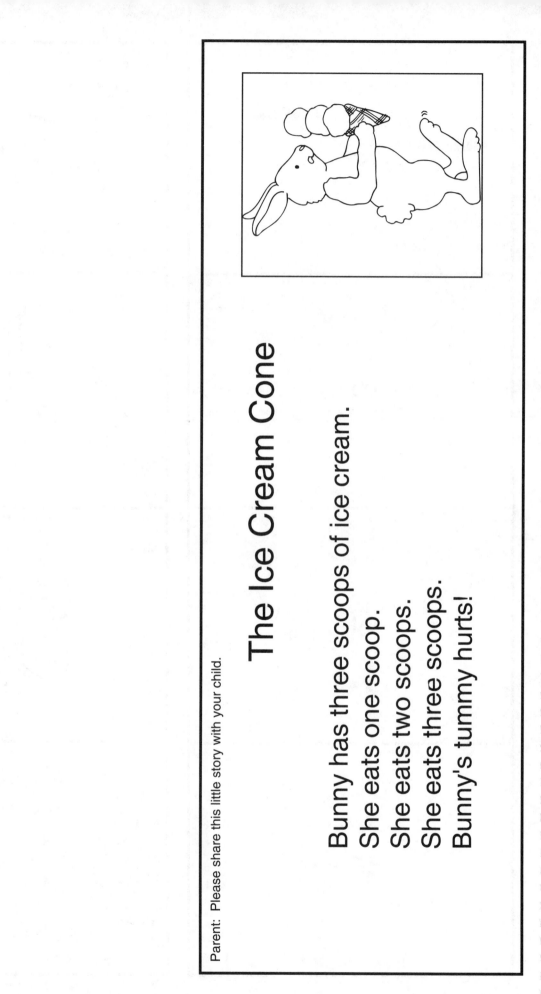

The Ice Cream Cone

Bunny has three scoops of ice cream.
She eats one scoop.
She eats two scoops.
She eats three scoops.
Bunny's tummy hurts!

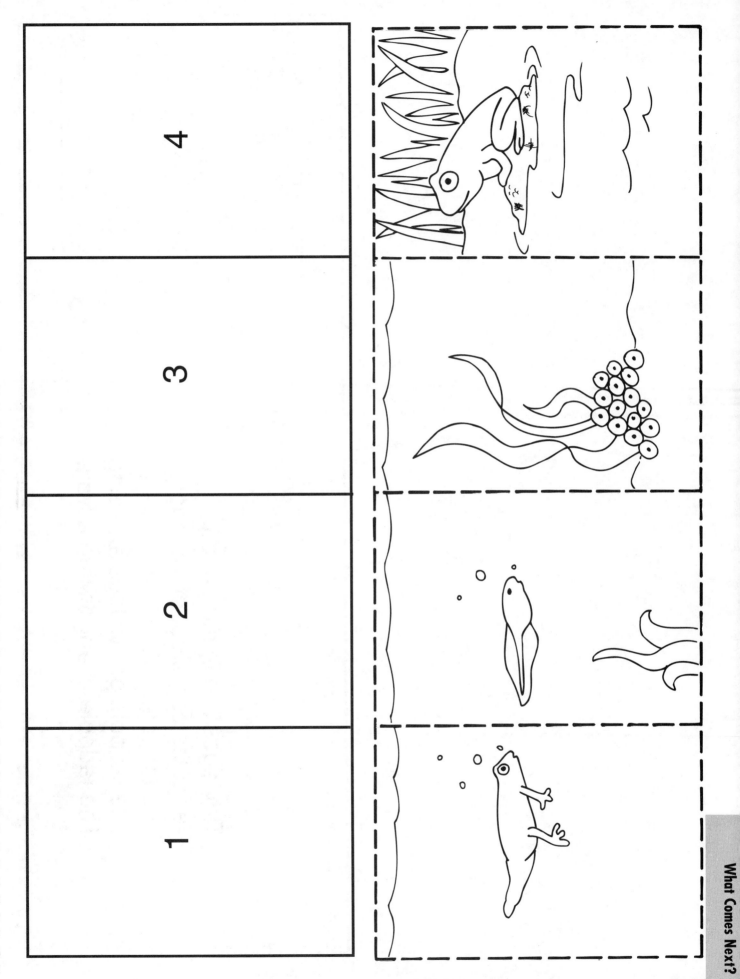

Putting pictures in correct order

Parent: Please share this little story with your child.

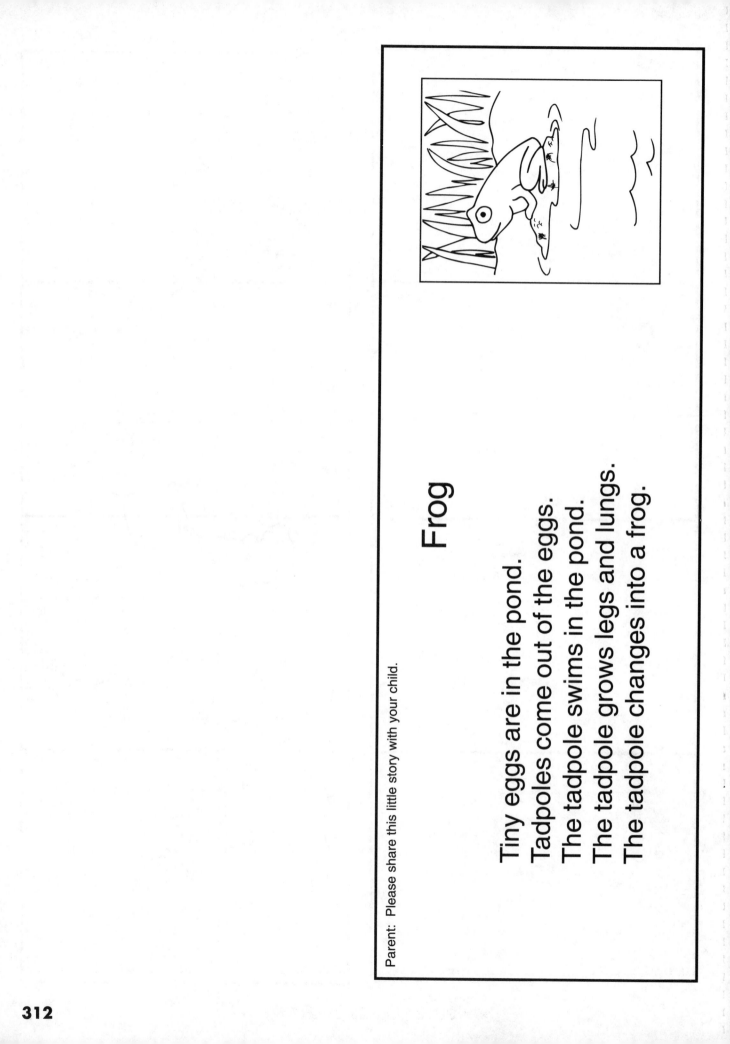

Frog

Tiny eggs are in the pond.
Tadpoles come out of the eggs.
The tadpole swims in the pond.
The tadpole grows legs and lungs.
The tadpole changes into a frog.

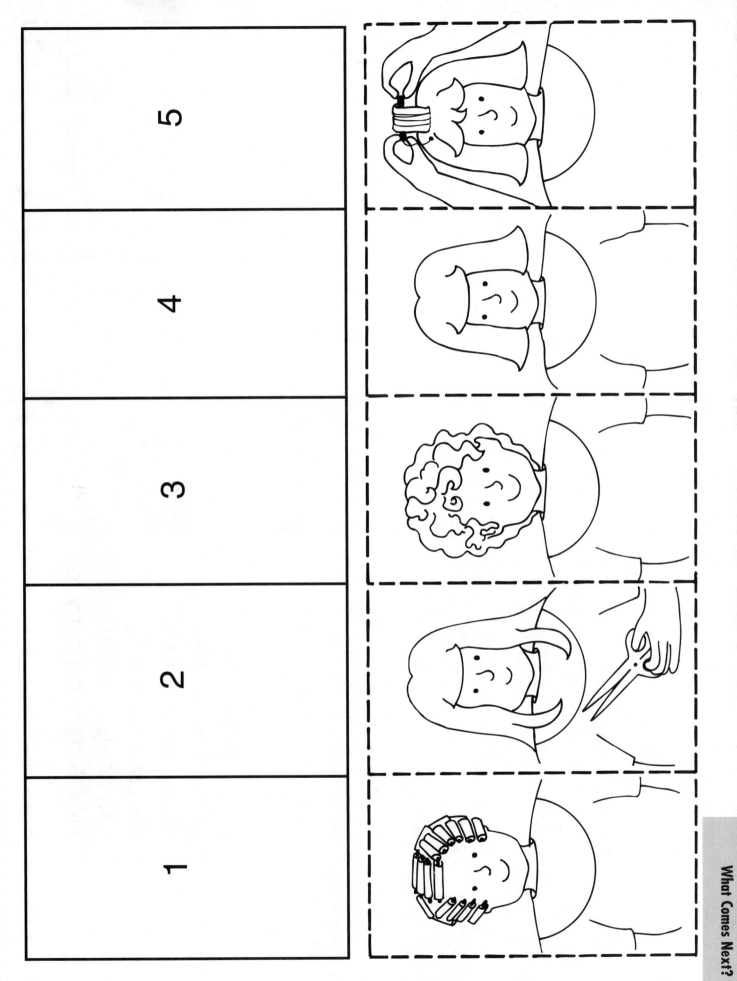

1	2	3	4	5

Putting pictures in correct order

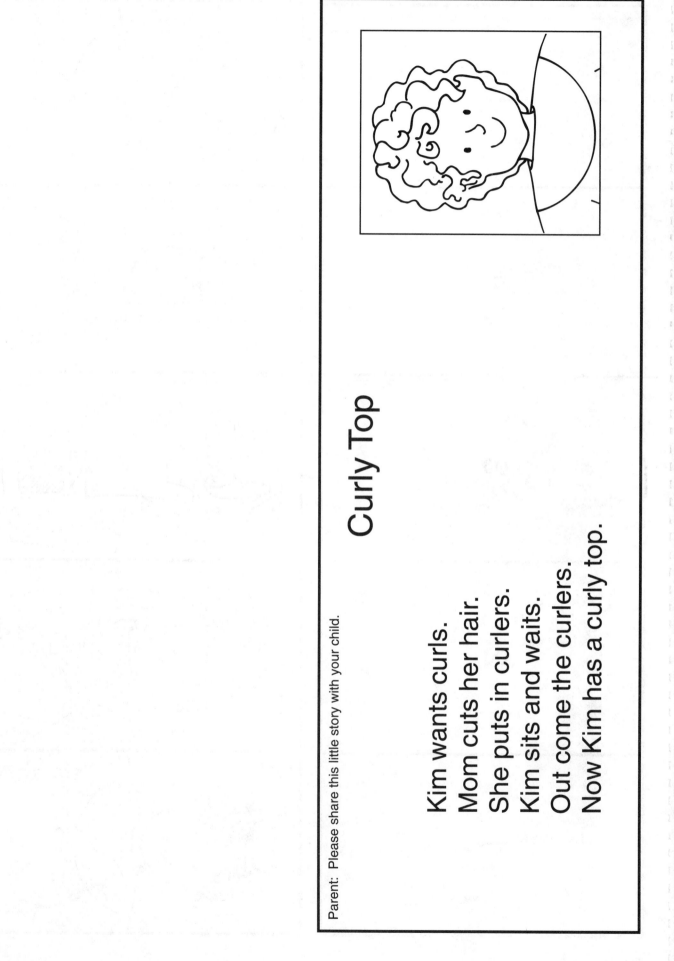

Curly Top

Kim wants curls.
Mom cuts her hair.
She puts in curlers.
Kim sits and waits.
Out come the curlers.
Now Kim has a curly top.

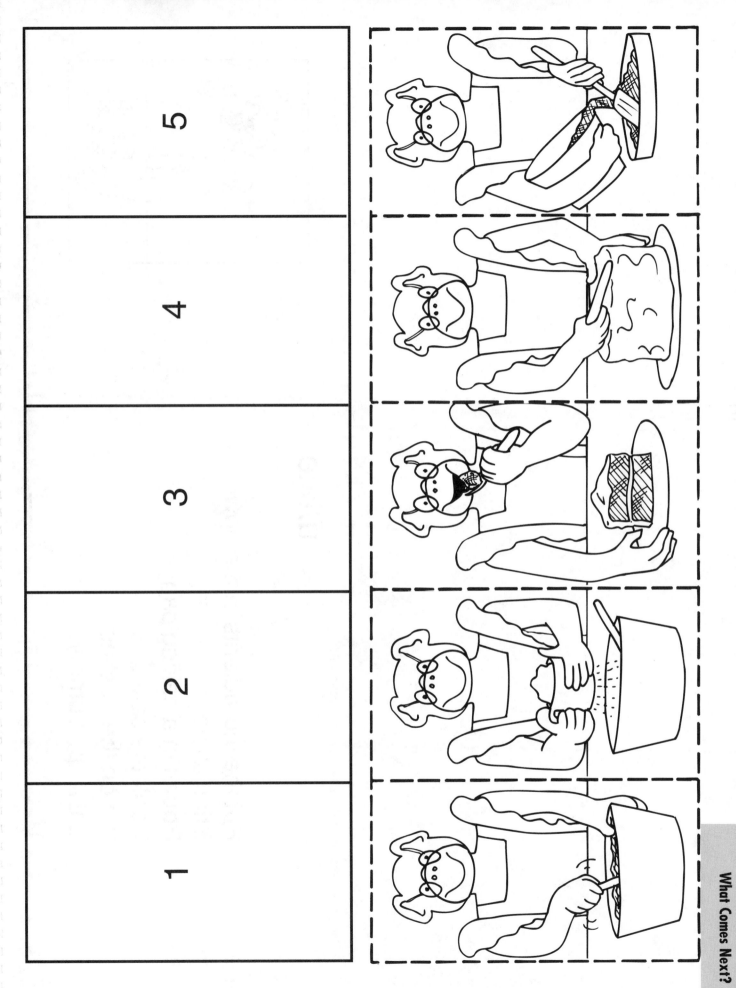

1	2	3	4	5

What Comes Next?

Parent: Please share this little story with your child.

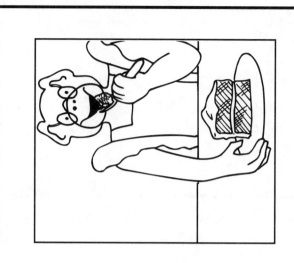

Cake

Put the ingredients in the bowl.
Stir it all up.
Pour it in a baking pan.
Cook the cake.
Put on the frosting.
Eat it up. Yummy!

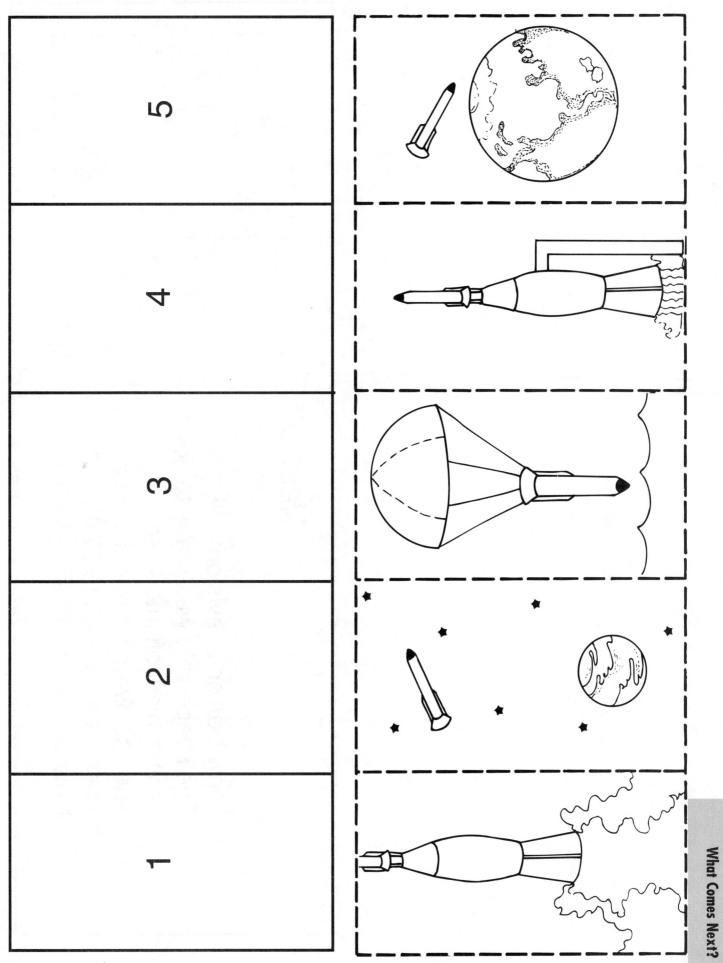

What Comes Next?

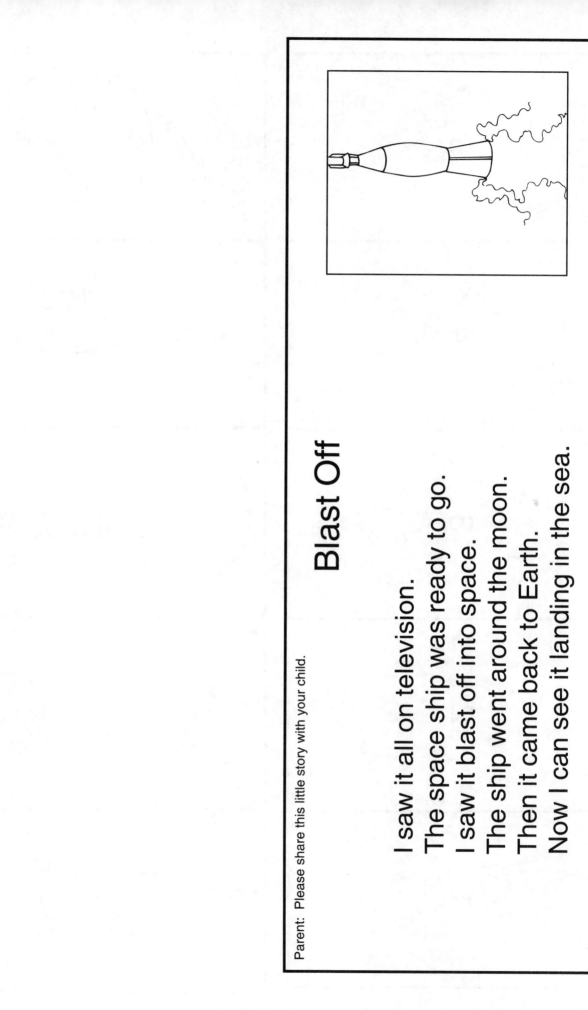

Blast Off

I saw it all on television.

The space ship was ready to go.

I saw it blast off into space.

The ship went around the moon.

Then it came back to Earth.

Now I can see it landing in the sea.

Answer Key

Please take time to go over the work your child has completed. Ask your child to explain what he/she has done. Praise both success and effort. If mistakes have been made, explain what the answer should have been and how to find it. Let your child know that mistakes are a part of learning. The time you spend with your child helps let him/her know you feel learning is important.

2   3   1

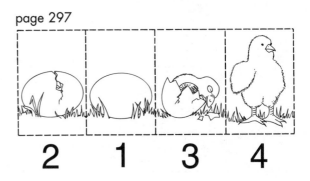

2   1   3   4

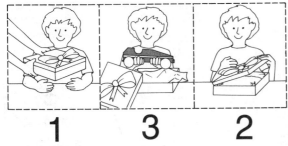

1   3   2

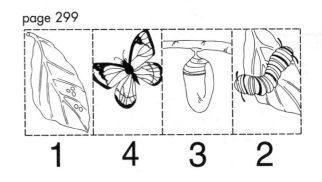

1   4   3   2

3   2   1

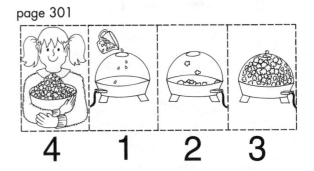

4   1   2   3

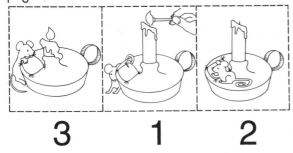

3   1   2

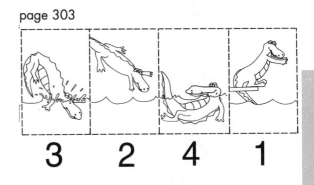

3   2   4   1

What Comes Next?

Answers

319

page 305

4   2   3   1

page 307

4   3   2   1

page 309

2   4   1   3

page 311

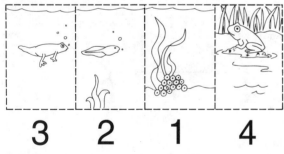

3   2   1   4

page 313

4   1   5   2   3

page 315

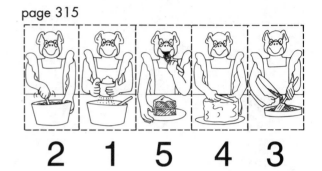

2   1   5   4   3

page 317

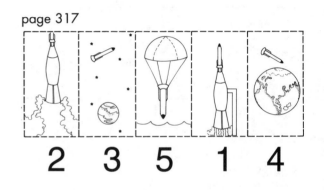

2   3   5   1   4